COURSE 2

A

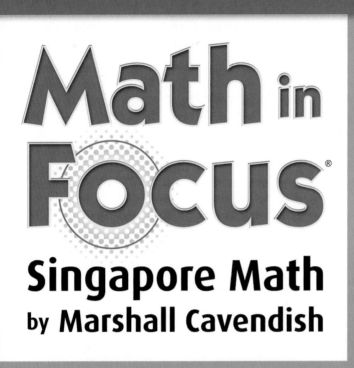

Math in FOCUS®

Singapore Math
by Marshall Cavendish

Authors
Dr. Chee-Chong Lai
May-Kuen Leong
Wai-Cheng Low

U.S. Consultants
Dr. Richard Bisk
Andy Clark

mc **Marshall Cavendish**
Education

U.S. Distributor

Houghton
Mifflin
Harcourt

COMMON
CORE

© 2013 Marshall Cavendish International (Singapore) Private Limited

Published by Marshall Cavendish Education
An imprint of Marshall Cavendish International (Singapore) Private Limited
Times Centre, 1 New Industrial Road, Singapore 536196
Customer Service Hotline: (65) 6213 9444
E-mail: tmesales@sg.marshallcavendish.com
Website: www.marshallcavendish.com/education

Distributed by
Houghton Mifflin Harcourt
222 Berkeley Street
Boston, MA 02116
Tel: 617-351-5000
Website: www.hmheducation.com/mathinfocus

Cover: © Tim Laman/Getty Images

First published 2013

Math in Focus® Course 2 Student Book A
ISBN 978-0-547-56007-6

Printed in United States of America

9   10   11   12   1401   18   17   16   15   14
4500457790   B C D E

Course 2A Contents

In Student Book A and Student Book B, look for

Practice and Problem Solving	**Assessment Opportunities**
• **Practice** in every lesson • Real-world and mathematical problems in every chapter • **Brain @ Work** in every chapter • *Math Journal* exercises	• **Quick Check** at the beginning of every chapter to assess chapter readiness • **Guided Practice** after every Example to assess readiness to continue lesson • **Chapter Review/Test** in every chapter to review or test chapter material • **Cumulative Reviews** four times during the year

CHAPTER

2 Rational Number Operations

3 Algebraic Expressions

4 Algebraic Equations and Inequalities

5

Direct and Inverse Proportion

Welcome to

Math in Focus®

Singapore Math®
by Marshall Cavendish

What makes
Math in Focus® different?

This world-class math program comes to you from the country of Singapore. We are sure that you will enjoy learning math with the interesting lessons you will find in these books.

▶ **Two books** The textbook is divided into 2 semesters. Chapters 1–5 are in Book A. Chapters 6–10 are in Book B.

▶ **Longer lessons** More concepts are presented in a lesson. Some lessons may last more than a day to give you time to understand the math.

▶ **Multiple representations** will help you make sense of new concepts and solve real-world and mathematical problems with ease.

About the book Here are the main features in this book.

Chapter Opener

Introduces chapter concepts and big ideas through a story or example. There is also a chapter table of contents.

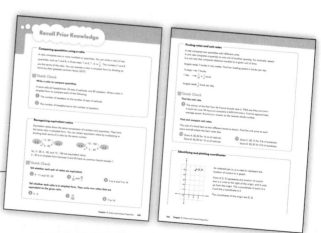

Recall Prior Knowledge

Assesses previously learned concepts, definitions, vocabulary, and models relevant to the chapter.

Quick Check assesses readiness for the chapter.

Look for these features in each lesson.

 Instructions make use of multiple representations to help you become familiar with new ideas.

 Model mathematics.

Use a Graph to Interpret Direct Proportion.

Each time the wheel on Mike's unicycle goes around, th
2 meters. The distance the unicycle moves forward is d
number of revolutions.

The table and the graph show the relationship betwee
and distance the wheel moves.

Revolutions (*x*)	1	2	3
Distance (*y* meters)	2	4	6

Example 1 **Tell whether quantities are in direct**

a) A pet store owner uses a table to decide how man
put in an aquarium. Tell whether the number of fish
the volume of the water, *g* gallons. If so, give the
tell what it represents in this situation. Then write

Volume of Water (*g* gallons)	4
Number of Fish (*f*)	6

Solution

For each pair of values, *f* and *g*:

Examples and **Guided Practice** provide step-by-step guidance through solutions.

Guided Practice

Copy and complete to determine whether *y* is directly proportional to *x*.

1 The table shows the distance traveled by a school bus, *y* miles, after *x* hours.

Time (*x* hours)	2	3	4
Distance Traveled (*y* miles)	100	150	200

Caution ////////

Make sure that both ratios compare quantities in the same order when you write a proportion. In this case, each ratio compares dollars to T-shirts.

Cautions alert you to common mistakes and misconceptions related to the topics.

 Structure, reasoning, and precision.

Math Notes are helpful hints and reminders.

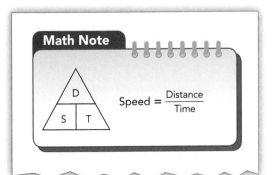

Math Note

$$\text{Speed} = \frac{\text{Distance}}{\text{Time}}$$

Think Math

In the equation $y = 2x$, *x* represents pounds of strawberries, and *y* represents the cost of strawberries. How can you use the equation to find the cost of buying 10 pounds of strawberries?

Think Math questions help you reason and explain mathematical situations.

Tell whether each graph represent a direct proportion. If so, find the constant of proportionality.

1

2

Practice and **Math Journal** are included in practice sets.

6 *Math Journal* Explain how you can tell whether a line represents a direct proportion.

Hands-On or **Technology Activities** provide opportunities for investigation, reinforcement, and extension.

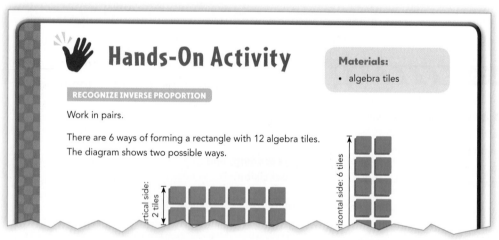

Hands-On Activity

Materials:
• algebra tiles

RECOGNIZE INVERSE PROPORTION

Work in pairs.

There are 6 ways of forming a rectangle with 12 algebra tiles. The diagram shows two possible ways.

vertical side: 2 tiles

horizontal side: 6 tiles

Brain @ Work

1 Tom is French, but lives in United States. On a visit to Germany, he saw a book that cost 25.99 euros plus 7% VAT (value-added tax). At that time, one euro

Brain@Work problems, found at the end of each chapter, are challenging and promote critical thinking.

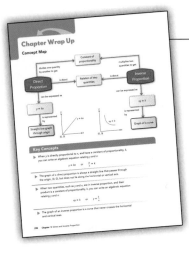

Chapter Wrap Up

Key concepts, definitions, and formulas are summarized for easy review.

The Chapter Wrap Up summaries contain concept maps like the one shown below.

The lines and arrows show how all the concepts in the chapter are related to one another and to the big ideas.

There may be more than one way to draw a concept map. With practice, you should be able to draw your own.

The red center boxes contain the big idea.

Other boxes represent key concepts of the chapter.

Structure, reasoning, and precision.

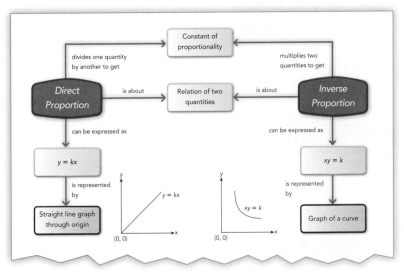

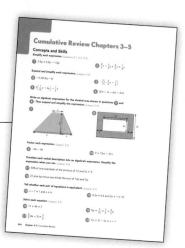

Chapter Review/Test

A practice test is found at the end of each chapter.

Cumulative Review

Cumulative review exercises can be found after Chapters 2, 5, 8, and 10.

CHAPTER

1

The Real Number System

How far is it to the next exit?

Have you ever been on a long road trip? As you go along, you see road signs telling you how far it is to the next town or exit. But have you noticed the smaller mile marker signs on interstate highways? They indicate the distance from one of the state lines.

If you have ever noticed those small green signs that only contain a number, it's likely a mile-marker. Emergency workers use the mile marker system to locate accidents, or drivers can estimate how far away an exit is. These signs are like the tick marks on a real number line and can be used to estimate or measure distances.

BIG IDEA

▶ Real numbers are represented as points on an infinite line and are used to count, measure, estimate, or approximate quantities.

Recall Prior Knowledge

Recognizing types of numbers

Type of Number	Whole numbers	Negative numbers	Fractions	Decimals
Examples	0, 1, 2, 3	−1, −2, −3	$\frac{1}{4}, \frac{3}{5}, \frac{19}{10}$	1.3, 2.71

Graph the numbers in the table on a horizontal number line.

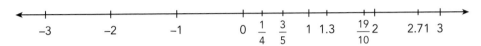

You can also graph the numbers on a vertical number line.

✓ Quick Check

Order the numbers from least to greatest. Use the < symbol. Graph each number on a horizontal number line.

1 $\frac{11}{17}, 1\frac{3}{5}, 0.3, 1.6, \frac{19}{10}$

Comparing decimals

When comparing two decimals, 1.945 and 1.954, you may use a place value chart to determine which decimal is greater.

	Ones		Tenths	Hundredths	Thousandths
1.945	1	·	9	4	5
1.954	1	·	9	5	4

The two decimals have the same values in ones and tenths. In the hundredths place, 4 < 5. So, 1.954 is greater than 1.945.

You can also use a number line to compare the decimals.

From the number line, you can see that 1.954 lies to the right of 1.945. So, 1.954 > 1.945.

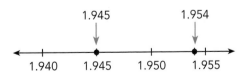

✓ Quick Check

Compare. Copy and complete each ? with <, >, or =.

2 3.87 ? 3.68

3 0.982 ? 0.982

4 5.23 ? 5.235

Rounding numbers

Sometimes a quantity is estimated by rounding its value to a given place value. Look at the digit to the right of the given place value to decide whether to round up or round down.

For example, to round a number to the tenths place, look at the digit in the hundredths place.

a) If the digit in the hundredths place is less than 5, round down.

b) If the digit in the hundredths place is 5 or greater, round up.

1,234.0564 is written as
- 1,200 when rounded to the nearest hundred because, looking at the tens place, $3 < 5$.
- 1,230 when rounded to the nearest ten because, looking at the ones place, $4 < 5$.
- 1,234 when rounded to the nearest whole number because, looking at the tenths place, $0 < 5$.
- 1,234.1 when rounded to nearest tenth because, looking at the hundredths place, $5 \geq 5$.
- 1,234.06 when rounded to 2 decimal places because, looking at the third decimal place, $6 \geq 5$.
- 1,234.056 when rounded to 3 decimal places because, looking at the fourth decimal place, $4 < 5$.

☑ Quick Check

Round each number.

5 1,456 to the nearest hundred.

6 849.58 to the nearest whole number.

7 4,923 to the nearest ten.

8 23.84 to 1 decimal place.

9 306.128 to the nearest hundredth.

Round 9,909.937 as indicated.

10 To 2 decimal places

11 To the nearest tenth

12 To the nearest whole number

13 To the nearest ten

Finding squares, cubes, square roots, and cube roots

Find the square and cube of 4. The square of a number is its second power and the cube of a number is its third power.

$$4^2 = 4 \cdot 4$$
$$= 16$$

$$4^3 = 4 \cdot 4 \cdot 4$$
$$= 64$$

The square of 4 is 16.

The cube of 4 is 64.

Find the square root of 4 and the cube root of 27.

$$\sqrt{4} = 2$$
$$\sqrt[3]{27} = 3$$

The square root of 4 is 2, because $2^2 = 4$.
The cube root of 27 is 3, because $3^3 = 27$.

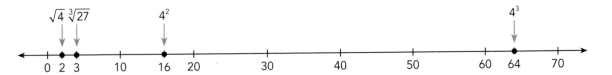

On the number line, $\sqrt{4}$ is closest to 0 and 4^3 is farthest from 0. To describe these numbers in relation to one another, you may express them as follows:

$$\sqrt{4} < \sqrt[3]{27} < 4^2 < 4^3$$

✓ Quick Check

Find the square of each number.

14 3

15 12

Find the cube of each number.

16 5

17 6

Find the square root and cube root of each number.

18 64

19 729

Order the numbers from greatest to least. Use the > symbol.

20 $\sqrt{81}$, 8^2, 3^3

Determining absolute values

The absolute value of a number n is denoted by $|n|$.

Examples: $|2| = 2$, $|-3| = 3$

The absolute value of a number is a measure of its distance from 0.

The distance from -3 to 0 is 3 units.

The distance from 2 to 0 is 2 units.

✔ Quick Check

Use the following set of numbers for questions 21 to 25.

34, −23, −54, 54, −60

21 Find the absolute value of each number.

22 Which number is closest to 0?

23 Which number is farthest from 0?

24 Name two numbers with the same absolute value.

25 Which number has the greatest absolute value?

Use the number line to find the absolute value of each of the following numbers.

26 $|-15|$

27 $|6|$

28 $|-2.1|$

Copy and complete each ? with >, =, or <.

29 $|-7|$? $|-72|$

30 $|5|$? $|-5|$

31 $|-26|$? $|5|$

Lesson Objectives

- Find the absolute values of rational numbers.
- Express numbers in $\frac{m}{n}$ form.
- Locate rational numbers on the number line.

Vocabulary

opposites	positive integers
set of integers	negative fractions
negative integers	rational numbers

Find the Absolute Values of Positive Fractions.

Previously, you learned how to graph whole numbers and negative numbers on a number line. The set of whole numbers and their **opposites** is called the **set of integers**.

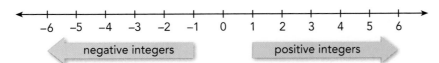

The numbers on the right of 0 are called **positive integers**. The numbers on the left of 0 are called **negative integers**. The number 0 itself is neither positive nor negative.

There are gaps between the integers on the number line. These gaps contain fractions.

In the gap between 0 and 1, you can write proper fractions such as $\frac{1}{4}$, $\frac{1}{2}$, $\frac{3}{5}$, and $\frac{9}{10}$.

The integer 1 is one unit from 0. So, the fraction $\frac{1}{2}$ must be $\frac{1}{2}$ unit from 0. You can write this distance as $\left|\frac{1}{2}\right|$. The measure of the distance of other fractions from 0 is defined in the same way.

> The absolute value of a positive fraction is just the fraction itself.

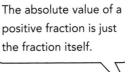

Examples: $\left|\frac{1}{4}\right| = \frac{1}{4}$, $\left|\frac{3}{5}\right| = \frac{3}{5}$, and $\left|2\frac{5}{8}\right| = \frac{21}{8}$, because $2\frac{5}{8} = \frac{21}{8}$.

Find the Absolute Values of Negative Fractions and Decimals.

You might imagine that a mirror is placed on the number line at the number 0.

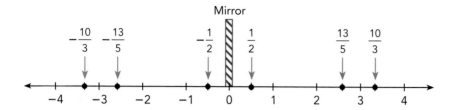

As you look into the mirror, you see the images of the positive integers. These images are the negative integers.

In the same way, fractions such as $\frac{1}{2}$, $\frac{13}{5}$, and $\frac{10}{3}$ each has an opposite in the mirror. The negative fractions are $-\frac{1}{2}$, $-\frac{13}{5}$, and $-\frac{10}{3}$.

In a mirror, the distance of an *image* from the mirror and the distance of the *object* from the mirror are equal.

The absolute value of a negative fraction is defined as the distance of the negative fraction from 0. You find the absolute value of the negative fractions as you do negative integers.

Examples:

$$\left|-\frac{10}{3}\right| = \frac{10}{3}$$

$$\left|-\frac{13}{5}\right| = \frac{13}{5}$$

$$|-1.35| = 1.35$$

So, the distance of $-\frac{10}{3}$ from 0 is $\frac{10}{3}$ units. In the same way, $-\frac{13}{5}$ is $\frac{13}{5}$ units from 0 and -1.35 is 1.35 units from 0.

Example 1 **Find the absolute values of fractions.**

Solve. Show your work.

a) Find the absolute values of $-\frac{11}{12}$ and $\frac{26}{15}$.

Solution

$\left|-\frac{11}{12}\right| = \frac{11}{12}$ and $\left|\frac{26}{15}\right| = \frac{26}{15}$.

b) Using a number line, show how far $-\frac{11}{12}$ and $\frac{26}{15}$ are from 0. Which number is closer to 0?

Solution

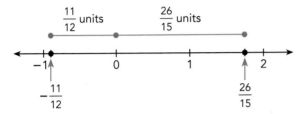

$-\frac{11}{12}$ is $\frac{11}{12}$ units to the left of 0. $\frac{26}{15}$ is $\frac{26}{15}$ units to the right of 0.

Because the distance $\frac{11}{12} < 1$ unit and $\frac{26}{15} > 1$ unit, $-\frac{11}{12}$ is closer to 0.

Guided Practice

Solve.

1 Find the absolute values of $3\frac{2}{7}$ and $-\frac{18}{5}$.

2 Graph the two numbers on a number line and indicate their distances from 0. Which number is farther from 0?

Express Integers and Fractions in $\frac{m}{n}$ Form.

A **rational number** is a number which can be written as $\frac{m}{n}$ where m and n are integers with $n \neq 0$. The definition of rational numbers comes from the concept of fractions.

Think Math

You cannot write a rational number $\frac{m}{n}$ with $n = 0$. Why?

Examples: $1\frac{1}{2} = \frac{3}{2}$. So, $1\frac{1}{2}$ is a rational number.

$3 = \frac{3}{1}$. So, 3 is a rational number.

To express 0 in the form $\frac{m}{n}$, you can write 0 as $\frac{0}{1}$.

Example 2 **Express integers and fractions in $\frac{m}{n}$ form.**

Write each number in $\frac{m}{n}$ form where m and n are integers.

a) 23

b) -45

c) $11\frac{7}{9}$

d) $-\frac{16}{21}$

Solution

a) $23 = \frac{23}{1}$ Whole numbers have 1 in the denominator.

b) $-45 = \frac{-45}{1}$ Negative integers have 1 in the denominator.

c) $11\frac{7}{9} = \frac{11 \cdot 9}{9} + \frac{7}{9}$ Write $11\frac{7}{9}$ as an improper fraction.

$= \frac{106}{9}$

d) $-\frac{16}{21} = \frac{-16}{21}$ Write the negative integer in either the numerator or denominator.

or $= \frac{16}{-21}$

For negative fractions, the negative integer may be placed in either the numerator or the denominator.

Examples: $-\frac{2}{9} = \frac{-2}{9} = \frac{2}{-9}$

$-3 = \frac{-3}{1} = \frac{3}{-1}$

Guided Practice

Write each number in $\frac{m}{n}$ form where m and n are integers.

3 $11\frac{1}{6}$

4 48

5 $-5\frac{4}{12}$

6 $-\frac{25}{10}$

Express Decimals in $\frac{m}{n}$ Form.

You have learned how to express decimals as fractions. Decimals also have their negative counterparts on the number line. So, you can write decimals in $\frac{m}{n}$ form.

Example 3   **Express decimals in $\frac{m}{n}$ form.**

Write each decimal as $\frac{m}{n}$ where m and n are integers with $n \neq 0$.

a)   0.4   b) -0.186

c)   30.5   d) -1.48

Solution

a) $0.4 = \frac{4}{10}$ 4 is in the tenths place. Use 10 as the denominator.

        $= \frac{2}{5}$ Simplify.

b) $-0.186 = -\frac{186}{1,000}$ 6 is in the thousandths place. Use 1,000 as the denominator.

           $= \frac{-93}{500}$ Simplify.

c) $30.5 = 30\frac{1}{2}$ Write the integer, 30. Write 0.5 as $\frac{1}{2}$.

          $= \frac{61}{2}$ Write as an improper fraction.

d) $-1.48 = -1\frac{48}{100}$ Write the integer, -1. 8 is in the hundredths place.
                                  Use 100 as the denominator.

           $= \frac{-148}{100}$ Write as an improper fraction.

           $= \frac{-37}{25}$ Simplify.

Guided Practice

Write each decimal as $\frac{m}{n}$ where m and n are integers with $n \neq 0$.

7   11.5   **8** -7.8

9   0.36   **10** -0.125

Locate Rational Numbers on the Number Line.

Rational numbers can be located on the number line easily.

Locate rational numbers on the number line.

Locate the rational numbers $\frac{3}{5}$ and -2.4 on the number line.

Solution

STEP 1 Find the integers that the rational number lies between.

$\frac{3}{5}$ is a proper fraction so it is located between 0 and 1.

-2.4 is located between -3 and -2.

> ## Caution
>
> -2.4 can be written as a mixed number $-2\frac{2}{5}$ or $-2\frac{4}{10}$. Remember that it is a negative mixed number.
>
> Make sure that you do not graph -2.4 by counting to the right of 0.

STEP 2 Graph a number line and label the integers.

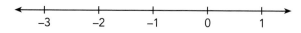

STEP 3 Divide the distance between the integers into equal segments.

You divide the distance between 0 and 1 into 5 equal segments and the distance between -3 and -2 into 10 equal segments.

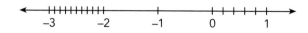

STEP 4 Use the segments to locate $\frac{3}{5}$ and -2.4.

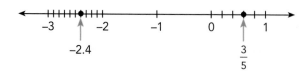

Guided Practice

Copy and complete.

11 Locate the rational numbers -1.5 and $\frac{15}{4}$ on the number line.

STEP 1   Find the integers that the rational number lies between.

$\frac{15}{4}$ can be written as a mixed number, $3\frac{3}{4}$, and $3\frac{3}{4}$ lies between 3 and 4.
The negative decimal -1.5 lies between -2 and -1.

STEP 2   Graph a number line and label the integers.

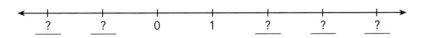

STEP 3   Divide the distance between the integers into equal segments.

You divide the distance between -2 and -1 into __?__ segments and
the distance between 3 and 4 into __?__ segments.

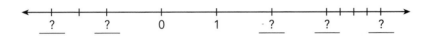

STEP 4   Use the segments to locate -1.5 and $3\frac{3}{4}$.

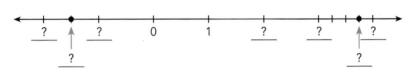

Locate the following rational numbers on the number line.

12 $\frac{1}{6}$ and $\frac{15}{3}$

13 -0.4 and $\frac{11}{5}$

14 $\frac{12}{15}$ and -1.8

15 $-\frac{5}{15}$ and $-\frac{25}{30}$

Practice 1.1

Find the absolute value of each fraction. Use a number line to show how far the fraction is from 0. Write fractions in simplest form.

1 $\dfrac{7}{10}$

2 $\dfrac{18}{8}$

3 $-\dfrac{5}{13}$

4 $-\dfrac{48}{15}$

Write each integer or fraction as $\dfrac{m}{n}$ in simplest form where m and n are integers.

5 67

6 −345

7 $\dfrac{25}{80}$

8 $-\dfrac{264}{90}$

9 $-\dfrac{14}{70}$

10 $\dfrac{600}{480}$

Write each mixed number or decimal as $\dfrac{m}{n}$ in simplest form where m and n are integers.

11 $7\dfrac{7}{9}$

12 $-5\dfrac{1}{10}$

13 $2\dfrac{5}{12}$

14 $-10\dfrac{11}{36}$

15 0.4

16 −0.625

17 5.80

18 9.001

19 −10.68

Copy and complete.

20 Locate the following rational numbers correctly on the number line.

$-\dfrac{1}{4}, -1.5, 0.8, \dfrac{5}{2}$

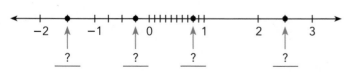

21 Locate the following rational numbers correctly on the number line.

$$1\frac{7}{10}, -\frac{13}{5}, 2.25, -0.7$$

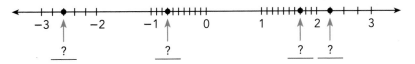

Graph each rational number on a separate number line.

22 $67\frac{1}{8}$

23 $\frac{305}{20}$

24 $\frac{98}{28}$

25 $-\frac{21}{12}$

26 -25.8

27 -45.3

A video game gives you 10 minutes to find a treasure. The results of your first 8 games show the amount of time left unused when you have found the treasure. A negative time means you have gone beyond the 10 minutes allotted. Use these data for questions 28 to 35.

$$\frac{23}{8}, 0, -7\frac{1}{5}, 6, -\frac{17}{4}, 8, 7.8, -9.1$$

28 Order the times left from most to least time using the symbol >.

29 Write the absolute value of each number.

30 Which number has the greatest absolute value?

31 Order the absolute values from least to greatest. Use the symbol <.

32 Graph the original numbers on a number line.

33 Which negative number in the list is farthest from 0?

34 Which positive number in the list is closest to 10?

35 Which time is closest to −5 minutes?

1.2 Writing Rational Numbers as Decimals

Lesson Objectives

- Write rational numbers as terminating or repeating decimals using long division.
- Compare rational numbers on the number line.

Vocabulary

terminating decimal

repeating decimal

Write Rational Numbers as Terminating Decimals Using Long Division.

In a previous course, you learned to write some rational numbers as decimals.

Examples: $\frac{3}{10} = 0.3$, $\frac{21}{100} = 0.21$, and $5\frac{323}{1,000} = 5.323$.

Any rational number may be written in decimal form using long division. You write $\frac{1}{4}$ as a decimal using long division, because $\frac{1}{4}$ means 1 divided by 4.

$$
\begin{array}{r}
0.25 \\
4\overline{)1.00} \\
\underline{8} \\
20 \\
\underline{20} \\
0
\end{array}
$$

Divide 1 by 4.
Add zeros after the decimal point.

The remainder is 0.

So, $\frac{1}{4} = 0.25$.

The fraction $\frac{1}{4}$ is written as 0.25.

Notice that the long division ends with a remainder of zero. A decimal, such as 0.25, is called a terminating decimal, because it has a finite number of nonzero decimal places.

Think Math

Any fraction whose denominator has only 2s and 5s in its prime factorization can be written as a terminating decimal. Why?

Example 5 **Use long division to write rational numbers as terminating decimals.**

Using long division, write each rational number as a terminating decimal.

a) $\dfrac{3}{8}$

Solution

```
    0.375
8 ) 3.000
    2 4
    ───
     60
     56
    ───
     40
     40
    ───
      0
```

Divide 3 by 8.
Add zeros after the decimal point.

The remainder is 0.

So, $\dfrac{3}{8} = 0.375$.

b) $6\dfrac{2}{25}$

Solution

```
     0.08
25 ) 2.00
     2 00
    ────
       0
```

Divide 2 by 25.
Add zeros after the decimal point.

The remainder is 0.

So, $6\dfrac{2}{25} = 6.08$.

You could also write $6\dfrac{2}{25}$ as the improper fraction $\dfrac{152}{25}$ and then divide: $152 \div 25$. The answer is the same.

Guided Practice

Using long division, write each rational number as a terminating decimal.

1 $\dfrac{7}{8}$

2 $\dfrac{19}{4}$

3 $\dfrac{52}{40}$

4 $10\dfrac{13}{25}$

Write Rational Numbers as Repeating Decimals Using Long Division.

You can also write the fraction $\frac{1}{3}$ as a decimal using long division because $\frac{1}{3}$ means 1 divided by 3.

$$
\begin{array}{r}
0.333 \\
3\overline{)1.000} \\
\underline{9} \\
10 \\
\underline{9} \\
10 \\
\underline{9} \\
1
\end{array}
$$

Divide 1 by 3.
Add zeros after the decimal point.

The remainder will not terminate with 0.

So, $\frac{1}{3} = 0.333\ldots$

When you divide 1 by 3, the division process will not terminate with a remainder of 0. The digit 3 keeps repeating infinitely. A decimal, such as 0.333..., is called a repeating decimal.

> A repeating decimal, such as 0.333...,
> has a group of one or more digits that
> repeat endlessly.

Example 6 **Use long division or a calculator to write rational numbers as repeating decimals.**

Write each rational number as a repeating decimal. Use long division for a) and b).

 Use a calculator for c) and d).

a) $\frac{1}{11}$

b) $\frac{13}{12}$

c) $\frac{82}{333}$

d) $\frac{2}{7}$

Solution

a)
```
        0.0909
   11 ) 1.0000
        99
        ───
        100
         99
        ───
          1
```
Divide 1 by 11.
Add zeros after the decimal point.

The remainder will not terminate with 0.

Stop dividing when you see the digits continue to repeat themselves.

So, $\frac{1}{11} = 0.0909\ldots$

b)
```
          1.0833
   12 ) 13.0000
        12
        ───
        1 00
          96
        ────
          40
          36
        ────
          40
          36
        ────
           4
```
Divide 13 by 12.
Add zeros after the decimal point.

The remainder will not terminate with 0.

So, $\frac{13}{12} = 1.0833\ldots$

c) From the calculator, $\frac{82}{333} = 0.246246246\ldots$

d) From the calculator, $\frac{2}{7} = 0.285714285714\ldots$

Guided Practice

Using long division, write each rational number as a repeating decimal.

5 $\frac{2}{9}$

6 $\frac{11}{6}$

 Using a calculator, write each rational number as a repeating decimal.

7 $\frac{23}{54}$

8 $\frac{78}{37}$

Write Repeating Decimals Using Bar Notation.

For the repeating decimal 0.333..., you see that the digit 3 repeats itself. You write 0.333... as $0.\overline{3}$ with a bar above the repeating digit 3. So, 0.333... = $0.\overline{3}$.

For the repeating decimal 0.0909..., you see that 0 and 9 repeat as a group of digits. You write 0.0909... as $0.\overline{09}$. In the repeating decimal 1.068181..., 8 and 1 repeat as a group of digits. So, you write 1.068181... as $1.06\overline{81}$.

You write 0.246246... and 0.285714285714... as repeating decimals using the bar notation as shown below.

0.246246... = $0.\overline{246}$ The digits 2, 4, and 6 form a repetitive group.

0.285714285714 = $0.\overline{285714}$ The digits 2, 8, 5, 7, 1, and 4 form a repetitive group.

Guided Practice

Using long division, write each rational number as a repeating decimal. Use bar notation to indicate the repeating digits.

 9 $\dfrac{5}{6}$

10 $\dfrac{17}{12}$

 Technology Activity

Materials:
- spreadsheet software

CLASSIFY RATIONAL NUMBERS IN DECIMAL FORM

Work in pairs.

 STEP 1 On a spreadsheet, label four columns with the following column heads.

| Sheets | Charts | SmartArt Graphics | WordArt |

	A	B	C	D
1	Rational Numbers in Decimal Form	Terminating, Repeating, or Neither	Number of Decimal Digits (Terminating Decimal)	Digits that Repeat (Repeating Decimal)
2				

 STEP 2 Enter each rational number below in the first column, labeled "**Rational Numbers in Decimal Form**". Make sure that the cells in this column are formatted to display decimals up to 8 decimal places.

$$\dfrac{5}{16}, \dfrac{141}{25}, -\dfrac{40}{111}, -\dfrac{15}{16}, \dfrac{14}{5}, \dfrac{1}{8}, -\dfrac{9}{44}, \dfrac{2}{11}, \dfrac{5}{4}, \text{ and } -\dfrac{40}{9}.$$

For example, if you enter $\dfrac{5}{16}$ into the spreadsheet, the entry will show the decimal form of this fraction.

3 Determine whether the decimal is terminating, repeating, or neither. Enter either "**Terminating**", "**Repeating**", or "**Neither**" in the second column.

4 If the decimal terminates, record the number of decimal digits in the third column. If the decimal repeats, record the repeating digits in the fourth column.

Example:

	Sheets	Charts	SmartArt Graphics	WordArt	
	A	B	C	D	

	Rational Numbers in Decimal Form	Terminating, Repeating, or Neither	Number of Decimal Digits (Terminating Decimal)	Digits that Repeat (Repeating Decimal)
1				
2	0.3125	Terminating	?	?

Math Journal Did you find any decimals that neither terminated nor repeated? What can you conclude about the decimal form of a rational number?

Compare Rational Numbers.

Suppose you have to compare the two rational numbers $\frac{3}{4}$ and $\frac{4}{5}$. You write each rational number as a decimal first.

$$\frac{3}{4} = 0.75, \qquad \frac{4}{5} = 0.8$$

To compare the rational numbers, you compare their decimal forms. That is, you compare 0.75 with 0.8.

0.7**5**
0.8**0**

Because 7 tenths < 8 tenths, 0.75 < 0.8.

You may also use a number line to compare these decimals.

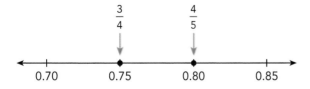

0.75 lies to the left of 0.80. So, 0.75 < 0.80.

So, $\frac{3}{4} < \frac{4}{5}$.

You compare the corresponding place value of two decimals from left to right. You stop at the first pair of digits which are different.

Example 7 **Compare two positive rational numbers.**

Compare the positive rational numbers using the symbols < or >. Use the number line to help you.

a) $\frac{11}{8}$ and $\frac{15}{11}$

Solution

$\frac{11}{8} = 1.375$ Write each rational number as a decimal.

$\frac{15}{11} = 1.3636\ldots$

     $= 1.\overline{36}$

Compare the decimals, 1.375 and 1.$\overline{36}$.

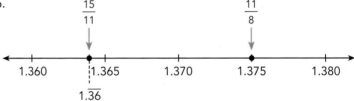

1.375 lies to the right of 1.$\overline{36}$.
So, 1.375 > 1.$\overline{36}$

     $\frac{11}{8} > \frac{15}{11}$

b) When 17 blue bottles and 14 white bottles are completely filled with liquid, the blue bottles hold a total volume of 228 liters while the white bottles hold a total volume of 222 liters. On average, which bottle holds less?

Solution

$\frac{228}{17} = 13.4117\ldots$ liters   Find the average amount of liquid in one blue bottle.

$\frac{222}{14} = 15.8571\ldots$ liters   Find the average amount of liquid in one white bottle.

So, 13.4117… < 15.8571…

     $\frac{228}{17} < \frac{222}{14}$

So, the blue bottle holds less liquid on average.

Guided Practice

Compare the positive rational numbers using the symbols < or >. Use a number line to help you.

11 $\frac{7}{10}$ [?] $\frac{13}{16}$

12 $\frac{24}{7}$ [?] $\frac{10}{3}$

Example 8 **Compare two negative rational numbers.**

Compare the negative rational numbers using the symbols $<$ or $>$. Use a number line to help you.

a) $-\dfrac{1}{8}$ and $-\dfrac{3}{16}$

Solution

Method 1

Compare using a number line.

$-\dfrac{1}{8} = -0.125$ Write each rational number as a decimal.

$-\dfrac{3}{16} = -0.1875$

Use the absolute values of -0.125 and -0.1875 to help you graph the decimals on a number line.

$|-0.125| = 0.125$
$|-0.1875| = 0.1875$

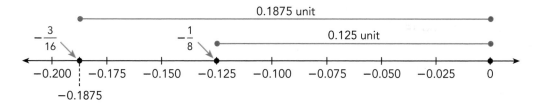

From the number line, you see that -0.1875 lies farther to the left of 0 than -0.125.

So, $-0.125 > -0.1875$

$$-\dfrac{1}{8} > -\dfrac{3}{16}$$

Method 2

Compare using place value.

You can also write an inequality using the absolute value of the two numbers.

$|-0.125| < |-0.1875|$

The two numbers are negative so the number with the greater absolute value is farther to the left of 0. It is the lesser number.

$-0.125 > -0.1875$

$$-\dfrac{1}{8} > -\dfrac{3}{16}$$

Continue on next page

b) $-\dfrac{56}{11}$ and $-\dfrac{17}{5}$

Solution

Method 1

Compare using a number line.

$-\dfrac{56}{11} = -5.0909\ldots$ Write each rational number as a decimal.

$\quad\quad = -5.\overline{09}$

$-\dfrac{17}{5} = -3.4$

Use the absolute values of $-5.\overline{09}$ and -3.4 to help you graph the decimals on a number line.

$|-5.\overline{09}| = 5.\overline{09}$

$|-3.4| = 3.4$

From the number line, you see that $-5.\overline{09}$ lies farther left of 0 than -3.4.

So, $-5.\overline{09} < -3.4$

$\quad -\dfrac{56}{11} < -\dfrac{17}{5}$

Method 2

Compare using place value.

You can also write an inequality using the absolute value of the two numbers.

$|-5.\overline{09}| > |-3.4|$

The two numbers are negative so the number with the greater absolute value is farther to the left of 0. It is the lesser number.

$-5.\overline{09} < -3.4$

$-\dfrac{56}{11} < -\dfrac{17}{5}$

Guided Practice

Compare the negative rational numbers using the symbols $<$ or $>$. Use a number line to help you.

13 $-\dfrac{3}{5}$? $-\dfrac{4}{5}$

14 $-10\dfrac{3}{4}$? $-\dfrac{41}{5}$

15 -4.063 ? $-4\dfrac{1}{6}$

Practice 1.2

Using long division, write each rational number as a terminating decimal.

1 $76\frac{1}{2}$

2 $-39\frac{2}{5}$

3 $-\frac{47}{10}$

4 $\frac{5}{16}$

5 $\frac{7}{20}$

6 $\frac{7}{8}$

Simplify each rational number. Then use long division to write each rational number as a terminating decimal.

7 $\frac{99}{36}$

8 $\frac{12}{15}$

9 $\frac{9}{48}$

10 $-\frac{132}{8}$

11 $-\frac{48}{50}$

12 $-\frac{14}{128}$

Using long division, write each rational number as a repeating decimal with 3 decimal places. Identify the pattern of repeating digits using bar notation.

13 $\frac{5}{6}$

14 $-8\frac{2}{3}$

Write each rational number as a repeating decimal using bar notation. You may use a calculator.

15 $\frac{8}{55}$

16 $\frac{456}{123}$

17 $-\frac{987}{110}$

18 $\frac{11}{14}$

19 $-\frac{10}{13}$

20 $\frac{4,005}{101}$

Refer to the list of rational numbers below for questions 21 to 23. You may use a calculator.

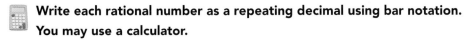

$$-\frac{23}{32}, \frac{7}{15}, -\frac{368}{501}, -\frac{19}{26}, \frac{37}{44}$$

21 Write each rational number as a decimal with at most 6 decimal places.

22 Using your answers in **21**, list the numbers from least to greatest using the symbol <. Graph a number line between −1 and 1 with 0 in the middle. Then, place each rational number on the number line.

23 *Math Journal* Margo tries to compare $-\frac{2}{3}$ and $-\frac{5}{8}$ using absolute values. She finds their decimal equivalents to be $-0.\overline{6}$ and -0.625, and she knows $|-0.\overline{6}| > |-0.625|$. Explain why she must reverse the inequality in her final answer, $-\frac{2}{3} < -\frac{5}{8}$.

Lesson Objectives

- Understand irrational numbers and how they fill the number line.
- Use rational numbers to locate irrational numbers approximately on the number line.

Understand 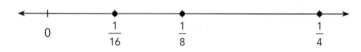 on the Number Line.

Consider a small portion of the number line close to 0. If $\frac{1}{4}$ is close to 0, then $\frac{1}{8}$ is even closer to 0 than $\frac{1}{4}$. In the same way, $\frac{1}{16}$ is closer to 0 than $\frac{1}{8}$. If you carry on in a similar manner, you can see that there are infinitely many rational numbers clustering very close to 0. In fact, this phenomenon appears at every other point on the number line.

However, there are holes in the number line. There are numbers which are on the number line but they are not rational numbers. One such example is $\sqrt{2}$, because it cannot be written in $\frac{m}{n}$ form.

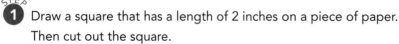

Hands-On Activity

Materials:
- paper
- ruler
- scissors

 **FIND THE VALUE OF $\sqrt{2}$ USING A SQUARE**

Work in pairs.

STEP 1 Draw a square that has a length of 2 inches on a piece of paper. Then cut out the square.

STEP 2 Find the area of the square (square A).

STEP 3 Fold the four vertices of square A towards the center to form square B as shown below.

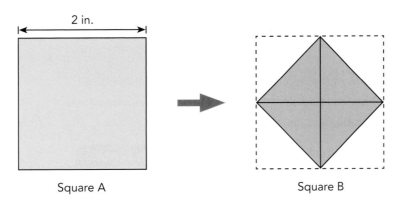

Square A

Square B

STEP 4 State how the areas of square A and square B are related. State the area of square B. How can you represent the length of a side of square B?

STEP 5 Using your answer in **STEP 4**, find the length of a side of square B with a calculator. Round your answer to 2 decimal places.

Math Journal Place an edge of square B alongside a ruler to measure its length. Explain why the reading from the ruler is different from the answer in **STEP 5**.

Locate $\sqrt{2}$ on the Number Line.

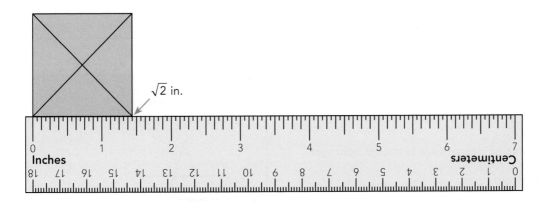

$\sqrt{2}$ in.

The readings from the calculator and from the ruler give **approximate** values of $\sqrt{2}$, the length of a side of square B. You may also regard the marking of $\sqrt{2}$ on the ruler as a point on the right side of the number line.

Continue on next page

All nonzero multiples of $\sqrt{2}$, such as $2\sqrt{2}$, $3\sqrt{2}$, $4\sqrt{2}$, and so on, are also not rational numbers.

In other words, the positive side of the number line has many holes that do not contain rational numbers. There are also similar holes on the negative side of the number line. So, the entire number line has many holes!

To make a complete number line, you have to fill the number line with numbers such as $\sqrt{2}$ and many others. These numbers are called irrational numbers.

An irrational number cannot be expressed as a ratio of two integers. So, it has a decimal value which does not terminate or repeat.

So $-\sqrt{2}$ is a negative irrational number.

Examples of Irrational Numbers.

Many square roots of positive integers are irrational numbers.

Examples: $\sqrt{2}$, $\sqrt{3}$, $\sqrt{5}$, $\sqrt{7}$, and $\sqrt{10}$.

Many cube roots of integers are irrational numbers.

Examples: $\sqrt[3]{2}$, $\sqrt[3]{9}$, $\sqrt[3]{11}$, and $\sqrt[3]{16}$.

The ratio of the circumference of a circle to its diameter, π, and the golden ratio, φ, are also examples of irrational numbers.

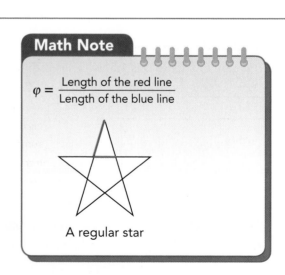

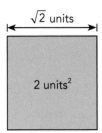

Use Area of Squares to Locate Irrational Numbers Approximately.

You know how to find the square root of a perfect square. These perfect squares enable you to estimate the location of an irrational number on the number line without using a calculator.

Consider $\sqrt{2}$. When you square $\sqrt{2}$, you get 2. You may regard the area of square B as 2 square units.

$\sqrt{2}$ units

2 units^2

Square B

Note that 2 is more than 1 but less than 4. Both 1 and 4 are perfect squares and so $1^2 < 2 < 2^2$. You read $1^2 < 2 < 2^2$ as 2 is between 1^2 and 2^2.

That means the area of square B is more than the area of square C but less than the area of square A.

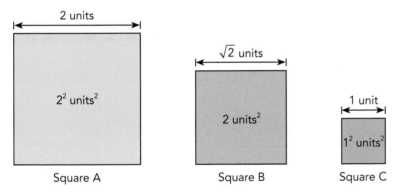

Square A   Square B   Square C

Compare the side lengths of squares A, B, and C. You get $1 < \sqrt{2} < 2$.

To approximate the location of $\sqrt{2}$, consider another square D with side length 1.5 units. The area of square D is 1.5^2 which is 2.25 square units. You can identify $1^2 < 2 < 1.5^2$. Compare the side lengths of squares B, C, and D. You get $1 < \sqrt{2} < 1.5$.

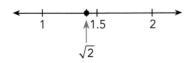

This method only gives you an estimation of the location of $\sqrt{2}$ on the number line. A calculator gives a better approximation.

Use Rational Approximations to Locate Irrational Numbers.

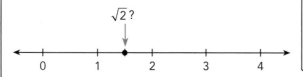

How do you locate $\sqrt{2}$ on the number line?

$\sqrt{2}$?

Because $1^2 = 1$ and $2^2 = 4$, you need to find some number x between 1 and 2 so that x^2 is about 2.

You use a calculator to locate $\sqrt{2}$ more precisely on the number line.

STEP 1   **Find an approximate value of $\sqrt{2}$ using a calculator.**

Enter $\sqrt{2}$ in your calculator. You will see 1.414213562 on the display. The decimal shown is only an approximate value of $\sqrt{2}$. Using this approximate value, you can identify the numbers, to the nearest tenth, that $\sqrt{2}$ lies between: $1.4 < \sqrt{2} < 1.5$.

STEP 2   **Graph the interval from 1.4 to 1.5 on a number line.**

So, $\sqrt{2}$ is located somewhere in this interval.

STEP 3   **Use the approximate value of $\sqrt{2}$ to 2 decimal places.**

The approximate value of $\sqrt{2}$ to two decimal places is 1.41. It is a rational number, because any decimal with a finite number of decimal places is a rational number. 1.41 is closer to 1.4 than to 1.5. So, $\sqrt{2}$ is located closer to 1.4 on the number line.

STEP 4   **Use 1.41 to locate $\sqrt{2}$ approximately on the number line.**

The approximate value of $\sqrt{2}$ on the number line is shown below.

Example 9 **Use rational numbers to locate a positive irrational number approximately.**

Graph $\sqrt{15}$ on the number line using rational approximations.

Solution

Because 15 is just a little less than 16, $\sqrt{15}$ should be just a little less than $\sqrt{16}$, or 4.

STEP 1  Find an approximate value of $\sqrt{15}$ by using a calculator.

$\sqrt{15} = 3.872983346\ldots$

$\sqrt{15}$ lies between 3.8 and 3.9. So, $3.8 < \sqrt{15} < 3.9$.

STEP 2 Graph the interval from 3.8 to 3.9 on a number line.

STEP 3 Use the approximate value of $\sqrt{15}$ with two decimal places.

3.87 is closer to 3.9 than to 3.8. So, $\sqrt{15}$ is located closer to 3.9.

STEP 4 Use 3.87 to locate $\sqrt{15}$ approximately on the number line.

Guided Practice

Copy and complete.

1 Graph $\sqrt{5}$ on the number line using rational approximations.

Which two whole numbers is $\sqrt{5}$ between? Justify your reasoning.
Using a calculator, $\sqrt{5} = \underline{\ ?\ }$.

Graph an interval where $\sqrt{5}$ is located.
The value of $\sqrt{5}$ with two decimal places is $\underline{\ ?\ }$.

$\underline{\ ?\ }$ is closer to $\underline{\ ?\ }$ than to $\underline{\ ?\ }$. So, $\sqrt{5}$ is located
closer to $\underline{\ ?\ }$.

By using an approximate value of $\sqrt{5}$, locate $\sqrt{5}$ on
the number line.

Example 10 **Use rational numbers to locate a negative irrational number approximately.**

Graph $-\sqrt{3}$ **on the number line using rational approximations.**

Solution

Because $1^2 = 1$ and $2^2 = 4$, $\sqrt{3}$ is between 1 and 2, and $-\sqrt{3}$ is between -1 and -2.

> **Math Note**
>
> Just as -1 means "the opposite of 1," $-\sqrt{3}$ means the opposite of $\sqrt{3}$.

STEP 1 Find an approximate value of $-\sqrt{3}$ by using a calculator.

$-\sqrt{3} = -1.732050808\ldots$

$-\sqrt{3}$ lies between -1.8 and -1.7. So, $-1.8 < -\sqrt{3} < -1.7$.

STEP 2 Graph the interval from -1.8 to -1.7 on a number line.

STEP 3 Use the approximate value of $-\sqrt{3}$ with two decimal places.
-1.73 is closer to -1.7 than to -1.8. So, $-\sqrt{3}$ is located closer to -1.73

STEP 4 Use -1.73 to locate $-\sqrt{3}$ approximately on the number line.

Guided Practice

Copy and complete.

2 Graph $-\sqrt{2}$ on the number line using rational approximations.

 Which two integers is $-\sqrt{2}$ between? Justify your reasoning.
Using a calculator, $-\sqrt{2} = \underline{\quad?\quad}$.

Graph an interval where $-\sqrt{2}$ is located.
The value of $-\sqrt{2}$ with two decimal places is $\underline{\quad?\quad}$.

$\underline{\quad?\quad}$ is closer to $\underline{\quad?\quad}$ than to $\underline{\quad?\quad}$. So, $-\sqrt{2}$ is located closer to $\underline{\quad?\quad}$.

By using an approximate value of $-\sqrt{2}$, locate $-\sqrt{2}$ on the number line.

Solve.

3 Graph $-\sqrt{7}$ on the number line using rational approximations.

Practice 1.3

Locate each positive irrational number on the number line using rational approximations. First tell which two whole numbers the square root is between.

1 $\sqrt{3}$

2 $\sqrt{7}$

3 $\sqrt{11}$

4 $\sqrt{26}$

5 $\sqrt{34}$

6 $\sqrt{48}$

Locate each negative irrational number on the number line using rational approximations. First tell which two integers the square root is between.

7 $-\sqrt{5}$

8 $-\sqrt{6}$

9 $-\sqrt{17}$

10 $-\sqrt{26}$

11 $-\sqrt{53}$

12 $-\sqrt{80}$

Use a calculator. Locate each irrational number to 3 decimal places on the number line using rational approximations.

13 $\sqrt{47}$

14 $-\sqrt{15}$

15 $\sqrt[3]{94}$

Locate each irrational number on the number line using rational approximations.

16 $\sqrt{101}$

17 $-\sqrt{132}$

18 $\sqrt{2,255}$

Solve.

19 Locate the value of the constant, π, on the number line using rational numbers.

20 3.1416 and $\dfrac{22}{7}$ are two rational approximate values of π.

    a) Graph 3.1416, $\dfrac{22}{7}$, and π on the number line.

    b) Which of the two rational approximate values is closer to π?

21 A triangle is cut from a square as shown in the diagram. The area of the square is 59 square inches. Approximate the height of the triangle to 3 decimal places.

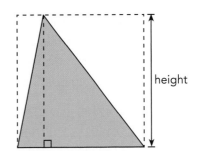
height

22 *Math Journal* When do you need to approximate an irrational number with a rational value? Explain and illustrate with an example.

1.4 Introducing the Real Number System

Lesson Objectives

- Show that irrational numbers are characterized by a nonterminating and nonrepeating decimal representation.
- Introduce the real number system and the real number line.

Vocabulary

real number

real number line

Extend the Concept of Absolute Values to All Irrational Numbers.

You have seen that irrational numbers can be located on the number line. So you can use their absolute values to indicate their distances from 0.

$$|-\sqrt{15}| = |\sqrt{15}|$$

This equation is true because $\sqrt{15}$ and $-\sqrt{15}$ are equidistant from 0.

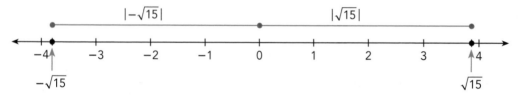

The absolute value of a rational number can be measured exactly. The absolute value of an irrational number cannot. It can only be approximated. In Example 9 on page 31, the value of $\sqrt{15}$ is only approximated by 3.87, a value correct to two decimal places.

Decimal Forms of Irrational Numbers.

You have seen that rational numbers can be written as terminating or repeating decimals. It can be shown algebraically that every repeating decimal is also a rational number. All nonterminating and nonrepeating decimals are irrational numbers.

Some decimal approximations of a few irrational numbers are shown below. For each irrational number, you can see that the digits after the decimal point do not terminate or have a repeating pattern in the first 32 digits. Mathematicians have also shown that no matter how many digits you calculate, they still will not terminate or repeat.

Examples: $\sqrt{2} = 1.41421356237309504880168887242096\ldots$
$\pi = 3.14159265358979323846264338327950\ldots$
$\varphi = 1.61803398874989484820458683436538\ldots$

Introduce the **Real Number** System and the **Real Number Line.**

You have seen that the number line is made up of rational and irrational numbers. Together, these numbers can be used to label every point on the number line.

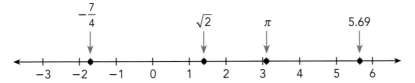

Rational and irrational numbers are collectively known as real numbers. The number line containing all real numbers is called the real number line. The diagram below summarizes the relationship among the types of numbers you have learned. You can see that a real number is either rational or irrational.

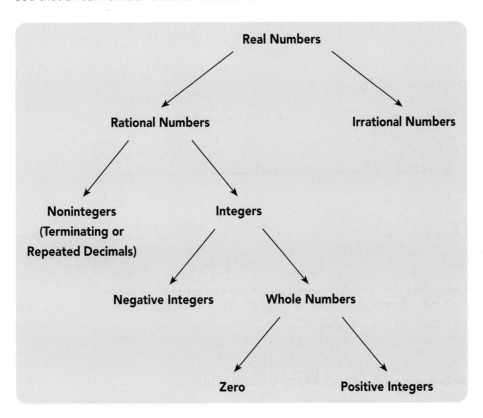

Order **Real Numbers** on the **Real Number Line.**

Real numbers appear in many forms such as fractions, negative decimals, or irrational numbers. When placing real numbers on a number line, it is easiest to compare and place them using their decimal forms.

Example 11 **Order real numbers on the real number line.**

Refer to the list of real numbers below for a) to c).

$$5\frac{11}{13}, \sqrt{30}, -\frac{84}{25}, -8.2\overline{83}, \pi^2$$

a) 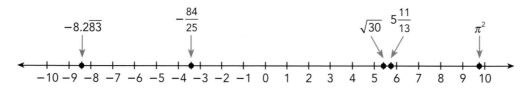 Represent each real number in decimal form with 3 decimal places.

Solution

From the calculator,

$$5\frac{11}{13} \approx 5.846, \sqrt{30} \approx 5.477, -\frac{84}{25} = -3.360$$
$$-8.2\overline{83} \approx -8.284, \pi^2 \approx 9.870$$

> **Math Note**
>
> The symbol ≈ means "approximately equal to."

b) Order the real numbers from least to greatest using the symbol <.

Solution

Ordering the real numbers from least to greatest,

$$-8.2\overline{83} < -\frac{84}{25} < \sqrt{30} < 5\frac{11}{13} < \pi^2$$

c) Locate each real number approximately on the real number line.

Solution

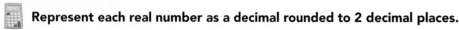

Guided Practice

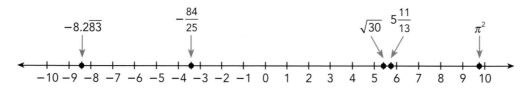 **Represent each real number as a decimal rounded to 2 decimal places.**

1 $208\frac{12}{19}$

2 $-\frac{456}{37}$

3 4π

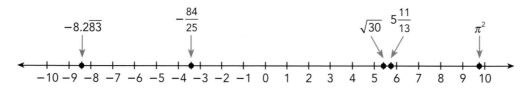 **Represent each real number below as a decimal rounded to 4 decimal places when necessary. Locate each number on a real number line.**

4 $\frac{199}{23}, -12.054, -\pi^3, \frac{\pi}{2}, \sqrt{200}, -\sqrt{289}$

Practice 1.4

 Use a calculator. Compare each pair of real numbers using either < or >.

1 $\sqrt{18}$ and $\sqrt{19}$

2 -2.23 and $-\sqrt{5}$

3 6.1640 and $\sqrt{38}$

4 -87.09812 and $-87.098126\ldots$

Use the irrational numbers below for questions 5 to 7.

$\sqrt{26}$, $\sqrt[3]{311}$, π , $\sqrt{\pi}$

5 Find the absolute value of each irrational number with 3 decimal places.

6 Graph each irrational number on a real number line.

7 Order the irrational numbers from greatest to least using the symbol >.

Use the real numbers below for questions 8 and 9.

$\sqrt{10}$, $\sqrt{100}$, $\sqrt{1,000}$, $\sqrt{10,000}$, $\sqrt[3]{27}$, $\sqrt{25}$, $\sqrt[3]{64}$, $\sqrt[3]{125}$, $-\sqrt{8}$, $\sqrt[3]{8}$

8 Copy and complete the table using the real numbers above.

Rational Numbers	Irrational Numbers
?	?

9 Order the real numbers from least to greatest using the symbol <.

Solve.

10 Using a formula from physics, a sky diver knows that she can free fall $\sqrt{875}$ seconds before opening her parachute.

  a)   About how many seconds (to the nearest 0.01 second) can she free fall?

  b)   For her next jump, she can free fall for 29.55 seconds. Does she have more time on her first or second jump? Explain using a number line.

Lesson Objectives

- Introduce rules to identify significant digits in a given number.
- Determine if trailing zeros of an integer are significant.
- Round integers and decimals to a specified number of significant digits.

Introduce Significant Digits.

Approximation is about finding a suitable decimal value close to a measured value. So, nonterminating decimals are usually approximated by rounding.

When you measure a quantity, such as length, weight, volume, or temperature, you do not always get an exact measurement. It is an approximation, rounded either to the degree of precision of your instrument, or the number of digits you want. For example, you might not be able to read the liquid level in the measuring cylinder accurately. You may not be sure whether the measurement should be 39 milliliters or 40 milliliters.

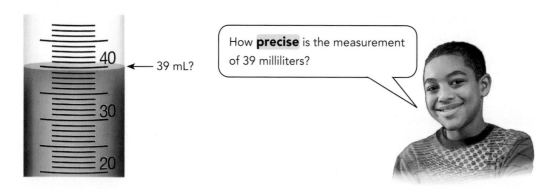

39 mL?

How **precise** is the measurement of 39 milliliters?

The word "precision" means that you will get a consistent measurement each time you measure the quantity. Look at the measurement of the liquid in the cylinder. You are certain of the digits 3 and 9 but are unsure of the quantity between 39 and 40 milliliters on the scale. You observe that the liquid level is closer to 40 milliliters, and you estimate the level to be 39.8 milliliters. Here 8 is an estimated digit.

The digits that you are certain of and the digit that you estimate are called significant digits. Significant digits are important to scientists who must keep track of how precise each measurement is in order to draw justifiable conclusions.

Apply Rules to Identify Significant Digits in a Given Number.

A given number may contain both significant and nonsignificant digits. The rules for determining which digits in a given number are significant are as follows.

RULE 1: All nonzero digits are significant.

Number	Significant Digits	Number of Significant Digits
487	4, 8, and 7	3
65.211	6, 5, 2, 1, and 1	5
12,345,678.54	1, 2, 3, 4, 5, 6, 7, 8, 5, and 4	10
9,700	9 and 7	2

RULE 2: Zeros in between nonzero digits are significant.

Number	Significant Digits	Number of Significant Digits
1,006	1, 0, 0, and 6	4
2,309,005	2, 3, 0, 9, 0, 0, and 5	7
51.0007	5, 1, 0, 0, 0, and 7	6

RULE 3: Trailing zeros in a decimal are significant.

Number	Significant Digits	Number of Significant Digits
21.30	2, 1, 3, and 0	4
798.00	7, 9, 8, 0, and 0	5
40.0	4, 0, and 0	3

> **Math Note**
>
> Trailing zeros are significant when there is a decimal point in the number.

RULE 4: Zeros on the left of the first nonzero digit are NOT significant.

Number	Significant Digits	Number of Significant Digits	Nonsignificant Digits
0.123	1, 2, and 3	3	0
0.04	4	1	The two 0s
0.060	6 and 0	2	The first two 0s
0.000385	3, 8, and 5	3	The first four 0s

RULE 5: Trailing zeros in an integer may or may not be significant due to rounding.

Number After Rounding	Rounded from 298	Significant Digits	Number of Significant Digits	Nonsignificant Digits
300	To the nearest 10	3 and 0	2	The last 0
300	To the nearest 100	3	1	The two 0s

Example 12   **Identify significant digits.**

Complete the table. List the significant digits for each number. Then, count the number of significant digits.

Number	Significant Digits	Number of Significant Digits
0.0401	?	?
3.1208	?	?
20	?	?
3.56780	?	?
70.0	?	?

Solution

Number	Significant Digits	Number of Significant Digits
0.0401	4, 0, and 1	3
3.1208	3, 1, 2, 0, and 8	5
20	2	1
3.56780	3, 5, 6, 7, 8, and 0	6
70.0	7, 0, and 0	3

Guided Practice

List the significant digits for each number. Then write the number of significant digits.

1 23,005

The two zeros are in between nonzero digits. Using **RULES 1** and **2**, __?__ are significant digits.

There are __?__ significant digits.

2 367.9410

The trailing zero in the decimal is __?__. Using **RULES 1** and **3**, __?__ are significant digits.

There are __?__ significant digits.

3 0.094

4 450.0

Round Integers and Decimals to a Given Number of Significant Digits.

When you round an integer or a decimal to a given number of significant digits, you must check that the answer has the exact number of significant digits stated. You will also apply the rules of rounding which you have already learned.

Example 13 **Round integers to the given number of significant digits.**

Round each integer to the number of significant digits given.

a) 4,321   (3 significant digits)

Solution

The fourth significant digit is 1, which is less than 5.
4,321 is closer to 4,320 than to 4,330.

So, the integer rounded to 3 significant digits is 4,320.

b) 872,090   (4 significant digits)

Solution

The fifth significant digit is 9, which is greater than 5.
872,090 is closer to 872,100 than to 872,000.

So, the integer rounded to 4 significant digits is 872,100.

c) 869,700   (2 significant digits)

Solution

The third significant digit is 9, which is greater than 5.
869,700 is closer to 870,000 than to 860,000.

So, the integer rounded to 2 significant digits is 870,000.

d) 119,800,145   (8 significant digits)

Solution

The ninth significant digit is 5.
119,800,145 is exactly halfway between 119,800,150 and 119,800,140.

So, the integer rounded to 8 significant digits is 119,800,150.

Guided Practice

Complete.

5 Round 346 to 2 significant digits.

The third significant digit is 6, which is __?__ than 5.
346 is closer to __?__ than to __?__.

So, the integer rounded to 2 significant digits is __?__.

Round each integer to the number of significant digits given.

6 16,890   (3 significant digits)

7 96,500,100   (2 significant digits)

8 8,253,611   (4 significant digits)

9 7,462   (1 significant digit)

Example 14 **Identify significant digits of a rounded integer with trailing zeros.**

Identify the significant digits in each number. Tell how many significant digits each number has.

a) The population of Medville is 84,000 and the population of Alberton is 130,000. Both numbers have been rounded to the nearest 1,000.

Solution

In this case, 84,000 has two significant digits, 8 and 4. The number 130,000 has three significant digits: 1, 3, and the first 0.

$$8\ 4,\ 0\ 0\ 0 \qquad\qquad 1\ 3\ 0,\ 0\ 0\ 0$$

significant not significant   significant not significant

b) In the recent year, there were 140,000 miles of railroad tracks and 46,900 miles of interstate highways in the United States. Both numbers have been rounded to the nearest 100.

Solution

The number 140,000 has four significant digits: 1, 4, 0, and 0. The number 46,900 has three significant digits: 4, 6, and 9.

$$1\ 4\ 0,\ 0\ 0\ 0 \qquad\qquad 4\ 6,\ 9\ 0\ 0$$

significant   not significant   significant not significant

c) The height of Mount Everest to the nearest 10 feet is 29,030 feet.

Solution

This number has 4 significant digits: 2, 9, 0, and 3. The last 0 is not a significant digit.

$$2\;9,\;0\;3\;\;0$$

significant   not significant

Guided Practice

Solve.

The integer 6,590,000 is obtained after rounding a number to the hundreds place.
The integer 200,000 is obtained after rounding another number to the ten thousands place.

10 List the significant digits in each integer.

11 State the number of significant digits in each integer.

Example 15 **Round decimals to a given number of significant digits.**

Use the rules of significant digits to round each decimal.

a) Round 0.03468 to 3 significant digits.

Solution

Using **RULE 4**, the first two zeros of 0.03468 are not significant.

Only 3 significant digits are required. The fourth significant digit is 8, which is greater than 5.

So, the decimal rounded to 3 significant digits is 0.0347.

b) Round 0.07614 to 2 significant digits.

Solution

Using **RULE 4**, the first two zeros of 0.07614 are not significant.

Only 2 significant digits are required. The third significant digit is 1, which is less than 5.

So, the decimal rounded to 2 significant digits is 0.076.

Continue on next page

c) Round 14.0408 to 5 significant digits.

Solution

Using **RULE 2**, all the digits in 14.0408 are significant.

Only 5 significant digits are required. The sixth significant digit is 8, which is greater than 5.

So, the decimal rounded to 5 significant digits is 14.041.

d) Round 28.702 to 4 significant digits.

Solution

Using **RULE 2**, all the digits in 28.702 are significant.

Only 4 significant digits are required. The fifth significant digit is 2, which is less than 5.

So, the decimal rounded to 4 significant digits is 28.70.

e) Round 119.99990 to 6 significant digits.

Solution

Using **RULE 3**, all the digits in 119.99990 are significant.

Only 6 significant digits are required. The seventh significant digit is 9, which is greater than 5.

So, the decimal rounded to 6 significant digits is 120.000.

Guided Practice

Complete.

12 Round 1,230.320 to 5 significant digits.

Using **RULE 3**, all the digits in 1,230.320 are significant. Only 5 significant digits are required. The sixth significant digit is 2, which is __?__ than 5. So, the decimal rounded to 5 significant digits is __?__.

13 Round 0.8765421 to 3 significant digits.

Using **RULES 1** and **4**, only the digits after the decimal point are significant. Only 3 significant digits are required. The fourth significant digit is 5, which is __?__ 5. So, the decimal rounded to 3 significant digits is __?__.

Round each decimal to the number of significant digits given.

14 35.0997   (4 significant digits)

15 0.008010002   (5 significant digits)

16 74.015   (3 significant digits)

Example 16 **Understand the meaning of significant digits in a real-world situation.**

Greg wants to know the circumference of the base of a cylinder. He places a paper strip around the base of the cylinder. He then measures the length of the paper strip with a ruler.

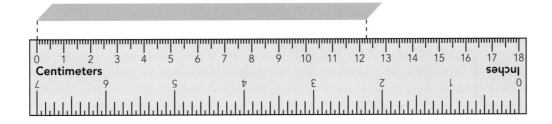

a) List the digits in the length that are certain.

Solution

From the ruler, the length seems to be between 12.2 centimeters and 12.3 centimeters. Greg knows the length is at least 12.2 centimeters. So, the digits in 12.2 are certain.

b) List the digit that is not certain, the estimated digit. Write an approximate length to two decimal places.

Solution

Greg estimates that the digit in the second decimal place is 5, since the length seems to be between 12.2 centimeters and 12.3 centimeters. The approximate length is 12.25 centimeters, where the digit 5 is estimated.

c) State the number of significant digits the length has.

Solution

The approximate length 12.25 centimeters has 4 significant digits.

Guided Practice

Solve.

17 A reading of a thermometer in Celsius is shown.

a) List the digits in the reading that are certain.

b) List the digit that is not certain, the estimated digit. Write an approximate reading with two decimal places.

c) State the number of significant digits the reading has.

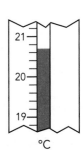

Example 17 **Use significant digits in a real-world situation.**

Gavin measured the base to be 12.64 centimeters and the height of a triangle to be 7.15 centimeters.

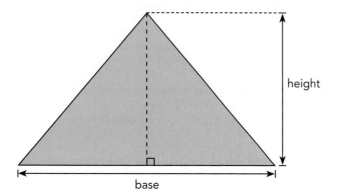

a) Calculate the area of the triangle.

Solution

Area of triangle $= \dfrac{1}{2} \cdot 12.64 \cdot 7.15$

$= 45.188 \text{ cm}^2$

The area of the triangle is 45.188 square centimeters.

b) State the area of the triangle correct to 3 significant digits.

Solution

The area of the triangle correct to 3 significant digits is 45.2 square centimeters.

Guided Practice

Solve.

18 The area of a circle is given by the expression πr^2. The radius of a circle is 4.13 centimeters.

a) Calculate the area of the circle.

b) State the area of the circle correct to 3 significant digits.

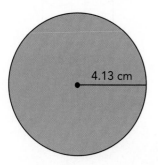

4.13 cm

Practice 1.5

List the significant digits for each number. Then count the number of significant digits.

1 0.0017

2 82.005

3 300.0

4 0.0600

5 45.13

6 2.002

Round each integer to the number of significant digits stated in the parentheses.

7 8,496 (to 2 significant digits)

8 187,204 (to 3 significant digits)

9 39,148 (to 3 significant digits)

10 40,100 (to 2 significant digits)

11 5,300,924 (to 4 significant digits)

12 111,111 (to 4 significant digits)

13 99,000 (to 3 significant digits)

14 820,635 (to 1 significant digit)

Round each decimal to the given number of significant digits.

15 0.7621 (to 1 significant digit)

16 1.0087 (to 2 significant digits)

17 45.91082 (to 5 significant digits)

18 0.08507 (to 3 significant digits)

19 520.8 (to 3 significant digits)

20 4.381 (to 2 significant digit)

Solve.

21 Round 0.09845 and 109,530 to the given number of significant digits.

a) 1 significant digit

b) 2 significant digits

c) 3 significant digits

22 The touchpad that Mike hits at the end of a swimming race is calibrated to measure the time to the nearest hundredth of a second. John claims that Mike won the race by 0.005 second. Jacqui says that Mike won by 0.05 second. Whose claim is more reliable? State your reason.

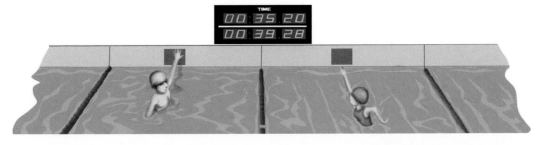

23 Table A measures 2 feet long and table B measures 2.0 feet long.

  a) How many significant digits are there in each measurement?

  b) Do you think that the measurements are rounded values? Explain your answer.

24 A bag of potatoes weighs 9.42 pounds on a weighing scale. Which of the significant digits in the scale reading is the least reliable? Explain your answer.

25 The thickness of a ream of 500 sheets of paper is 57.15 millimeters. What is the thickness of one sheet of paper correct to 2 significant digits?

26 Given a rectangle of length 36.80 centimeters and width 13.4 centimeters, find the area of the rectangle correct to 3 significant digits.

27 The temperature ranges from 43.5°C to 44.5°C in an experiment. You want to find the average of the two extreme temperature readings.

  a) What would you write as the value of the average temperature?

  b) How many significant digits will the value of the average temperature have?

28 The average distance of the Sun from the Earth is about 93,000,000 miles. How many of the trailing zeros could be significant? State your reason.

Brain @ Work

Use the decimal representation of π, 3.141592653…, to answer the following questions.

  a) Describe an irrational number, a, which is at a distance of 0.0001 unit from π.

  b) Describe another irrational number, b, which is even closer to π than the previous answer.

  c) Graph the positions of π and the two irrational numbers on a real number line.

  d) What can you conclude about the irrational numbers on the real number line?

Chapter Wrap Up

Concept Map

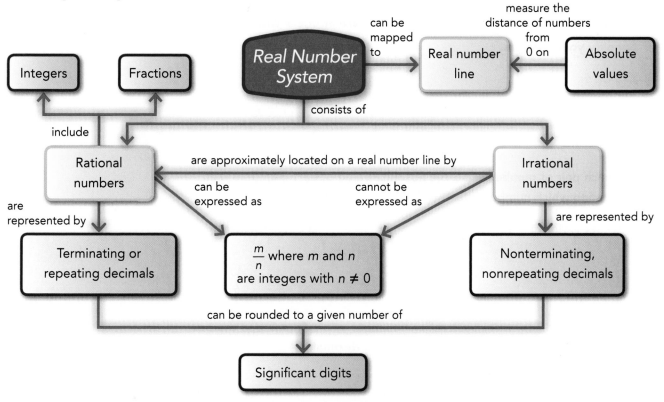

Key Concepts

▶ Rational numbers are found in every segment on the number line.

▶ Numbers that cannot be expressed in the form $\frac{m}{n}$ are called irrational numbers. These numbers fill holes in the number line.

▶ An irrational number can be located on a segment defined by two rational numbers between which the irrational number lies.
Example: $1.41 < \sqrt{2} < 1.42$.

▶ The decimal form of a rational number is either terminating or repeating. The decimal form of an irrational number is nonterminating and nonrepeating.

▶ Significant digits tell you how precise a measurement or rounded number is. The rules for identifying significant digits are on page 39.

▶ The number of significant digits of an integer depends on the place value to which a number has been rounded.

Chapter Review/Test

Concepts and Skills

Write each number in $\dfrac{m}{n}$ form where m and n are integers with $n \neq 0$.
Simplify your answers.

1 20.75

2 −0.48

3 $4\dfrac{6}{13}$

4 $-\dfrac{39}{56}$

5 1.34

6 60%

For each pair of numbers, find the absolute value of each number. Then,
determine which number is farther from 0 on the number line.

7 −16 and −18

8 $-\dfrac{15}{4}$ and $\dfrac{18}{7}$

9 2.36 and −2.7

10 $\dfrac{31}{3}$ and $\dfrac{40}{6}$

Using long division, write each rational number as a decimal. Use the bar
notation if the rational number is a repeating decimal.

11 $\dfrac{7}{56}$

12 $9\dfrac{13}{20}$

13 $\dfrac{100}{11}$

14 $-\dfrac{5}{12}$

15 $-2\dfrac{9}{55}$

16 47%

Problem Solving

Use the irrational numbers below for questions **17** to **20**.

$$\sqrt{31}, \ -\sqrt{112}, \ \sqrt[3]{142}, \ -\dfrac{1}{4}\pi^3$$

17 Using rational numbers, find a segment with a distance of not more than 0.1
to locate each irrational number approximately on the real number line.

18 Write a rational approximation of each irrational number correct to
2 decimal places.

19 Graph on a real number line the interval and the approximate location of
each irrational number.

20 Order the irrational numbers from greatest to least using the symbol >.

Use the real numbers below for questions 21 to 24.

$-12\frac{3}{8}, \frac{90}{7}, -\sqrt{49}, \sqrt{164}, -8.207$

21 Find the absolute value of each real number in decimal form, correct to three decimal places.

22 Graph each real number on a real number line.

23 Order the numbers from least to greatest using the symbol $<$.

24 *Math Journal* Explain why the product of a nonzero rational number and an irrational number is irrational.

Solve.

25 Round each number to the given number of significant digits.

Number	Number of Significant Digits	Answer
0.1350	2	?
3,004	3	?
22.5	1	?
9.03	2	?
4,567	3	?
507.01	4	?
9,820.036	5	?
6.999	3	?

26 The distance between New York City, New York, and Sydney, Australia, is about 15,989 kilometers. What is this distance when rounded to 2 significant digits?

27 A dime has a mass of 2.268 grams. Round the mass of the dime to 3 significant digits.

28 In 2009, the population of New York City was estimated at 8,391,881. Round this population estimation to the given number of significant digits.

   a) 2 significant digits

   b) 3 significant digits

   c) 4 significant digits

29 A square has an area of 72 square inches. What is the length of a side of the square correct to 2 significant digits?

CHAPTER 2

Rational Number Operations

Do you ever experience temperature extremes?

Is it hot where you live? Does it get very cold in the winter? Among the U.S. states, Hawaii has the smallest range of recorded temperatures. It has the lowest maximum temperature in the nation: 100°F. It also has the highest minimum temperature: 12°F. Some states have very drastic temperature changes. For example, Spearfish, South Dakota, experienced the fastest temperature change ever, from −4°F to 45°F in two minutes. Loma, Montana, had the greatest temperature change over a 24-hour period when the temperature rose from −54°F to 49°F. In this chapter, you will learn to add, subtract, multiply, and divide rational numbers so that you can solve problems such as finding ranges in temperature.

BIG IDEA

▶ The operations of addition, subtraction, multiplication, and division can be applied to rational numbers, including negative numbers.

Recall Prior Knowledge

Comparing numbers on a number line

A number line can be used to represent the set of real numbers.

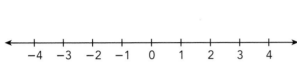

Horizontal Number Line

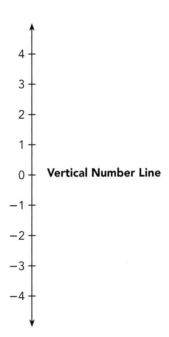

Vertical Number Line

You can use a number line to compare numbers. On a horizontal number line, the lesser number lies to the left of the greater number. On a vertical number line, the lesser number lies below the greater number.

$-1 < 4$, because -1 is to the left of 4 on the horizontal number line, and -1 is below 4 on the vertical number line.

✓ Quick Check

Complete each ? with > or <.

1 -3 ? 5

2 -7 ? -12

3 10 ? -16

4 -28 ? 0

5 $\frac{1}{2}$? $\frac{3}{4}$

6 $-1\frac{1}{4}$? $2\frac{2}{3}$

7 0.15 ? 0.13

8 -1.23 ? -1.25

Using order of operations to simplify numerical expressions

STEP 1   Perform operations within parentheses.

STEP 2   Evaluate exponents.

STEP 3   Multiply and divide from left to right.

STEP 4   Add and subtract from left to right.

Evaluate $(58 - 16) + 7 \cdot 3$.

$$(58 - 16) + 7 \cdot 3$$

=	**42** $+ 7 \cdot 3$	Perform operations in parentheses.
=	42 $+ 21$	Then multiply.
=	63	Then add.

✔ Quick Check

Evaluate each expression.

9 $75 - (18 + 2) \cdot 3$

10 $15 \cdot (40 \div 8) + 72$

Expressing improper fractions and mixed numbers in other forms

You can express improper fractions as mixed numbers.

$\dfrac{19}{4} = \dfrac{16}{4} + \dfrac{3}{4}$	Rewrite as a sum.
$= 4 + \dfrac{3}{4}$	Write the improper fraction as a whole number.
$= 4\dfrac{3}{4}$	Then write the sum as a mixed number.

You can express mixed numbers as improper fractions.

$2\dfrac{1}{5} = 2 + \dfrac{1}{5}$	Rewrite as a sum.
$= \dfrac{10}{5} + \dfrac{1}{5}$	Write the whole number as a fraction.
$= \dfrac{11}{5}$	Then write the sum as an improper fraction.

✔ Quick Check

Express each improper fraction as a mixed number.

11 $\dfrac{12}{7}$

12 $\dfrac{19}{3}$

Express each mixed number as an improper fraction.

13 $4\dfrac{3}{5}$

14 $6\dfrac{7}{9}$

Adding and subtracting fractions

You can add and subtract fractions with unlike denominators as shown.

$5\frac{2}{3} + 1\frac{3}{4} = 5 + \frac{2}{3} + 1 + \frac{3}{4}$ Rewrite the sum.

$= 6 + \frac{2}{3} + \frac{3}{4}$ Add the whole numbers.

$= 6 + \frac{2 \cdot 4}{3 \cdot 4} + \frac{3 \cdot 3}{4 \cdot 3}$ Rewrite the fractions as fractions with a common denominator.

$= 6 + \frac{8}{12} + \frac{9}{12}$ Simplify the products.

$= 6 + \frac{17}{12}$ Add the fractions.

$= 6 + 1\frac{5}{12}$ Write the improper fraction as a mixed number.

$= 7\frac{5}{12}$ Write the sum as a mixed number.

✓ Quick Check

Add or subtract. Express your answer in simplest form.

15 $\frac{2}{3} + \frac{5}{4}$ **16** $\frac{7}{8} - \frac{2}{3}$ **17** $1\frac{1}{4} + 3\frac{2}{5}$

Multiplying and dividing fractions

You can multiply two fractions as shown.

Method 1

$\frac{2}{3} \cdot \frac{3}{4} = \frac{2 \cdot 3}{3 \cdot 4}$ Multiply the numerators. Multiply the denominators.

$= \frac{6}{12}$ Simplify the product.

$= \frac{1}{2}$ Write the fraction in simplest form.

Method 2

$\frac{2}{3} \cdot \frac{3}{4} = \frac{\overset{1}{2}}{3} \cdot \frac{3}{\underset{2}{4}}$ Divide a numerator and a denominator by the common factor, 2.

$= \frac{1}{\underset{1}{3}} \cdot \frac{\overset{1}{3}}{2}$ Divide a numerator and a denominator by the common factor, 3.

$= \frac{1 \cdot 1}{1 \cdot 2}$ Multiply the numerators. Multiply the denominators.

$= \frac{1}{2}$ Simplify the product.

Continue on next page

You can divide a fraction by another fraction as shown.

$$\frac{3}{4} \div \frac{3}{8} = \frac{3}{4} \cdot \frac{8}{3}$$ Rewrite using the reciprocal of the divisor.

$$= \frac{3}{{}_1\cancel{4}} \cdot \frac{\cancel{8}^{\,2}}{3}$$ Divide a numerator and a denominator by the common factor, 4.

$$= \frac{\cancel{3}^{\,1}}{1} \cdot \frac{2}{{}_1\cancel{3}}$$ Divide a numerator and a denominator by the common factor, 3.

$$= \frac{1 \cdot 2}{1 \cdot 1}$$ Multiply the numerators. Multiply the denominators.

$$= 2$$ Simplify the product.

✓ Quick Check

Multiply or divide. Express your answer in simplest form.

18 $\dfrac{2}{9} \cdot \dfrac{3}{4}$

19 $1\dfrac{2}{3} \cdot \dfrac{1}{5}$

20 $\dfrac{5}{8} \div \dfrac{21}{4}$

21 $\dfrac{3}{4} \div 1\dfrac{1}{2}$

Multiplying and dividing decimals

You ignore the decimal as you multiply. Then you decide where to place the decimal point in the product.

$$
\begin{array}{r}
\overset{1}{}3.6\,2 \\
\times \quad\ 0.3 \\
\hline
1\,0\,8\,6 \\
0\,0\,0 \\
\hline
1.0\,8\,6
\end{array}
$$

← 2 decimal places
← + 1 decimal place

← 3 decimal places

You can express the division expression as a fraction when you divide by a decimal. Then multiply the dividend and divisor by the same power of 10.

$$17.8 \div 0.25 = \frac{17.8}{0.25}$$ Write division as a fraction.

$$= \frac{17.8 \cdot 100}{0.25 \cdot 100}$$ Multiply both the numerator and the denominator by 100 to make the denominator a whole number.

$$= \frac{1,780}{25}$$ Simplify the product.

$$= 71.2$$ Divide as with whole numbers.

✓ Quick Check

Multiply or divide.

22 $15.8 \cdot 2.7$

23 $8.82 \div 0.6$

Using percents

Percents compare one quantity to 100. The symbol for percent is written as %.

Find 10% of 20.

$$\frac{10}{100} \cdot 20 = 2$$

· ·

Sally had 50 rings to sell. By the end of one week, there were only 30 rings left.

a) Find the decrease in the number of rings by the end of one week.

Decrease in number of rings by the end of one week:
50 − 30 = 20

The decrease in the number of rings by the end of one week is 20.

b) Find the percent decrease in the number of rings by the end of one week.

Percent decrease:
$$\frac{20}{50} \cdot 100\% = 40\%$$

The percent decrease in the number of rings by the end of one week is 40%.

✓ Quick Check

Solve each percent problem.

24 25% of $420

25 115 is what percent of 345?

26 24 boys out of 64 classmates is what percent?

Solve.

27 A seedling that Jeffrey planted in 2009 was 50 centimeters tall. In 2010, it was 120 centimeters tall.

a) Find the increase in the height of the seedling Jeffrey planted.

b) Find the percent increase in the height of the seedling.

2.1 Adding Integers

Lesson Objectives

- Add integers with the same sign.
- Add integers to their opposites.
- Add integers with different signs.

Vocabulary

additive inverse

zero pair

Add Integers with the Same Sign.

You can show how to add two positive integers by moving to the right, or in the positive direction, on a number line.

Evaluate 2 + 3.

2 + 3 is a jump of **2 to the right of 0** followed by a jump of **3 to the right**.

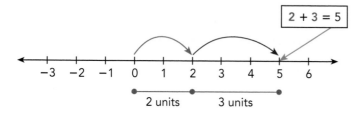

Distance of the sum from 0: $|2| + |3| = 5$

2 + 3 = 5

OR

You can also start at the first number of the sum, 2. Then you continue with a jump of **3 to the right** of the starting point, 2.

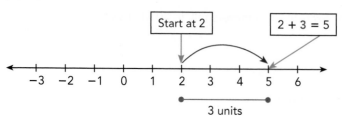

2 + 3 = 5

You have learned the commutative property of addition. Using the commutative property of addition, 2 + 3 gives the same answer as 3 + 2. So, 3 + 2 = 5.

You can use counters to model the adding of two positive integers, 2 + 3.

 represents +1.

2
+
3

Math Note

Commutative Property of Addition: Two or more numbers can be added in any order.

On a horizontal number line, the lesser number lies to the left of the greater number. On a vertical number line, the lesser number lies below the greater number.

For example, $-3 < 0$ because -3 is **to the left of 0** or **below 0**. You can locate -3 as a jump of 3 **to the left**, **below**, or in the **negative direction** of 0.

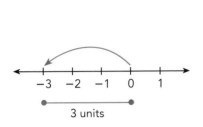

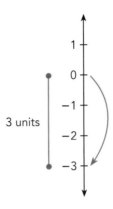

So, you can model adding two negative numbers by moving to the left, in the negative direction, on a horizontal number line, or down, in the negative direction, on a vertical number line.

Evaluate $-1 + (-3)$.

Method 1

Use a number line to model the sum of two negative integers.

Start at 0 and move to -1, which is **1 to the left of 0**.
Continue by adding -3 with a jump of **3 to the left** of -1.

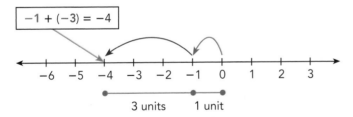

You can use counters to model the adding of two negative integers, $-1 + (-3)$.

⬤ represents -1.

⬤ -1
⬤⬤⬤ $+$
       -3

Using the commutative property of addition, $-1 + (-3)$ gives the same answer as $-3 + (-1)$.

Distance of sum from 0: $|-1| + |-3| = 1 + 3 = 4$

You move in a negative direction, so the sum is negative.

$-1 + (-3) = -4$

OR

You can also start at -1. Then add -3, a jump of **3 to the left**.

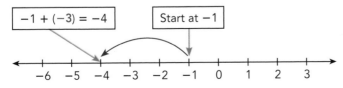

You can see that $-1 + (-3)$ is -4.

Continue on next page

Method 2

Use absolute values to find the sum of two negative integers.

First find the sum of the absolute values of the two negative integers.

$$|-1| = 1$$ Write the absolute value of each integer.
$$|-3| = 3$$

$$|-1| + |-3| = 1 + 3$$ Add the absolute values.
$$ = 4$$ This is the distance of the sum from 0.

Then decide whether this sum is negative or positive.

$$-1 + (-3) = -4$$ Use the common sign, a negative sign, for the sum.

You can see that the sum of negative integers is always negative, and the sum of positive integers is always positive.

Using a number line:
When you use a number line to add integers with the same sign,
- you move to the right, or in the positive direction, on the number line when you add a positive integer.
- you move to the left, or in the negative direction, on the number line when you add a negative integer.

Using absolute values:
When you use absolute values to add two integers with the same sign, you find the sum of their absolute values and then use the common sign.

The sum of positive integers is positive.
The sum of negative integers is negative.

Example 1 **Add two negative integers.**

Evaluate −2 + (−4).

Solution

Method 1

Use a number line to model the sum of two negative integers.

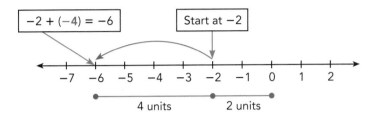

Start at −2. Then continue by adding −4, a jump of 4 to the left to reach −6.

−2 + (−4) = −6

Method 2

Use absolute values to find the sum of two negative integers.

First find the distance of the sum from 0. Then decide if the sum is positive or negative.

$|-2| = 2$ Write the absolute value of each integer.
$|-4| = 4$

$|-2| + |-4| = 2 + 4$ Add the absolute values.
$ = 6$ Simplify.

$-2 + (-4) = -6$ Use the common sign, a negative sign, for the sum.

Guided Practice

Copy and complete.

1 Evaluate $-3 + (-2)$.

Method 1

Use a number line to model the sum of two negative integers.

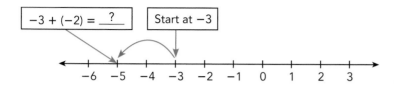

$$-3 + (-2) = \underline{}$$

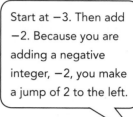

Start at -3. Then add -2. Because you are adding a negative integer, -2, you make a jump of 2 to the left.

Method 2

Use absolute values to find the sum of two negative integers.

$$|-3| = \underline{}$$
$$|-2| = \underline{}$$
Write the absolute value of each integer.

$$|-3| + |-2| = \underline{} + \underline{}$$
Add the absolute values.
$$= \underline{}$$
Simplify.

$$-3 + (-2) = \underline{}$$
Use the common sign, a $\underline{}$ sign, for the sum.

2 Evaluate $-15 + (-7)$.

Method 1

Use a number line to model the sum of two negative integers.

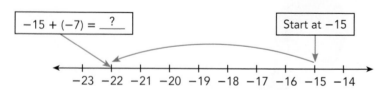

$$-15 + (-7) = \underline{}$$

Method 2

Use absolute values to find the sum of two negative integers.

$$|-15| = \underline{}$$
$$|-7| = \underline{}$$

$$|-15| + |-7| = \underline{} + \underline{}$$
$$= \underline{}$$

$$-15 + (-7) = \underline{}$$

Add Integers to Their Opposites.

You have learned that each integer has an opposite. For example, the opposite of 2 is −2.

On a horizontal number line, you move to the right, or the positive direction, when you add a positive integer. You move to the left, or the negative direction, when you add a negative integer. So, you can find the sum of an integer and its opposite using movement along a number line.

Evaluate 2 + (−2).

Use a number line to model the sum of integers with different signs.

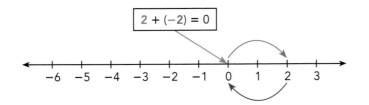

Start at 0 and move 2 to the right of 0. Then add −2, a jump of 2 to the left.

2 + (−2) = 0

You can see that the sum of an integer and its opposite is zero.

2 and −2 are called **additive inverses** because 2 and its opposite −2 have a sum of zero. They have two **zero pairs**.

 represents +1 and represents −1.

You can use counters to model 2 + (−2).

2
+
−2

Remove two zero pairs.

Using the commutative property of addition, 2 + (−2) and −2 + 2 give the same answer.

Think Math

Write a rule for the sum of a number and its additive inverse. How are the absolute values of a number and its additive inverse related?

Continue on next page

There are real-world situations in which opposite quantities combine to make zero.

Examples of real-world situations involving opposite quantities:

a) A hydrogen atom has a charge of zero, because it contains one positively charged proton and one negatively charged electron.

b) You put a stone that weighs 3 ounces on a weighing scale and then remove it. The overall change in weight on the scale is 0 ounces.

c) You heat up an oven, then turn it off so that it returns to room temperature. The overall change in temperature is 0°C.

d) You move 50 feet up in an elevator and move 50 feet back down. Overall, your change in position is 0 feet.

Example 2 Add integers and their opposites.

Evaluate 5 + (−5).

Solution

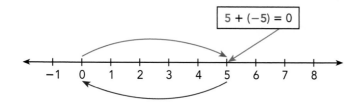

$5 + (−5) = 0$

Start at 0 and move 5 to the right of 0. Then add −5, a jump of 5 to the left.

$5 + (−5) = 0$

5
+
−5

Remove five zero pairs.

Guided Practice

Evaluate each sum.

3 9 + (−9)

4 −21 + 21

Hands-On Activity

Materials:
- counters

FIND THE SUM OF INTEGERS WITH DIFFERENT SIGNS

Work in pairs.

⬤ represents +1.

⬤ represents −1.

⬤ + ⬤ represent a zero pair.

A zero pair has a value of zero.

$(+1) + (−1) = (−1) + (+1)$
$\qquad\qquad = 0$

Removing a zero pair does not change the value of an expression. For example:

$(+1) + (−1) + 2 = 2$ because
$(+1) + (−1) + 2 = 0 + 2$
$\qquad\qquad\qquad = 2$

STEP 1 Use counters to model and find the sum of two integers with different signs.

a) Evaluate $3 + (−2)$.

$3 \qquad + \qquad (−2) \qquad = \qquad \underline{\;\;?\;\;}$

⬤⬤⬤ + ⬤⬤ → [⬤⬤⬤ / ⬤⬤]

Start with 3 ⬤ add 2 ⬤ becomes 1 ⬤ after removing two zero pairs.

b) Evaluate $(−3) + 2$.

$(−3) \qquad + \qquad 2 \qquad = \qquad \underline{\;\;?\;\;}$

⬤⬤⬤ + ⬤⬤ → [⬤⬤⬤ / ⬤⬤]

Start with 3 ⬤ add 2 ⬤ becomes 1 ⬤ after removing two zero pairs.

STEP 2 Use counters to model and find each sum.

a) $7 + (−2)$ and $(−7) + 2$

b) $(−8) + 5$ and $8 + (−5)$

 Math Journal Explain how to add two integers with different signs. How are the absolute values of the addends related to the sum?

Add Integers with Different Signs.

Suppose the temperature was −8°F at 7 A.M. Five hours later, the temperature had risen 10°F. Find the new temperature.

Because the temperature rose, you can find the new temperature by finding the sum −8 + 10.

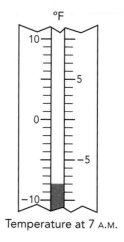

Temperature at 7 A.M.

Method 1

Use a number line to model the sum of integers with different signs.

−8 is a jump of 8 to the left of 0, because you add a negative integer.

Then continue with a jump of 10 to the right, because you add a positive integer.

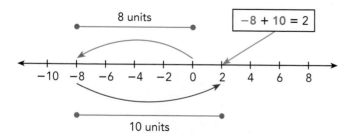

Distance of sum from 0: $|10| − |−8| = 2$

$−8 + 10 = −8 + 8 + 2$

$ = \quad 0 \quad + 2$

$ = 2$

You can think of −8 + 10 as −8 + 8 + 2. Then because −8 and 8 are opposites, their sum is 0.
So, −8 + 10 = −8 + 8 + 2 = 0 + 2.

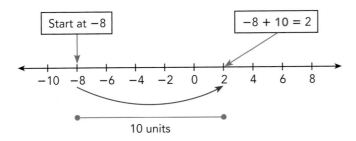

−8 + 10

Remove eight zero pairs.

OR

You can start at −8. Then continue by adding 10 with a jump of **10 to the right.**

Start at −8

−8 + 10 = 2

10 units

−8 + 10 = 2

The new temperature is 2°F.

Method 2

Use absolute values to find the sum of integers with different signs.

First find the distance of the sum from 0.

$$|-8| = 8$$ Write the absolute value of each integer.
$$|10| = 10$$

$$|10| - |-8| = 10 - 8$$ Subtract the lesser absolute value from the greater one.
$$= 2$$ Simplify.

Then use the sign of the addend with the greater absolute value.

$$-8 + 10 = 2$$ The sum is positive, because 10 has a greater absolute value.

The new temperature is 2°F.

When you use absolute values to add two integers with different signs, you subtract the lesser absolute value from the greater one, and use the sign of the integer with the greater absolute value.

Example 3 **Add two integers with different signs.**

Evaluate −12 + 6.

Solution

Method 1

Use a number line to model the sum of integers with different signs.

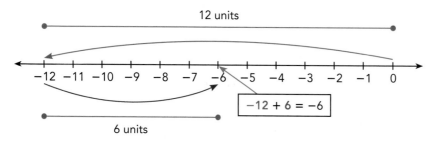

Start at 0 and move 12 to the left of 0. Then add 6, a jump of 6 to the right.

OR

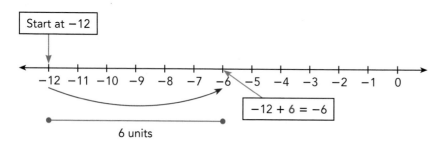

Start at −12. Then add 6, a jump of 6 to the right.

−12 + 6 = −6

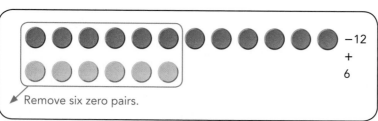

Remove six zero pairs.

Method 2

Use absolute values to find the sum of integers with different signs.

$|-12| = 12$ Write the absolute value of each integer.
$|6| = 6$

$|-12| - |6| = 12 - 6$ Subtract the lesser absolute value from the greater one.
$= 6$ Simplify.

$-12 + 6 = -6$ Use a negative sign, because −12 has a greater absolute value.

Guided Practice

Evaluate each sum.

5 −10 + 3

6 −9 + 2

7 11 + (−23)

Example 4 **Add more than two integers with different signs.**

Evaluate −9 + 2 + (−3).

Solution

Method 1

Use a number line to model the sum of integers with different signs.

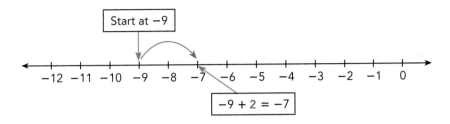

Start at −9. Then add 2, a jump of 2 to the right of 9.

$-9 + 2 = -7$

> You move to the right when adding a positive integer and move to the left when adding a negative integer.

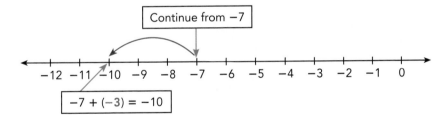

Continue by adding −3, a jump of 3 to the left of −7.

$-7 + (-3) = -10$

So, $-9 + 2 + (-3) = -7 + (-3)$
$\qquad\qquad\qquad = -10$

> When you add more than two integers, you add any two integers at a time until you arrive at an answer. This is the associative property of addition.
>
> You can also add 2 and −3 first. Then continue to add −9. So, $-9 + 2 + (-3) = -9 + (-1)$
> $\qquad\qquad\qquad\qquad\qquad = -10$

Continue on next page

Method 2

Use absolute values to find the sum of integers with different signs.
First group integers with the same sign.

$-9 + 2 + (-3) = -9 + (-3) + 2$ Commutative property of addition

Next add -9 and -3.

> Moving from left to right, you can add any two integers that have the same sign. Add their absolute values and use the sign of the two integers for the sum.

$|-9| = 9$ Write the absolute value of each integer.
$|-3| = 3$

$|-9| + |-3| = 9 + 3$ Add the absolute values.
$ = 12$ Simplify.

$-9 + (-3) = -12$ Use the common sign, a negative sign, for the sum.

Then continue by adding 2 to -12.

> You subtract the absolute values because the integers have different signs. Then use the sign of the greater absolute for the sum.

$|-12| = 12$ Write the absolute value of each integer.
$|2| = 2$

$|-12| - |2| = 12 - 2$ Subtract the lesser absolute value from the greater one.
$ = 10$ Simplify.

$-12 + 2 = -10$ Use a negative sign, because -12 has a greater absolute value.

So, $-9 + 2 + (-3) = -9 + (-3) + 2$
$ = -12 + 2$
$ = -10$

Guided Practice

Evaluate each sum.

8 $10 + (-3) + 6$

9 $-7 + (-23) + 15$

Example 5 **Add integers with different signs in a real-world situation.**

The water level in a large tank rises 5 feet, falls 9 feet, and then rises 3 feet. Overall, how far does the water level rise or fall?

Solution

Think of the water level rising as adding a positive integer and the water level falling as adding a negative integer.

So, the verbal description can be translated as $5 + (-9) + 3$.

Method 1

Use a number line to model the sum of integers with different signs.

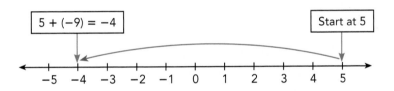

$5 + (-9) = -4$

Start at 5. Then add -9, a jump of 9 to the left of 5.

$5 + (-9) = -4$

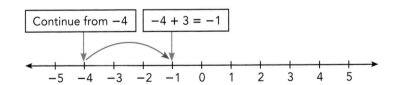

$-4 + 3 = -1$

Continue from -4 by adding 3, a jump of 3 to the right of -4.

$-4 + 3 = -1$

So, $5 + (-9) + 3 = -4 + 3$
$\qquad\qquad\qquad = -1$

Overall, the water level falls 1 foot.

Continue on next page

Method 2

Use absolute values to evaluate 5 + (−9) + 3.

> You perform the additions from left to right. First add 5 and (−9). Then continue by adding 3.

First add 5 and −9.

$\|5\| = 5$	Write the absolute value of each integer.
$\|-9\| = 9$	

$\|-9\| - \|5\| = 9 - 5$	Subtract the lesser absolute value from the greater one.
$= 4$	

$5 + (-9) = -4$	Use a negative sign, because −9 has a greater absolute value.

Then add −4 and 3.

$\|-4\| = 4$	Write the absolute value of each integer.
$\|3\| = 3$	

$\|-4\| - \|3\| = 4 - 3$	Subtract the lesser absolute value from the greater one.
$= 1$	Simplify.

$-4 + 3 = -1$	Use a negative sign, because −4 has a greater absolute value.

So, $5 + (-9) + 3 = -4 + 3$
$= -1$

Overall, the water level falls 1 foot.

Math Note

You can also use the commutative property of addition to group 5 and 3 together. Then use the associate property of addition to add 5 and 3 first.

$5 + (-9) + 3 = 5 + 3 + (-9)$
$= 8 + (-9)$
$= -1$

Guided Practice

Solve.

10 A submarine is at 400 feet below sea level. If it ascends 150 feet and then descends 320 feet, how far is it above or below sea level?

> You can think of the submarine ascending as an adding a positive integer, and descending as adding a negative integer.
>
> So, the verbal description can be translated as −400 + 150 + (−320).

Practice 2.1

Evaluate each sum using a number line.

1 −3 + (−9)

2 −8 + (−4)

3 7 + (−7)

4 −9 + 9

5 −10 + 6

6 −17 + 9

Evaluate each sum using the absolute values.

7 −23 + (−9)

8 −11 + (−34)

9 −15 + (−7)

10 12 + (−18)

11 −40 + 26

12 −75 + 19

Evaluate each sum.

13 −8 + 4 + 5

14 5 + (−10) + (−6)

15 −6 + (−8) + (−12)

16 −13 + (−17) + 7

17 −20 + 16 + (−7)

18 −11 + (−8) + 14

Solve. Show your work.

19 The temperature is originally recorded as −4°F. What will the temperature be if the temperature rises 20°F?

20 Mr. Lawson parked his car in a parking garage 33 feet below street level. He then got in an elevator and went up 88 feet to his office. How far above street level is his office?

21 A hiker starts hiking in Death Valley at an elevation of 143 feet below sea level. He climbs up 400 feet in elevation. What is his new elevation relative to sea level?

22 Elizabeth was playing a board game with her friends. On her first turn, she moved 6 spaces forward. On her second turn, she moved another 5 spaces forward. On her third turn, she moved 4 spaces backward. How many spaces forward or backward from her starting point was she after her third turn?

23 In the U.S. Open Golf Tournament, each qualifying golfer plays four rounds. The score for a round is recorded as positive (over par) or negative (under par). If a golfer scores −4, 6, 3, and −2 in the four rounds, what is the golfer's total score for the tournament?

24 *Math Journal* In a game, all scores with even numbers are recorded as positive numbers. Odd numbers are recorded as negative numbers. Explain how to find David's total score in this game if his individual scores during the game are 9, 12, 7, 18, and 19.

? ft above street level

Street level

33 ft below street level

Subtracting Integers

Lesson Objectives

- Subtract integers by adding their opposites.
- Find the distance between two integers on a number line.

 Hands-On Activity

Materials:
- counters

SUBTRACT INTEGERS

Work in pairs.

 represents +1.

represents −1.

+ represent a zero pair.

A zero pair can be added to any expression without changing its value. It is the same thing as adding 0 to a number.

Sometimes, you add zero pairs in order to subtract.

STEP 1 Use counters to model and complete the subtraction of a positive integer.

a) Evaluate 5 − (+2) and compare with 5 + (−2).

$$5 - (+2) \qquad = \qquad \underline{\ ?\ }$$

Start with 5 becomes ?

and remove 2

$$5 \qquad + \qquad (-2) \qquad = \qquad \underline{\ ?\ }$$

Start with 5 add 2 becomes ? after removing

two zero pairs

b) Evaluate −5 − (+2) and compare with −5 + (−2).

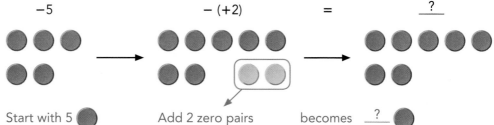

−5   − (+2)   =   <u>?</u>

Start with 5 ●   Add 2 zero pairs so that you can remove 2 ●   becomes <u>?</u> ●

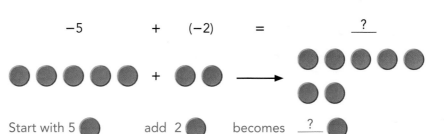

−5   +   (−2)   =   <u>?</u>

Start with 5 ●   add 2 ●   becomes <u>?</u> ●

STEP 2 Use counters to evaluate each expression.

a) 6 − 4 and 6 + (−4)   **b)** −6 − 4 and −6 + (−4)

STEP 3 Use counters to model and complete the subtraction of a negative integer.

a) Evaluate 5 − (−2) and compare with 5 + 2.

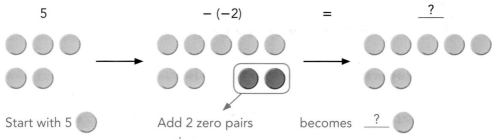

5   − (−2)   =   <u>?</u>

Start with 5 ●   Add 2 zero pairs so that you can remove 2 ●   becomes <u>?</u> ●

5   +   2   =   <u>?</u>

Start with 5 ●   add 2 ●   becomes <u>?</u> ●

Continue on next page

b) Find $-5 - (-2)$ and compare with $-5 + 2$.

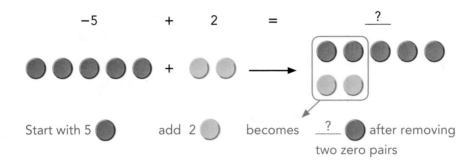

$$-5 - (-2) \qquad = \qquad \underline{\quad ? \quad}$$

Start with 5 ● becomes $\underline{\quad ? \quad}$ ●

and remove 2 ●

$$-5 \qquad + \qquad 2 \qquad = \qquad \underline{\quad ? \quad}$$

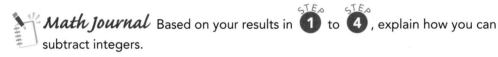

Start with 5 ●   add 2 ○   becomes $\underline{\quad ? \quad}$ ● after removing

two zero pairs

STEP 4 Use counters to evaluate each expression.

a) $7 - (-3)$ and $7 + 3$ **b)** $-7 - (-3)$ and $-7 + 3$

Math Journal Based on your results in **STEP 1** to **STEP 4**, explain how you can subtract integers.

Subtract Integers by Adding Their Opposites.

Addition and subtraction are inverse operations. So when you subtract an integer, you are adding its additive inverse or opposite.

For example, Michael scored 3 points in a game show for the first round and lost 5 points for the second round.

You can translate the verbal description into the numerical expression $3 - 5$. Instead of subtracting 5 from 3, you can add its opposite, which is -5.

$$3 - 5 = 3 + \underbrace{(-5)}_{\text{opposite of 5}}$$

$$= -2$$

So, $3 - 5$ can be rewritten as $3 + (-5)$. You can use either $3 - 5$ or $3 + (-5)$ to find Michael's final score, -2.

Using a number line,

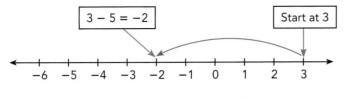

$3 - 5 = -2$ Start at 3

Start at 3. Then add -5, a jump of 5 to the left of 3.

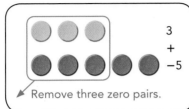

Remove three zero pairs.

$$3$$
$$+$$
$$-5$$

Michael's final score is -2 points.

You can use opposites to subtract negative integers.

For example, find $3 - (-5)$.

You know that the opposite of -5 is 5. Instead of subtracting -5 from 3, you can add its opposite, which is 5.

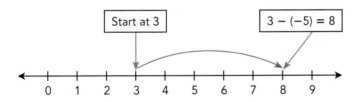

Start at 3 $3 - (-5) = 8$

$3 - (-5) = 3 + 5$
$\qquad\qquad\underbrace{}$
$\qquad\qquad$ opposite of -5

$\quad = 8$

So, $3 - (-5)$ can be rewritten as $3 + 5$ to give an answer of 8.

Instead of subtracting an integer, you can add its additive inverse or opposite as follows:
- Subtracting a positive integer b is the same as adding its opposite, $-b$.
  So, $a - b = a + (-b)$
- Subtracting a negative integer $-b$ is the same as adding its opposite, b.
  So, $a - (-b) = a + b$

To subtract integers on a horizontal number line,
- you move to the left when you subtract a positive integer.
- you move to the right when you subtract a negative integer.

Example 6 **Subtract positive integers.**

Evaluate each expression.

a) 10 − 25

Solution

You can change a subtraction expression to an addition expression using the additive inverse. Then you evaluate it using a number line, absolute values, or counters.

10 − 25 = 10 + (−25)   Rewrite subtraction as adding the opposite.

Using absolute values,

|−25| − |10| = 25 − 10   Subtract the absolute values, because the addends have different signs.

          = 15   Simplify.

10 − 25 = 10 + (−25)
        = −15   Use a negative sign, because −25 has a greater absolute value.

b) A diver went 24 feet below the surface of the ocean, and then 47 feet farther down. What is the diver's new position relative to the surface?

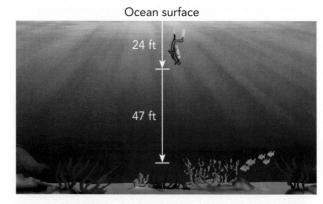

Ocean surface

24 ft

47 ft

Solution

−24 − 47 = −24 + (−47)   Rewrite subtraction as adding the opposite.

Using absolute values,

|−24| + |−47| = 24 + 47   Add the absolute values, because the addends have the same sign.

          = 71   Simplify.

−24 − 47 = −24 + (−47)
        = −71   Use the common sign, a negative sign, for the sum.

The diver's new position is 71 feet below the surface of the ocean.

Guided Practice

Copy and complete.

1 21 − 30

$$21 - 30 = 21 + \underline{\ ?\ }$$ Rewrite subtraction as adding the opposite.

Using absolute values,

$$|-30| - |21| = 30 - 21$$ Subtract the absolute values, because the addends have different signs.

$$= \underline{\ ?\ }$$ Simplify.

$$21 - 30 = 21 + \underline{\ ?\ }$$

$$= \underline{\ ?\ }$$ Use a negative sign, because −30 has a greater absolute value.

2 A fishing boat drags its net 35 feet below the ocean's surface. Then it lowers the net by an additional 12 feet. Find the new position relative to the surface of the fishing net.

$$-35 - \underline{\ ?\ } = -35 + \underline{\ ?\ }$$ Rewrite subtraction as adding the opposite.

Using absolute values,

$$\underline{\ ?\ } + \underline{\ ?\ } = \underline{\ ?\ }$$ Add the absolute values because the addends have the same sign.

$$-35 - \underline{\ ?\ } = -35 + \underline{\ ?\ }$$ Use the common sign, a negative sign, for the sum.

$$= \underline{\ ?\ }$$ Simplify.

The fishing net's new position is __?__ feet below the surface of the ocean.

Solve.

3 A submarine was at 1,200 feet below sea level. It then moved to 1,683 feet below sea level. How many feet did the submarine descend?

Sea level

1,200 ft below sea level

1,683 ft below sea level

Example 7 **Subtract negative integers.**

Evaluate each expression.

a)   32 − (−8)

Solution

8 is the additive inverse of –8.

32 − (−8) = 32 + 8   Rewrite subtraction as adding the opposite.
        = 40   Add.

b)   −15 − (−21)

Solution

  −15 − (−21) = −15 + 21   Rewrite subtraction as adding the opposite.

 Using absolute values,

|−21| − |−15| = 21 − 15   Subtract the absolute values.
          = 6   Simplify.

  −15 − (−21) = −15 + 21
          = 6   Use a positive sign, because 21 has a greater absolute value.

c)   −11 − (−5) − (−20)

Solution

5 is the additive inverse of −5, and 20 is the additive inverse of −20.

−11 − (−5) − (−20) = −11 + 5 + 20   Rewrite subtraction as adding the opposite.
            = −6 + 20   Add from left to right.
            = 14   Simplify.

Guided Practice

Copy and complete.

4 $17 - (-4)$

$17 - (-4) = 17 + \underline{\ ?\ }$ Rewrite subtraction as adding the opposite.
$\qquad\qquad\ \ = \underline{\ ?\ }$ Add.

Evaluate each expression.

5 $-25 - (-9)$

6 $-19 - (-7) - (-6)$

Find the Distance Between Two Integers on a Number Line.

You can find the distance between two integers. First plot the two integers on a number line. Then count the units between them.

For example, find the distance between 3 and 7.

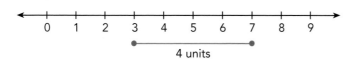

4 units

First plot the integers 3 and 7 on the number line. Then count the units from 3 to 7 or from 7 to 3.

Because you are finding the distance, and distance is always positive, it does not matter which integer you start counting from.

You can use absolute value to find the distance between two integers. It does not matter in which order you count, from 3 to 7 or from 7 to 3.

The distance between 3 and 7 can be represented as $|7 - 3| = |3 - 7| = 4$ units.

> For any two integers a and b, the distance between a and b is the absolute value of their difference, $|a - b|$. It does not matter which integer you decide to call a and which you decide to call b.

Example 8 | Find distance between two integers.

Find the distance between two integers.

a) Find the distance between 2 and −6.

Solution

Method 1

Use a number line to plot the points and count the units.

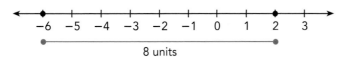

8 units

The distance between 2 and −6 is 8 units.

Method 2

Use absolute value to find the distance between integers with different signs.

Distance between 2 and −6:

$$|2 - (-6)| = |2 + 6|$$ Rewrite subtraction as adding the opposite.
$$= 8$$ Add.

The distance between 2 and −6 is 8 units.

You can also find the distance between 2 and −6 using $|-6 - 2|$.

b) Determine the difference in elevation between Death Valley, California, 282 feet below sea level, and the summit of California's Mount Davidson, 928 feet above sea level.

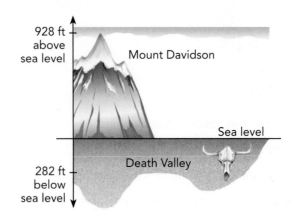

Solution

Elevation of Death Valley: −282 ft
Elevation of Mount Davidson: 928 ft
Difference between the two elevations:

$$|928 - (-282)| = |928 + 282|$$ Rewrite subtraction as adding the opposite.
$$= 1,210 \text{ ft}$$ Add.

The difference in elevation is 1,210 feet.

Guided Practice

Copy and complete.

7 Find the distance between 3 and −2.

Method 1

Use a number line to plot the points and count the units.

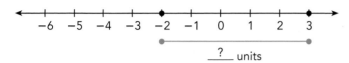

_____?_____ units

The distance between 3 and −2 is __?__ units.

Method 2

Use absolute value to find the distance between integers with opposite signs.

Distance between 3 and −2:

$|3 - \underline{}| = |\underline{}|$ Rewrite subtraction as adding the opposite.
$= \underline{}$ units   Add.

The distance between 3 and −2 is __?__ units.

8 A particular town has an elevation of 8 feet below sea level. Another town on top of a mountain has an elevation of 2,421 feet above sea level. What is the difference in the elevations of the two towns?

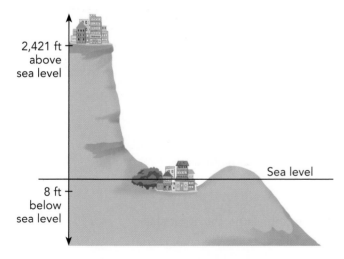

Elevation of town below sea level: __?__ ft
Elevation of town on top of mountain: __?__ ft

Difference between the two elevations:

$|\underline{} - \underline{}| = |\underline{}|$ Rewrite subtraction as adding the opposite.
$= \underline{}$ ft   Add.

The difference in the elevations of the two towns is __?__ feet.

Practice 2.2

Evaluate each expression.

1 7 − 18

2 20 − 30

3 53 − 109

4 45 − (−16)

5 −7 − (−5)

6 −94 − (−68)

7 −6 − 8 − 12

8 −23 − 17 − 7

9 −8 − (−4) − 5

10 −5 − (−10) − 6

11 −20 − (−16) − (−7)

12 −11 − (−8) − (−14)

Evaluate the distance between each pair of integers.

13 4 and 20

14 16 and 52

15 −15 and 36

16 −7 and 41

17 −28 and −3

18 −19 and −8

Solve. Show your work.

19 Rick leaves to go skiing in Burlington, Vermont, when the temperature is −4°C. The temperature drops 10°C when a cold front moves in. What is the new temperature?

20 The water level of the Dead Sea dropped from 390 meters below sea level in 1930 to 423 meters below sea level in 2010. By how much did the water level drop from 1930 to 2010?

21 *Math Journal* Florence has only $420 in her bank account. Describe how to find the amount in her account after she writes a check for $590.

22 *Math Journal* Darren has trouble simplifying 15 − (−36). Write an explanation to help him.

23 The wind-chill temperature at 10 P.M. was −8°F. One hour later, the wind-chill temperature had fallen to −28°F. Write an expression to represent the change in temperature. Then find the change in temperature.

24 The lowest point in North America is in Death Valley, California, which is 86 meters below sea level at its lowest point. The highest point is Denali, a mountain in Alaska, with an elevation of 6,198 meters above sea level. What is the difference in their elevations?

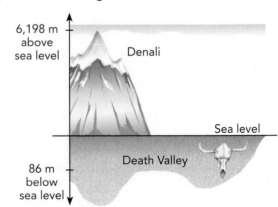

25 Belinda has two freezers. Freezer A keeps frozen foods at a temperature of −20°F, while Freezer B keeps frozen foods at a temperature of −4°F. She transferred a package of frozen food from one freezer to the other.

    a) What is the temperature difference between the two freezers?

    b) If the temperature of the package rises after the transfer, from which freezer was the package taken?

26 You and a friend are playing a video game. Your score so far is 340 points and your friend's score is −220 points. What is the difference between your scores?

27 Two record low monthly temperatures for Anchorage, Alaska, are −34°F in January and 31°F in August. Find the difference between these two temperatures.

28 Town X is 120 feet above sea level, Town Y is 25 feet below sea level, and Town Z is 30 feet below sea level. How high is

    a) Town X above Town Y?

    b) Town Y above Town Z?

    c) Town X above Town Z?

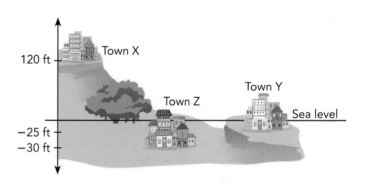

29 *Math Journal*

    a) Find |8 − 12| and |8| − |12|. Is |8 − 12| equal to |8| − |12|?

    b) Find |12 − 8| and |12| − |8|. Is |12 − 8| equal to |12| − |8|?

    c) Joe thinks that to find the distance between two integers m and n, he can write |m| − |n| or |n| − |m|. Use your answer in **a)** and **b)** to explain why you agree or disagree.

30 *Math Journal* Use the data in the following table. Which two gases have boiling points that are closest in value? Explain.

Gas	Temperature (°F)
Oxygen	−297
Hydrogen	−423
Nitrogen	−321

Multiplying and Dividing Integers

Lesson Objective

- Multiply and divide integers.

 Hands-On Activity

EXPLORE MULTIPLICATION RULES USING REPEATED ADDITION

Work individually.

You can think of multiplying integers as repeated addition.

STEP 1 Use a number line to model and complete the multiplication of integers as repeated addition.

a) Evaluate $3 \cdot 2$.

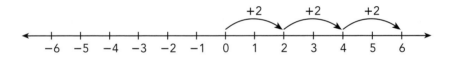

$3 \cdot 2$ means three groups of 2.

$3 \cdot 2 = 2 \cdot 3$
$\quad = 2 + 2 + 2$
$\quad = 6$

> **Commutative property of multiplication:**
>
> Two or more numbers can be multiplied in any order.

b) Evaluate $3 \cdot (-2)$.

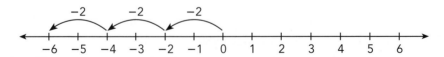

$3 \cdot (-2)$ means three groups of -2.

$3 \cdot (-2) = (-2) \cdot 3$
$\quad = -2 + (-2) + (-2)$
$\quad = \underline{\ ?\ }$

> The expression $3 \cdot (-2)$ can also be written as $3(-2)$.
>
> The expression $(-2) \cdot 3$ can also be written as $-2(3)$.

STEP 2 Copy and complete the table using repeated addition.

Product	Equivalent Sum	Answer	Sign
3(2)	2 + 2 + 2	6	+
3(−2)	−2 + (−2) + (−2)	?	?
2(5)	5 + 5	?	?
2(−5)	−5 + (−5)	?	?
4(3)	?	?	?
4(−3)	?	?	?

 Math Journal Study the pattern in the table from **STEP 2**.

a) What do you observe about the sign of the product of two positive integers?

b) What do you observe about the sign of the product of a positive and a negative integer?

STEP 3 Use a number line to model and complete the multiplication as addition of the opposite.

a) Evaluate $-3 \cdot 2$.

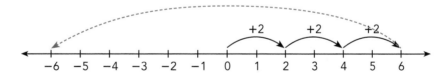

You can say that $-3 \cdot 2$ is the opposite of three groups of 2, 6.

$$-3 \cdot 2 = -(3)(2)$$
$$= \underline{}$$

b) Evaluate $-3 \cdot (-2)$.

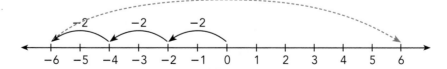

You can say that $-3 \cdot (-2)$ is the opposite of three groups of −2, −6.

$$-3 \cdot (-2) = -(3)(-2)$$
$$= -(\underline{})$$
$$= \underline{}$$

Continue on next page

Copy and complete the table using addition of the opposite and your results from .

Product	Use Addition of Opposite	Use Results from	Answer	Sign
−3(−2)	−(3)(−2)	−(−6)	6	+
−2(−5)	−(2)(−5)	−(−10)	?	?
−4(−3)	?	?	?	?

Math Journal Based on your observations in 1 to 4 ,

a) What do you observe about the sign of the product of two integers with the same sign?

b) What do you observe about the sign of the product of a positive integer and a negative integer? of integers with different signs?

Multiply Integers.

In the activity, you may have observed the following patterns:

When you multiply two integers with the same sign, the product is positive. For example, (2)(3) = 6 and (−2)(−3) = 6.

When you multiply two integers with different signs, the product is negative. For example, (−2)(3) = −6 and (2)(−3) = −6.

You can use a flow chart like the one below to find the product of two nonzero integers.

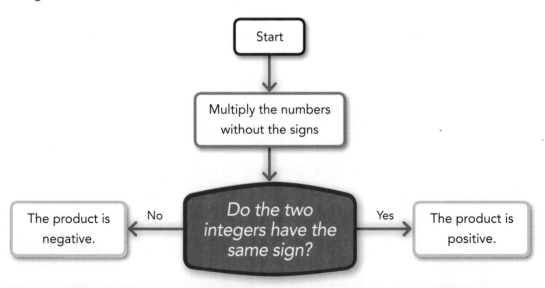

For example, evaluate $-2 \cdot 5$.

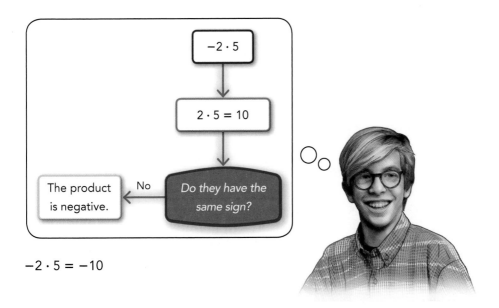

$-2 \cdot 5 = -10$

You can also use the flow chart to help you multiply more than two integers.
For example, evaluate $-1 \cdot 2 \cdot 3$.

Applying the associative property of multiplication, you can multiply any two integers at a time until you have found the product.

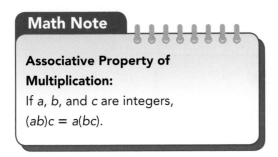

Math Note

Associative Property of Multiplication:
If a, b, and c are integers,
$(ab)c = a(bc)$.

Method 1

Multiply the first two numbers in the expression.

$-1 \cdot 2 \cdot 3$
$= -2 \cdot 3$ Multiply. Product of two integers with different signs is negative.
$= -6$ Multiply. Product of two integers with different signs is negative.

Method 2

Multiply the second two numbers in the expression.

$-1 \cdot 2 \cdot 3$
$= -1 \cdot 6$ Multiply. Product of two integers with the same sign is positive.
$= -6$ Multiply. Product of two integers with different signs is negative.

Example 9 Multiply two or more integers.

Evaluate each product.

a) $-5(4)$ b) $-3 \cdot (-9)$ c) $2(-3)(-7)$

Solution

a) $-5(4) = -20$ Product of two integers with different signs is negative.

b) $-3 \cdot (-9) = 27$ Product of two integers with the same sign is positive.

c) *Method 1*

$$2(-3)(-7) = -6(-7)$$ Product of two integers with different signs is negative.
$$= 42$$ Product of two integers with the same sign is positive.

Method 2

$$2(-3)(-7) = 2(21)$$ Product of two integers with the same sign is positive.
$$= 42$$ Product of two integers with the same sign is positive.

Guided Practice

Evaluate each product.

1 $9(-8)$

2 $-7 \cdot (-5)$

3 $3(-4)(6)$

> **Think Math**
>
> Will the product of three negative numbers be positive or negative? What about the product of four negative numbers? Explain your answers.

Example 10 Use multiplication in a real-world situation.

A helicopter's altitude is changing at a rate of -17 feet per second. Find the change in altitude of the helicopter after 4 seconds.

Solution

$$\text{Change in altitude} = \text{Rate} \cdot \text{Time}$$
$$= -17 \cdot 4$$ Substitute -17 for rate and 4 for time.
$$= -68 \text{ ft}$$ Multiply. Product of two integers with different signs is negative.

The change in altitude of the helicopter is -68 feet.

Guided Practice

Solve.

4 In a regional golf championship, Steven plays four rounds. The score for a round is recorded as positive (over par) or negative (under par). If Steven scores 6 points under par for all four rounds, what is his total score for his game?

$$\underline{\quad?\quad} \cdot (-6) = \underline{\quad?\quad}$$

His score is $\underline{\quad?\quad}$ points.

5 The price of a stock falls $2 each day for 9 days. Find the total change in the price of the stock during this time.

Divide Integers.

Division is the inverse (or reverse) of multiplication.

Multiplication	Division
$3(5) = 15$	$15 \div 5 = 3$
$3(-5) = -15$	$-15 \div (-5) = 3$
$(-3)5 = -15$	$-15 \div 5 = -3$
$(-3)(-5) = 15$	$15 \div (-5) = -3$

For the relationship between multiplication and division, you can conclude the following:

When you divide two integers with the same sign, the quotient is positive. For example, $2 \div 3 = \frac{2}{3}$ and $-2 \div (-3) = \frac{2}{3}$.

When you divide two integers with different signs, the quotient is negative. For example, $-2 \div 3 = -\frac{2}{3}$ and $2 \div (-3) = -\frac{2}{3}$.

Math Note

You have learned that for negative fractions, the negative integer may be placed in either the numerator or the denominator: $-\frac{m}{n} = \frac{-m}{n} = \frac{m}{-n}$, where m and n are integers with $n \neq 0$.

So,

$$-2 \div 3 \ = \frac{-2}{3} \quad \text{and} \quad 2 \div (-3) = \frac{2}{-3}$$
$$\qquad\quad = -\frac{2}{3} \qquad\qquad\qquad = -\frac{2}{3}$$

Continue on next page

You can use division in real-world situations.

A submarine descends 720 feet in 6 minutes. Find the submarine's change in elevation per minute.

A descent is in the negative direction. So, you translate the change in elevation as -720 feet.

Change in elevation per minute:

$$\frac{-720}{6} = -120 \text{ ft/min}$$

The submarine's change in elevation per minute is -120 feet per minute.

Example 11 Divide two integers.

Evaluate each quotient.

a) $-25 \div (-5)$

b) $-81 \div 3$

c) $96 \div (-4)$

Solution

a) $-25 \div (-5) = 5$ Divide. Quotient of two integers with the same sign is positive.

b) $-81 \div 3 = -27$ Divide. Quotient of two integers with different signs is negative.

c) $96 \div (-4) = -24$ Divide. Quotient of two integers with different signs is negative.

Guided Practice

Evaluate each quotient.

6 $-36 \div (-4)$

7 $-35 \div 5$

8 $45 \div (-3)$

Solve.

9 Find the change in elevation per minute of a hiker who descended 320 feet in 40 minutes.

Evaluate each product.

1 $5 \cdot (-7)$

2 $12 \cdot (-9)$

3 $-6 \cdot 8$

4 $-3 \cdot 15$

5 $-4 \cdot (-12)$

6 $-8 \cdot (-20)$

7 $-14 \cdot 0$

8 $0 \cdot (-50)$

9 $-3 \cdot 12 \cdot 7$

10 $8 \cdot (-4) \cdot 2$

11 $20 \cdot 5 \cdot (-5)$

12 $-4 \cdot 10 \cdot (-6)$

13 $-7 \cdot (-2) \cdot 10$

14 $9 \cdot (-6) \cdot (-4)$

15 $-2 \cdot (-8) \cdot (-7)$

16 $-5 \cdot (-12) \cdot (-3)$

17 $14 \cdot 0 \cdot (-15)$

18 $-30 \cdot (-2) \cdot 0$

19 $-6 \cdot (-7) \cdot 2 \cdot 5$

20 $-8 \cdot (-2) \cdot (-4) \cdot 12$

21 $-9 \cdot (-5) \cdot (-4) \cdot (-3)$

Evaluate each quotient.

22 $125 \div (-25)$

23 $300 \div (-15)$

24 $-100 \div 25$

25 $-32 \div 4$

26 $-480 \div (-12)$

27 $-144 \div (-24)$

28 $0 \div (-8)$

29 $0 \div (-111)$

Solve. Show your work.

30 While returning to the glider port, Laura descended at a rate of 380 feet per minute for 3 minutes. Calculate her change in altitude.

31 A scuba diver took 6 minutes to rise to the surface at a rate of 30 feet per minute. How far was he below sea level?

32 An elevator descends 1,500 feet in 60 seconds. Find the change in height per second.

33 A scientist measures the change in height per second of a diving osprey as −198 feet per second. Find the change in position of the osprey after 2 seconds.

34 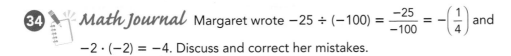 *Math Journal* Margaret wrote $-25 \div (-100) = \frac{-25}{-100} = -\left(\frac{1}{4}\right)$ and $-2 \cdot (-2) = -4$. Discuss and correct her mistakes.

35 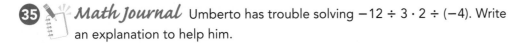 *Math Journal* Umberto has trouble solving $-12 \div 3 \cdot 2 \div (-4)$. Write an explanation to help him.

2.4 Operations with Integers

Lesson Objective

- Use addition, subtraction, multiplication, and division with integers.

Use Addition, Subtraction, Multiplication, and Division with Integers.

The order of operations for integers is the same as the order of operations for whole numbers, fractions, and decimals.

STEP 1 For expressions involving parentheses, evaluate expressions within parentheses first.

STEP 2 Evaluate exponents.

STEP 3 Working from left to right, perform multiplication and division.

STEP 4 Working from left to right, perform addition and subtraction.

For expressions with parentheses, there may be more than one way of solving. For example, evaluate $-13 + (-4) \cdot (2 - 10) + 8$.

Method 1

Follow the order of operations.

$$-13 + (-4) \cdot \underbrace{(2 - 10)} + 8 \qquad \text{Subtract within the parentheses.}$$

$$= -13 + \underbrace{(-4) \cdot (-8)} + 8 \qquad \text{Multiply.}$$

$$= -13 + \underbrace{32 + 8} \qquad \text{Use the associative property of addition.}$$

$$= \underbrace{-13 + 40} \qquad \text{Add.}$$

$$= 27 \qquad \text{Add.}$$

> **Math Note**
>
> **Associative Property of Addition:**
> If a, b, and c are integers,
> $(a + b) + c = a + (b + c)$.

Method 2

Use the distributive property first.

> **Caution** ///////
>
> $(-4)(2 - 10) \neq (-4)(2) + (-4)(10)$

$$-13 + (-4) \cdot (2 - 10) + 8$$

$$= -13 + (-4) \cdot (2) - (-4) \cdot (10) + 8 \qquad \text{Use the distributive property.}$$

$$= -13 + (-8) - (-40) + 8 \qquad \text{Multiply.}$$

$$= -13 + (-8) + 40 + 8 \qquad \text{Rewrite subtraction as adding the opposite.}$$

$$= -13 + 40 + (-8) + 8 \qquad \text{Use the commutative property of addition.}$$

$$= 27 \qquad \text{Add.}$$

Example 12 **Apply the order of operations with integers.**

Evaluate each expression.

a) $-9 - 32 \div 4 - 21$

> Evaluate from left to right. First multiply and divide. Then add and subtract.

Solution

$-9 - 32 \div 4 - 21$
$= -9 - 8 - 21$ Divide.
$= -9 + (-8) + (-21)$ Rewrite subtraction as adding the opposite.
$= -9 + (-21) + (-8)$ Use commutative property of addition.
$= -30 + (-8)$ Add.
$= -38$ Add.

b) $-5 + (8 - 12) \cdot (-4)$

> Evaluate from left to right. First evaluate within the parentheses. Next multiply and divide. Then add and subtract.

Solution

$-5 + \underbrace{(8 - 12)} \cdot (-4)$

$= -5 + \underbrace{(-4) \cdot (-4)}$ Simplify within the parentheses.

$= \underbrace{-5 + \quad 16}$ Multiply.

$= \quad\quad 11$ Add.

Guided Practice

Evaluate each expression.

1 $14 + 8 - 9 \cdot 6$

$14 + 8 - 9 \cdot 6 = 14 + 8 - \underline{\ ?\ }$ Multiply.
$= 14 + 8 + (\underline{\ ?\ })$ Rewrite subtraction as adding the opposite.
$= 14 + (\underline{\ ?\ }) + 8$ Use the commutative property of addition.
$= \underline{\ ?\ } + 8$ Add.
$= \underline{\ ?\ }$ Add.

2 $(-25 - 5) \div 6 - 21$

$(-25 - 5) \div 6 - 21 = \underline{\ ?\ } \div 6 - 21$ Subtract within the parentheses.
$= \underline{\ ?\ } - 21$ Divide.
$= \underline{\ ?\ }$ Subtract.

3 $-14 - (3 + 3) \cdot 2$

Angela is making a paper box using a piece of rectangular paper. The dimensions of the rectangular paper are 9 inches by 12 inches. To make the paper box, she cuts four identical rectangles from the corners of the paper. These cut-off rectangles are shown in the diagram on the right. What is the area of the paper that remains after these rectangles are cut off?

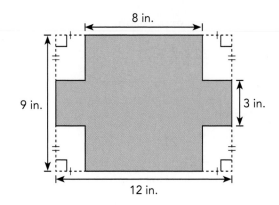

8 in.

9 in.

3 in.

12 in.

Solution

Length of 1 cut-off rectangle: $\left(\dfrac{9-3}{2}\right) = 3$ in.

Width of 1 cut-off rectangle: $\left(\dfrac{12-8}{2}\right) = 2$ in.

Area of remaining paper:

Area of original paper − Area of four cut-off rectangles

$= 12 \cdot 9 - 4(3 \cdot 2)$ Write an expression.

$= 108 - 24$ Multiply.

$= 84 \text{ in}^2$ Subtract.

The area of the remaining paper is 84 square inches.

Guided Practice

Solve.

4 Joseph drew a hexagon on a 3-inch square piece of paper. He cut four identical right triangles from the four corners of the paper. The height of each triangle is $\dfrac{1}{2}$ the length of the paper. The base of each triangle is $\dfrac{1}{3}$ the length of the paper. What is the area of the paper that remained after these triangles are cut off?

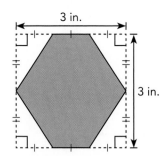

3 in.

3 in.

Height of a triangle: ___?___
Base of a triangle: ___?___

Area of remaining paper:

Area of original paper − Area of four cut-off triangles

$= 3 \cdot 3 - 4 \cdot \left(\dfrac{1}{2} \cdot \underline{} \cdot \underline{}\right)$ Write an expression.

$= \underline{} - \underline{}$ Multiply.

$= \underline{} \text{ in}^2$ Subtract.

The area of the remaining paper is ___?___ square inches.

Practice 2.4

Evaluate each expression.

1 $-3 \cdot 5 + 7$

2 $50 \div (-5) + (-4)$

3 $4 \cdot (-6) + (-3) \cdot 5$

4 $11 - 2 \cdot 8 - (-9)$

5 $-64 \div 4 \cdot 5 - 37$

6 $-28 - 350 \div 7 + 8$

7 $100 - (8 - 15) \cdot 9$

8 $70 \div (-4 - 3) + 60$

9 $(4 + 2) \cdot 3 - 8 \cdot (2 + 3)$

10 $-20 + 4 \cdot (2 + 7) - 35$

11 $15 \div (4 + 1) - 8 \cdot 3$

12 $24 \div 4 - (-13 + 3) \cdot 2$

13 $-12 + 50 \div (-2 - 3) + 72 \div (4 + 2)$

14 $180 \div (4 + 16) - 8 \cdot 3 + 7 \cdot (2 + 3)$

Solve. Show your work.

15 Emily made a sketch of an octagonal window on a 27-inch square piece of paper. First she cut four identical isosceles triangles from the corners of the paper. Then she cut a square from the center of the octagon. Each leg of a cut-off triangle is $\frac{1}{3}$ the length of the paper. The side length of the cut-out square is also $\frac{1}{3}$ the length of the paper. What is the area of the sketch after she removed the triangles and the square?

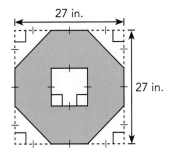
27 in.

27 in.

16 ✎ *Math Journal* Suppose that Lydia shows you some of her homework:

$$-2(6 - 8) = -2(6) - 2(8)$$
$$= -12 - 16$$
$$= -28$$

Lydia made a common error when she used the distributive property to evaluate the expression $-2(6 - 8)$. Evaluate the expression using the order of operations. Then explain how Lydia can correctly use the distributive property to evaluate the expression.

17 Sylvia took three turns in a video game. She scored -120 points during her first turn, 320 points during her second turn, and -80 points during her third turn. What was her average score for the three turns?

18 ✎ *Math Journal* Benjamin wrote: $-20 + 4 \cdot 2 + 7 - 35 = -19$. Where can he place the parentheses so that the equation will be a true statement?

2.5 Operations with Rational Numbers

Lesson Objectives

- Add and subtract rational numbers.
- Multiply and divide rational numbers.

Vocabulary

complex fraction   least common denominator

Add Rational Numbers.

A rational number is a number that can be written as $\frac{m}{n}$, where m and n are integers with $n \neq 0$.

If $\frac{m}{n}$ is negative, either m or n can be negative but not both m and n.

You may rewrite rational numbers with a common denominator before you add them.

> **Math Note**
>
> If $\frac{m}{n}$ is any rational number,
> then $-\frac{m}{n} = \frac{-m}{n} = \frac{m}{-n}$.
> For example, $\frac{-7}{15} = -\frac{7}{15} = \frac{7}{-15}$.

The sum of two rational numbers with the same denominator:

Let $\frac{a}{b}$ and $\frac{c}{b}$ be any rational numbers.

$$\frac{a}{b} + \frac{c}{b} = \frac{a+c}{b}$$

The sum of two rational numbers with different denominators:

Let $\frac{a}{b}$ and $\frac{c}{d}$ be any rational numbers.

$$\frac{a}{b} + \frac{c}{d} = \frac{ad + bc}{bd}$$

To add two rational numbers, such as $\frac{1}{5}$ and $\frac{-2}{3}$, you can apply the rules you know for adding integers.

First find the **least common denominator** (LCD) of $\frac{1}{5}$ and $\frac{-2}{3}$, which is 15. Then use the LCD to write equivalent fractions and evaluate.

$$\frac{1}{5} + \frac{-2}{3} = \frac{1 \cdot 3}{5 \cdot 3} + \frac{-2 \cdot 5}{3 \cdot 5}$$ Write equivalent fractions using the LCD.

$$= \frac{3}{15} + \frac{-10}{15}$$ Multiply all products.

$$= \frac{3 + (-10)}{15}$$ Simplify using a single denominator.

$$= \frac{-7}{15}$$ Add.

Example 14 **Add rational numbers.**

Evaluate each expression.

a) $\dfrac{-2}{7} + \dfrac{3}{-5}$

Solution

$$\dfrac{-2}{7} + \dfrac{3}{-5} = \dfrac{-2 \cdot (-5)}{7 \cdot (-5)} + \dfrac{3 \cdot 7}{-5 \cdot 7} \qquad \text{Write equivalent fractions using the LCD, } -35.$$

$$= \dfrac{10}{-35} + \dfrac{21}{-35} \qquad \text{Multiply all products.}$$

$$= \dfrac{10 + 21}{-35} \qquad \text{Simplify using a single denominator.}$$

$$= \dfrac{31}{-35} \qquad \text{Add.}$$

$$= -\dfrac{31}{35} \qquad \text{Write an equivalent fraction.}$$

b) $1\dfrac{2}{3} + \left(-2\dfrac{1}{6}\right)$

> **Caution** ////////
>
> The mixed number $-2\dfrac{1}{6}$ is the sum of -2 and $-\dfrac{1}{6}$. Both the fraction part and the integer part of the mixed number are negative.
>
> $$-2\dfrac{1}{6} = -2 + \left(-\dfrac{1}{6}\right) = -2 - \dfrac{1}{6}$$
>
> $$-2\dfrac{1}{6} \neq -2 + \dfrac{1}{6}$$

Solution

$$1\dfrac{2}{3} + \left(-2\dfrac{1}{6}\right) = 1\dfrac{2 \cdot 2}{3 \cdot 2} + \left(-2\dfrac{1}{6}\right) \qquad \text{Rewrite the fraction part of each mixed number using the LCD, 6.}$$

$$= 1\dfrac{4}{6} + \left(-2\dfrac{1}{6}\right) \qquad \text{Multiply all products.}$$

$$= 1 + \dfrac{4}{6} + (-2) + \left(-\dfrac{1}{6}\right) \qquad \text{Rewrite the sum.}$$

$$= 1 + (-2) + \dfrac{4}{6} + \left(-\dfrac{1}{6}\right) \qquad \text{Use the commutative property of addition.}$$

$$= -1 + \left(\dfrac{3}{6}\right) \qquad \text{Add the integers and the fractions.}$$

$$= \dfrac{-6}{6} + \dfrac{3}{6} \qquad \text{Write an equivalent fraction for the integer part using the same LCD.}$$

$$= -\dfrac{3}{6} \qquad \text{Add the like fractions.}$$

$$= -\dfrac{1}{2} \qquad \text{Write in simplest form.}$$

Continue on next page

c) $\frac{2}{5} + \left(\frac{-4}{15}\right) + \frac{1}{10}$

Solution

Method 1

Add two rational numbers at a time, working from left to right.

$\frac{2}{5} + \left(\frac{-4}{15}\right) + \frac{1}{10} = \frac{2 \cdot 3}{5 \cdot 3} + \left(\frac{-4}{15}\right) + \frac{1}{10}$

Write equivalent fractions for the first two fractions using the LCD.

$= \frac{6}{15} + \left(\frac{-4}{15}\right) + \frac{1}{10}$

Multiply all products.

$= \frac{6 + (-4)}{15} + \frac{1}{10}$

Write the first two fractions using a single denominator.

$= \frac{2}{15} + \frac{1}{10}$

Add.

$= \frac{2 \cdot 2}{15 \cdot 2} + \frac{1 \cdot 3}{10 \cdot 3}$

Write equivalent fractions using the LCD of the fractions in the new sum.

$= \frac{4}{30} + \frac{3}{30}$

Multiply all products.

$= \frac{7}{30}$

Add the like fractions.

Method 2

Use a common denominator for all three fractions.

Finding the LCD of $\frac{2}{5}$, $\frac{-4}{15}$, and $\frac{1}{10}$ is the same as finding the least common multiple (LCM) of 5, 15, and 10.

$5 \,\big|\, \underline{5, 10, 15}$
$\; 1, \;\; 2, \;\; 3$

Divide by the common prime factor 5. Stop dividing because 1, 2, and 3 have no common factor other than 1.

$5 \cdot 1 \cdot 2 \cdot 3 = 30$ Multiply the factors.

The LCM of 5, 10, and 15 is 30.

$\frac{2}{5} + \left(\frac{-4}{15}\right) + \frac{1}{10} = \frac{2 \cdot 6}{5 \cdot 6} + \frac{-4 \cdot 2}{15 \cdot 2} + \frac{1 \cdot 3}{10 \cdot 3}$

Write equivalent fractions using the LCD of all three fractions.

$= \frac{12}{30} + \left(\frac{-8}{30}\right) + \frac{3}{30}$

Multiply all products.

$= \frac{12 + (-8) + 3}{30}$

Rewrite using a single denominator.

$= \frac{7}{30}$

Add.

Guided Practice

Copy and complete.

1 $\dfrac{-1}{9} + \dfrac{2}{-5}$

$\dfrac{-1}{9} + \dfrac{2}{-5} = \dfrac{(-1)(?)}{9(-5)} + \dfrac{2(?)}{(-5)(9)}$ Write equivalent fractions using the LCD.

$= \dfrac{(-1)(?) + 2(?)}{9(-5)}$ Rewrite using a single denominator.

$= \dfrac{? + ?}{-45}$ Multiply all products.

$= \underline{\ ?\ }$ Add.

2 $-1\dfrac{1}{6} + 3\dfrac{4}{9}$

$-1\dfrac{1}{6} + 3\dfrac{4}{9} = -1\dfrac{?}{?} + 3\dfrac{?}{?}$ Rewrite the fraction part of each mixed number using the LCD.

$= (-1 + 3) + \dfrac{?}{?} + \dfrac{?}{?}$ Use the commutative property of addition to group the integers and then the fractions.

$= \underline{\ ?\ } + \dfrac{?}{?}$ Add.

$= \underline{\ ?\ }$ Write as a mixed number.

3 $\dfrac{1}{6} + \left(\dfrac{-5}{9}\right) + \left(\dfrac{-1}{3}\right)$

Method 1

Add two rational numbers at a time, working from left to right.

$\dfrac{1}{6} + \left(\dfrac{-5}{9}\right) + \left(\dfrac{-1}{3}\right) = \dfrac{?}{?} + \dfrac{?}{?} + \left(\dfrac{-1}{3}\right)$ Write equivalent fractions for first two fractions using the LCD.

$= \dfrac{?}{?} + \left(\dfrac{-1}{3}\right)$ Add the numerators of the first two fractions.

$= \dfrac{?}{?} + \dfrac{?}{?}$ Write equivalent fractions using the LCD.

$= \dfrac{? + ?}{?}$ Write using a single denominator.

$= \underline{\ ?\ }$ Add.

Method 2

Use a common denominator for all three fractions.

$\dfrac{1}{6} + \left(\dfrac{-5}{9}\right) + \left(\dfrac{-1}{3}\right) = \dfrac{?}{?} + \dfrac{?}{?} + \dfrac{?}{?}$ Write equivalent fractions using the LCD.

$= \dfrac{? + ? + ?}{?}$ Write using a single denominator.

$= \underline{\ ?\ }$ Add.

Subtract Rational Numbers.

As with fractions, you may need to rewrite rational numbers so that they have a common denominator before you subtract.

> **The difference of two rational numbers with the same denominator:**
>
> Let $\frac{a}{b}$ and $\frac{c}{b}$ be any rational numbers.
>
> $$\frac{a}{b} - \frac{c}{b} = \frac{a-c}{b}$$
>
> **The difference of two rational numbers with different denominators:**
>
> Let $\frac{a}{b}$ and $\frac{c}{d}$ be any rational numbers.
>
> $$\frac{a}{b} - \frac{c}{d} = \frac{ad-bc}{bd}$$

For example, subtract $\frac{1}{2}$ from $\frac{2}{5}$.

$\frac{2}{5} - \frac{1}{2} = \frac{2 \cdot 2}{5 \cdot 2} - \frac{1 \cdot 5}{2 \cdot 5}$ Write equivalent fractions using the LCD, 10.

$\qquad = \frac{4}{10} - \frac{5}{10}$ Multiply all products.

$\qquad = \frac{4-5}{10}$ Rewrite using a single denominator.

$\qquad = \frac{-1}{10}$ Subtract.

$\qquad = -\frac{1}{10}$ Write an equivalent fraction.

> Remember that subtracting a number is the same as adding its opposite.
>
> For example, $4 - 5 = 4 + (-5)$
> $$= -1$$

Caution /////////

The phrase "subtract a from b" does not mean $a - b$. It means $b - a$.

So, the phrase "subtract $\frac{1}{2}$ from $\frac{3}{5}$" does not mean $\frac{1}{2} - \frac{3}{5}$. It means $\frac{3}{5} - \frac{1}{2}$.

Example 15 **Subtract rational numbers.**

Evaluate each expression.

a) $\dfrac{1}{6} - \dfrac{3}{4}$

Solution

$\dfrac{1}{6} - \dfrac{3}{4} = \dfrac{1 \cdot 2}{6 \cdot 2} - \dfrac{3 \cdot 3}{4 \cdot 3}$ Write equivalent fractions using the LCD, 12.

$= \dfrac{2}{12} - \dfrac{9}{12}$ Multiply all products.

$= \dfrac{2 - 9}{12}$ Rewrite using a single denominator.

$= \dfrac{-7}{12}$ Subtract.

$= -\dfrac{7}{12}$ Rewrite an equivalent fraction.

b) $2\dfrac{1}{4} - 4\dfrac{2}{3}$

Solution

$2\dfrac{1}{4} - 4\dfrac{2}{3} = 2\dfrac{1 \cdot 3}{4 \cdot 3} - 4\dfrac{2 \cdot 4}{3 \cdot 4}$ Write equivalent fractions for the fraction part of each mixed number using the LCD, 12.

$= 2\dfrac{3}{12} - 4\dfrac{8}{12}$ Multiply all products.

$= 2 + \dfrac{3}{12} - 4 - \dfrac{8}{12}$ Rewrite the sum.

$= 2 - 4 + \left(\dfrac{3}{12} - \dfrac{8}{12} \right)$ Use the commutative property of addition.

$= -2 + \left(-\dfrac{5}{12} \right)$ Subtract the integers and the fractions.

$= -2\dfrac{5}{12}$ Simplify.

You can rewrite
$-4\dfrac{8}{12}$ as $-4 - \dfrac{8}{12}$ or $(-4) + \left(\dfrac{-8}{12} \right)$.

Continue on next page

c) $\dfrac{1}{3} - \dfrac{11}{12} - \dfrac{1}{2}$

Solution

Method 1

Subtract two rational numbers at a time, working from left to right.

$$\dfrac{1}{3} - \dfrac{11}{12} - \dfrac{1}{2} = \dfrac{1 \cdot 4}{3 \cdot 4} - \dfrac{11}{12} - \dfrac{1}{2}$$ Write equivalent fractions for the first two fractions using their LCD, 12.

$$= \dfrac{4}{12} - \dfrac{11}{12} - \dfrac{1}{2}$$ Multiply all products.

$$= \dfrac{4 - 11}{12} - \dfrac{1}{2}$$ Rewrite the first two fractions using a single denominator.

$$= \dfrac{-7}{12} - \dfrac{1}{2}$$ Subtract.

$$= \dfrac{-7}{12} - \dfrac{1 \cdot 6}{2 \cdot 6}$$ Write equivalent fractions using the LCD, 12.

$$= \dfrac{-7}{12} - \dfrac{6}{12}$$ Multiply all products.

$$= \dfrac{-7 - 6}{12}$$ Rewrite using a single denominator.

$$= \dfrac{-13}{12}$$ Subtract.

$$= -1\dfrac{1}{12}$$ Rewrite the improper fraction as a mixed number.

Method 2

Use a common denominator for all three fractions.

$$\dfrac{1}{3} - \dfrac{11}{12} - \dfrac{1}{2} = \dfrac{1 \cdot 4}{3 \cdot 4} - \dfrac{11}{12} - \dfrac{1 \cdot 6}{2 \cdot 6}$$ Write equivalent fractions using the LCD for all three fractions, 12.

$$= \dfrac{4}{12} - \dfrac{11}{12} - \dfrac{6}{12}$$ Multiply all products.

$$= \dfrac{4 - 11 - 6}{12}$$ Rewrite using a single denominator.

$$= \dfrac{-13}{12}$$ Subtract.

$$= -1\dfrac{1}{12}$$ Rewrite the improper fraction as a mixed number.

Guided Practice

Evaluate each expression.

4 $\dfrac{1}{4} - \dfrac{3}{10}$

5 $\dfrac{7}{8} - \dfrac{9}{10}$

6 $3\dfrac{1}{4} - 7\dfrac{5}{6}$

7 $\dfrac{3}{7} - \dfrac{27}{28} - \dfrac{3}{14}$

Example 16 **Subtract rational numbers in a real-world situation.**

Mr. Dawson has a partial roll of wire $18\frac{1}{4}$ feet long. He needs $25\frac{1}{2}$ feet of wire for a remodeling project. How many feet of wire is he short?

Solution

$18\frac{1}{4} - 25\frac{1}{2}$	Write an expression for this situation.
$= 18\frac{1}{4} - 25\frac{1 \cdot 2}{2 \cdot 2}$	Write equivalent fractions for the fraction parts using the LCD, 4.
$= 18\frac{1}{4} - 25\frac{2}{4}$	Multiply all products.
$= 18 + \frac{1}{4} - 25 - \frac{2}{4}$	Rewrite the sum.
$= 18 - 25 + \left(\frac{1}{4} - \frac{2}{4}\right)$	Use the commutative property of addition to group the integers and then the fractions.
$= -7 + \left(-\frac{1}{4}\right)$	Subtract the integers and then the fractions.
$= -7\frac{1}{4}$	Subtract.

He is short $7\frac{1}{4}$ feet of wire.

Guided Practice

Solve.

8 Philadelphia suffered a severe snowstorm in 1996 that left $30\frac{7}{10}$ inches of snow on the ground. Another severe snowstorm occured in 2010, when $28\frac{1}{2}$ inches of snow fell.

a) Write a subtraction expression for the difference in depth of these two record snowfalls.

b) Rewrite the expression as an addition expression.

c) Find the difference in these two record snowfalls.

Multiply Rational Numbers.

You have learned how to multiply positive fractions and how to multiply positive and negative integers. So, you can multiply both positive and negative rational numbers using the same rules for the signs of the products.

Multiply rational numbers with the same sign.

Examples:

$$\frac{1}{2} \cdot \frac{3}{4} = \frac{1 \cdot 3}{2 \cdot 4} = \frac{3}{8}, \text{ and } \left(-\frac{1}{2}\right) \cdot \left(-\frac{3}{4}\right) = \frac{1 \cdot 3}{2 \cdot 4} = \frac{3}{8}.$$

Multiply rational numbers with different signs.

Examples:

$$\frac{1}{2} \cdot \left(-\frac{3}{4}\right) = -\frac{1 \cdot 3}{2 \cdot 4} = -\frac{3}{8}, \text{ and } \left(-\frac{1}{2}\right) \cdot \frac{3}{4} = -\frac{1 \cdot 3}{2 \cdot 4} = -\frac{3}{8}.$$

> **Math Note**
>
> **Multiplying Positive and Negative Rational Numbers:**
>
> Two signs are the same:
> $(+) \cdot (+) = (+)$
> $(-) \cdot (-) = (+)$
> The product is positive.
>
> Two signs are different:
> $(+) \cdot (-) = (-)$
> $(-) \cdot (+) = (-)$
> The product is negative.

Example 17 Multiply rational numbers.

Evaluate each product.

a) $-\frac{3}{7} \cdot \frac{8}{15}$

Solution

$$-\frac{3}{7} \cdot \frac{8}{15} = \frac{-3 \cdot 8}{7 \cdot 15}$$

Multiply the numerators, and multiply the denominators.

$$= \frac{^{-1}\cancel{-3} \cdot 8}{7 \cdot \cancel{15}_{\,5}}$$

Divide the numerator and denominator by their greatest common factor (GCF), 3.

$$= -\frac{8}{35}$$

Simplify.

b) $-2\frac{3}{5} \cdot \left(-1\frac{1}{4}\right)$

Solution

$$-2\frac{3}{5} \cdot \left(-1\frac{1}{4}\right) = -\frac{13}{5} \cdot \left(-\frac{5}{4}\right)$$

Write as improper fractions.

$$= \frac{13 \cdot \cancel{5}^{\,1}}{_{1}\cancel{5} \cdot 4}$$

Divide the numerator and denominator by their GCF, 5.

$$= \frac{13}{4}$$

Simplify.

$$= 3\frac{1}{4}$$

Write as a mixed number.

Guided Practice

Copy and complete.

9 $-\dfrac{4}{5} \cdot \dfrac{20}{21}$

$$-\dfrac{4}{5} \cdot \dfrac{20}{21} = \dfrac{?}{?}$$ Multiply the numerators, and multiply the denominators.

$$= \dfrac{?}{?}$$ Divide the numerator and denominator by their GCF, __?__.

$$= \underline{?}$$ Simplify.

10 $-3\dfrac{1}{4} \cdot \left(-2\dfrac{2}{3}\right)$

$$-3\dfrac{1}{4} \cdot \left(-2\dfrac{2}{3}\right) = -\dfrac{?}{4} \cdot \left(-\dfrac{?}{3}\right)$$ Write as improper fractions.

$$= \dfrac{?}{?}$$ Divide the numerator and denominator by their GCF, __?__.

$$= \dfrac{?}{?}$$ Simplify.

$$= \underline{?}$$ Write as a mixed number.

Divide Rational Numbers.

You have learned that dividing by a fraction is the same as multiplying by the reciprocal of the fraction.

You can use this same method to divide rational numbers, but you need to apply what you know about dividing numbers with the same or different signs.

Math Note

Dividing Positive and Negative Rational Numbers:

Two signs are the same:
$(+) \div (+) = (+)$
$(-) \div (-) = (+)$
The quotient is positive.

Two signs are different:
$(+) \div (-) = (-)$
$(-) \div (+) = (-)$
The quotient is negative.

Two numbers are reciprocals if their product is 1.

3 and -3 are not reciprocals, because their product is -9, not 1.

-5 and $-\dfrac{1}{5}$ are reciprocals because their product is 1.

So, $3 \div \dfrac{1}{5} = 3 \cdot 5$.

Continue on next page

The quotient of two rational numbers may be written as a **complex fraction**. A complex fraction is a fraction in which the numerator, the denominator, or both the numerator and denominator contain a fraction.

An example of a complex fraction whose both numerator and denominator contain a fraction is

$$\left(\dfrac{1}{3}\right) \longrightarrow \text{Numerator}$$

$$\overline{\left(\dfrac{5}{6}\right)} \longrightarrow \text{Denominator}$$

Other examples of complex fractions include $\dfrac{\left(\frac{2}{7}\right)}{8}$, $\dfrac{3}{-\left(\frac{5}{2}\right)}$, and $\dfrac{-\left(4\frac{1}{2}\right)}{-\left(1\frac{5}{16}\right)}$.

To simplify a complex fraction, you rewrite the fraction using a division symbol '÷'.

$$\dfrac{\frac{1}{3}}{\frac{5}{6}} = \dfrac{1}{3} \div \dfrac{5}{6} \qquad \text{Rewrite as a division expression.}$$

$$= \dfrac{1}{3} \cdot \dfrac{6}{5} \qquad \text{Multiply } \dfrac{1}{3} \text{ by the reciprocal of } \dfrac{5}{6}.$$

$$= \dfrac{1 \cdot 6}{3 \cdot 5} \qquad \text{Multiply the numerators and the denominators.}$$

$$= \dfrac{1 \cdot \cancel{6}^{\,2}}{{}_{1}\cancel{3} \cdot 5} \qquad \text{Divide the numerator and the denominator by the GCF, 3.}$$

$$= \dfrac{2}{5} \qquad \text{Simplify.}$$

Example 18 | **Divide rational numbers.**

Evaluate each quotient.

a) $\quad -\dfrac{5}{6} \div \dfrac{1}{24}$

Solution

$$-\dfrac{5}{6} \div \dfrac{1}{24} = -\dfrac{5}{6} \cdot \dfrac{24}{1} \qquad \text{Multiply } -\dfrac{5}{6} \text{ by the reciprocal of } \dfrac{1}{24}.$$

$$= \dfrac{-5 \cdot 24}{6 \cdot 1} \qquad \text{Multiply the numerators and denominators.}$$

$$= \dfrac{-5 \cdot \cancel{24}^{\,4}}{{}_{1}\cancel{6} \cdot 1} \qquad \text{Divide the numerator and denominator by the GCF, 6.}$$

$$= \dfrac{-20}{1} \qquad \text{Simplify.}$$

$$= -20 \qquad \text{Write as a negative integer.}$$

b) $-5\dfrac{1}{3} \div \left(-2\dfrac{2}{5}\right)$

Solution

$-5\dfrac{1}{3} \div \left(-2\dfrac{2}{5}\right) = \dfrac{-16}{3} \div \dfrac{-12}{5}$ Write as improper fractions.

$= \dfrac{-16}{3} \cdot \dfrac{5}{-12}$ Multiply $\dfrac{-16}{3}$ by the reciprocal of $\dfrac{-12}{5}$.

$= \dfrac{\overset{4}{\cancel{16}} \cdot 5}{3 \cdot \underset{3}{\cancel{12}}}$ Multiply numerators and denominators. Divide the numerators and denominators by the GCF, 4.

$= \dfrac{20}{9}$ Simplify.

$= 2\dfrac{2}{9}$ Write as a mixed number.

c) $\dfrac{-\left(\frac{1}{4}\right)}{\left(\frac{1}{2}\right)}$

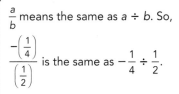 $\dfrac{a}{b}$ means the same as $a \div b$. So, $\dfrac{-\left(\frac{1}{4}\right)}{\left(\frac{1}{2}\right)}$ is the same as $-\dfrac{1}{4} \div \dfrac{1}{2}$.

Solution

$\dfrac{-\left(\frac{1}{4}\right)}{\left(\frac{1}{2}\right)} = -\dfrac{1}{4} \div \dfrac{1}{2}$ Rewrite as a division expression.

$= -\dfrac{1}{4} \cdot \dfrac{2}{1}$ Multiply $\dfrac{1}{4}$ by the reciprocal of $\dfrac{1}{2}$.

$= -\dfrac{2}{4}$ Multiply numerators and denominators.

$= -\dfrac{1}{2}$ Write in simplest form.

Guided Practice

Evaluate each quotient.

11 $\dfrac{3}{20} \div \left(-\dfrac{6}{35}\right)$

12 $-3\dfrac{1}{3} \div \left(-1\dfrac{1}{4}\right)$

13 $\dfrac{\left(\frac{1}{4}\right)}{-\left(\frac{3}{8}\right)}$

Solve. Show your work.

14 A pancake recipe requires $1\dfrac{2}{3}$ cups of flour to make 20 pancakes and you have 9 cups of flour.

   a)   How many pancakes can you make with 1 cup of flour?

   b)   How many pancakes can you make with 9 cups of flour?

   c)   Do you have enough to make 100 pancakes? Explain your reasoning.

Practice 2.5

Evaluate each expression. Give your answer in simplest form.

1 $\frac{1}{2} + \left(-\frac{5}{6}\right)$

2 $\frac{-6}{7} + \frac{3}{14}$

3 $-\frac{1}{7} + \left(\frac{-3}{5}\right)$

4 $\frac{1}{2} + \left(-\frac{2}{5}\right) + \frac{1}{4}$

5 $\frac{-1}{7} + \left(\frac{-5}{6}\right) + \left(\frac{-1}{3}\right)$

6 $\frac{3}{5} - \frac{2}{3}$

7 $\frac{-1}{7} - \frac{3}{14}$

8 $-\frac{1}{5} - \left(\frac{-2}{7}\right)$

9 $\frac{1}{3} - \left(-\frac{2}{5}\right) - \frac{3}{4}$

Evaluate each product. Give your answer in simplest form.

10 $-\frac{7}{25} \cdot \frac{5}{14}$

11 $\frac{5}{8} \cdot \left(-\frac{4}{15}\right)$

12 $\frac{7}{30} \cdot \left(-\frac{6}{7}\right)$

13 $-\frac{8}{27} \cdot \left(-\frac{9}{40}\right)$

14 $-\frac{11}{16} \cdot \left(-\frac{4}{33}\right)$

15 $\frac{5}{8} \cdot \left(-2\frac{4}{5}\right)$

16 $-\frac{3}{22} \cdot 1\frac{5}{6}$

17 $3\frac{1}{8} \cdot \left(-\frac{3}{10}\right)$

18 $-4\frac{1}{2} \cdot \left(-1\frac{8}{9}\right)$

Evaluate each quotient. Give your answer in simplest form.

19 $-10 \div \left(-\frac{5}{6}\right)$

20 $\frac{9}{25} \div (-18)$

21 $-\frac{3}{8} \div \left(-\frac{1}{8}\right)$

22 $-\frac{1}{4} \div \frac{3}{8}$

23 $\frac{5}{12} \div \left(-\frac{1}{6}\right)$

24 $-1\frac{1}{4} \div \frac{3}{4}$

25 $\frac{8}{15} \div \left(-2\frac{2}{3}\right)$

26 $3\frac{3}{4} \div \left(-\frac{1}{4}\right)$

27 $2\frac{1}{2} \div \left(-1\frac{2}{3}\right)$

28 $-2\frac{2}{7} \div \left(-1\frac{3}{7}\right)$

29 $\dfrac{-7}{-\left(\frac{7}{3}\right)}$

30 $\dfrac{-\left(\frac{2}{3}\right)}{4}$

31 $\dfrac{-\left(\frac{3}{4}\right)}{-\left(\frac{5}{8}\right)}$

32 $\dfrac{-\left(\frac{1}{5}\right)}{\left(1\frac{2}{15}\right)}$

Solve. Show your work.

33 David biked $15\frac{9}{10}$ miles on Saturday and $6\frac{7}{10}$ miles on Sunday. How much farther did David bike on Saturday than on Sunday?

34 A recipe calls for $\frac{3}{4}$ cup of flour, but Kelli has only $\frac{1}{3}$ cup of flour. How much more flour does she need?

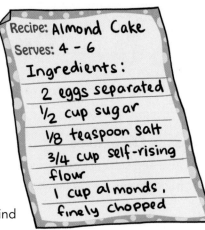

35 A weather report showed that the rainfall in Janesville was $2\frac{2}{3}$ inches during the first half of January. At the end of January, the total rainfall was $3\frac{1}{4}$ inches. How much did it rain in the second half of January?

36 The sum of two rational numbers is $5\frac{1}{2}$. If one of the numbers is $6\frac{3}{14}$, find the other number.

37 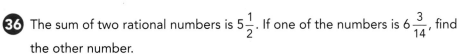 *Math Journal* Peter adds $\frac{1}{a} + \left(-\frac{1}{b}\right)$ and says the answer is $\frac{1}{a-b}$. Give an example to show that Peter is wrong.

38 *Math Journal* Jo multiplies two mixed numbers, $-4\frac{3}{5}$ and $1\frac{2}{7}$, as follows:

$$-4\frac{3}{5} \cdot 1\frac{2}{7} = -4 \cdot 1 \cdot \frac{3}{5} \cdot \frac{2}{7}$$
$$= -4 \cdot \frac{3 \cdot 2}{5 \cdot 7}$$
$$= -4\frac{6}{35}$$

Describe Jo's mistakes. What is the correct answer?

39 A clock's battery is running low. Every 6 hours, it slows down by $\frac{1}{2}$ hour. By how much does it slow down in 1 hour?

40 Package A weighs $5\frac{1}{2}$ pounds and package B weighs $1\frac{1}{4}$ pounds. Find the average weight of the two packages.

41 A scientist measured the weight of some damp soil. After exposing the soil to the air for $4\frac{1}{2}$ weeks, the scientist found that the weight had decreased by $5\frac{5}{8}$ ounces. Find the average weight loss per week.

42 A plank measures $4\frac{3}{4}$ feet. Elizabeth cuts off $\frac{2}{5}$ of the plank. How long is the plank now?

Operations with Decimals

Lesson Objectives

- Add and subtract decimals.
- Multiply and divide numbers in decimal or percent form.

Add and Subtract Decimals.

You have learned how to add and subtract positive decimals, and how to apply rules for adding and subtracting integers. You can combine these skills to add and subtract decimals.

The table shows the monthly profits and losses in dollars of a company for the first three months of one year.

January	February	March
−$2.14 million	−$1.5 million	$2.17 million

From the table, the negative decimals mean that the company lost money doing business in January and February.

It made a profit in March.

> **Math Note**
>
> A company has a profit if its income is more than its expenses. It has a loss if the income is less than its expenses.
>
> Income and expenses are always positive, but business losses can be represented by negative numbers.

You can find the company's combined loss for January and February, as well as the net profit or loss the company made at the end of the three months.

To find the combined loss for January and February, evaluate the sum of −2.14 and −1.5. In this case, you are adding two negative decimals, −2.14 + (−1.5).

Using absolute values,

$|-2.14| + |-1.5| = 2.14 + 1.5$ Add the absolute values.
              $= 3.64$ Simplify.

You add the absolute values because you are adding two negative decimals.

Align decimal points

$$\begin{array}{r} 2.1\,4 \\ +\ 1.5\,0 \\ \hline 3.6\,4 \end{array}$$ ← Insert zero

$-2.14 + (-1.5) = -3.64$ Use the common sign, a negative sign.

The combined loss for January and February is $3.64 million.

To find the net profit or loss of the company at the end of the three months, evaluate the sum of −2.14, −1.5, and 2.17. Since −2.14 + (−1.5) = −3.64, you only need to find −3.64 + 2.17. In this case, you are adding two decimals with different signs.

Using absolute values,

$|-3.64| - |2.17| = 3.64 - 2.17$ Subtract the lesser absolute value from the greater one.
              $= 1.47$ Simplify.

You subtract the absolute values because you are adding two decimals with different signs.

Align decimal points

$$\begin{array}{r} 3.\overset{5\ \ 14}{\cancel{6}\,\cancel{4}} \\ -\ 2.1\,7 \\ \hline 1.4\,7 \end{array}$$

$-3.64 + 2.17 = -1.47$ Use a negative sign, because −3.64 has a greater absolute value.

Because −1.47 is negative, you know that the company had a net loss at the end of the three months. The company had a net loss of $1.47 million.

Example 19 | **Add and subtract decimals.**

Evaluate each expression.

a)   −4.52 + 3.26

Solution

Using absolute values,

$|-4.52| - |3.26| = 4.52 - 3.26$ Subtract the lesser absolute value from the greater one.

$= 1.26$ Simplify.

$-4.52 + 3.26 = -1.26$ Use a negative sign, because −4.52 has a greater absolute value.

b)   −7.4 − 5.18

Solution

$-7.4 - 5.18 = -7.4 + (-5.18)$ Rewrite subtraction as adding the opposite.

Using absolute values,

$|-7.4| + |-5.18| = 7.4 + 5.18$ Add the absolute values.

$= 12.58$ Simplify.

$-7.4 - 5.18 = -12.58$ Use the common sign, a negative sign.

Guided Practice

Copy and complete.

1 2.35 + (−6.13)

Using absolute values,

$\underline{\ ?\ } - \underline{\ ?\ } = \underline{\ ?\ } - \underline{\ ?\ }$ Subtract the lesser absolute value from the greater absolute value.

$= \underline{\ ?\ }$ Simplify.

$2.35 + (-6.13) = \underline{\ ?\ }$ Use a $\underline{\ ?\ }$ sign, because $\underline{\ ?\ }$ has a greater absolute value.

Solve.

2 −8.6 − 3.27

3 3.38 + (−5.6)

Example 20 **Add and subtract decimals in a real-world situation.**

A diver went 30.65 feet below the surface of the ocean, and then 46.5 feet farther down. He then rose 52.45 feet. Find the diver's new depth.

Solution

$-30.65 - 46.5 + 52.45$	Write an expression.
$= -30.65 + (-46.5) + 52.45$	Rewrite subtraction as adding the opposite.

Using absolute values to add the first two numbers,

$\|-30.65\| + \|-46.5\| = 30.65 + 46.5$	Add the absolute values of the first two numbers.
$= 77.15$	Simplify.
$-30.65 - 46.5 = -77.15$	Use the common sign, a negative sign.

Using absolute values to add the sum of the first two numbers to the third,

$\|-77.15\| - \|52.45\| = 77.15 - 52.45$	Subtract the lesser absolute value.
$= 24.7$	Simplify.
$-77.15 + 52.45 = -24.7$	Use a negative sign, because -77.15 has a greater absolute value.

$-30.65 - 46.5 + 52.45 = -24.7$

The diver's new depth is 24.7 feet below the surface of the ocean.

Guided Practice

Solve.

4 At noon, the temperature was 2.7°F. By midnight, the temperature had dropped 7.5°F. Then, during the morning, the temperature rose 3.8°F. Find the final temperature.

Multiply Numbers in Decimal or Percent Form.

The rules for multiplying integers also apply to multiplying numbers in decimal form. For example, evaluate the product of -2.05 and 1.2.

First you multiply the two decimals without their signs. Then apply what you know about multiplying numbers with the same or different signs.

The product of -2.05 and 1.2 has a negative sign because the two decimals have different signs. So, the product of -2.05 and 1.2 is -2.46.

$-2.05 \cdot 1.2 = -2.46.$

$$
\begin{array}{r}
\overset{1}{2}.0\ 5 \quad \leftarrow \text{ 2 decimal places} \\
\times \quad 1.2 \quad \leftarrow \text{ + 1 decimal place} \\
\hline
4\ 1\ 0 \\
2\ 0\ 5 \quad\ \\
\hline
2.4\ 6\ 0 \quad \leftarrow \text{ 3 decimal places}
\end{array}
$$

Example 21 **Multiply decimals.**

Evaluate each product.

a)   6.72 · (−0.4)

Solution

```
    ²
    6.7 2  ←——  2 decimal places
  ×    0.4  ←——  + 1 decimal place
    2 6 8 8                            Multiply the numbers without their signs.
      0 0 0
    2.6 8 8  ←——  3 decimal places     Add.
```

6.72 · (−0.4) = −2.688   Product of two decimals with different signs is negative.

b)   −51 · (−8.5)

Solution

```
      5 1  ←——  0 decimal place
  ×   8.5  ←——  + 1 decimal place
    2 5 5                              Multiply the numbers without their signs.
  4 0 8
  4 3 3.5  ←——  1 decimal place        Add.
```

−51 · (−8.5) = 433.5   Product of two decimals with the same sign is positive.

c)   6% of 530

> **Math Note**
>
> Percent is written as %, which means out of 100. It can be written as a decimal. So, $6\% = \frac{6}{100} = 0.06$

Solution

```
      ¹
      5 3 0  ←——  0 decimal place
  ×   0.0 6  ←——  + 2 decimal places
    3 1 8 0                            Multiply the numbers without their signs.
    0 0 0
  0 0 0
  0 3 1.8 0  ←——  2 decimal places     Add.
```

6% · 530 = 31.8   Product of two decimals with the same sign is positive.

Guided Practice

Evaluate each product.

 −7.23 · 4.6   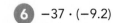 −37 · (−9.2)   **7** 8% of $230

Divide Numbers in Decimal or Percent Form.

The rules for dividing integers also apply to dividing numbers in decimal form.

For example, evaluate $-24.18 \div 2.6$.

First you divide the two decimals without their signs. Then use what you know about dividing numbers with the same or different signs.

$$2.6\overline{)24.18}$$

Make the divisor a whole number by multiplying both the divisor and the dividend by 10.

$$\begin{array}{r} 9.3 \\ 26\overline{)241.8} \\ \underline{234} \\ 7\ 8 \\ \underline{7\ 8} \\ 0 \end{array}$$

Place the decimal point in the quotient above the decimal point in the dividend.

$-24.18 \div 2.6 = -9.3$

You use a negative sign because the two decimals have different signs.

Example 22 **Divide a decimal by a decimal.**

Evaluate $13.14 \div (-1.8)$.

Solution

$$1.8\overline{)13.14}$$

Make the divisor a whole number by multiplying both the divisor and the dividend by 10.

$$\begin{array}{r} 7.3 \\ 18\overline{)131.4} \\ \underline{126} \\ 5\ 4 \\ \underline{5\ 4} \\ 0 \end{array}$$

Place the decimal point in the quotient above the decimal point in the dividend.

$13.14 \div (-1.8) = -7.3$

Guided Practice

Tell whether each quotient is positive or negative. Then evaluate the quotient.

8 $-21.7 \div 0.7$

9 $-31.92 \div (-4.2)$

Example 23 Apply the order of operations to decimals.

a) A hot air balloon ascended at 0.7 meter per second for 8 seconds. It then descended at 0.5 meter per second for 6 seconds. Find the overall change in altitude.

Solution

$$0.7 \cdot 8 - 0.5 \cdot 6 = 5.6 - 3.0 \qquad \text{Multiply.}$$
$$= 2.6 \qquad \text{Subtract.}$$

The overall change in altitude is 2.6 meters.

b) An electronic game system set costs $399 plus a 4% sales tax. What is the total cost of the game system?

Solution

Method 1

$$\$399 + 0.04 \cdot \$399 = \$399 + \$15.96 \qquad \text{Multiply.}$$
$$= \$414.96 \qquad \text{Add.}$$

The total cost of the game system is $414.96.

The total cost is more than $399 because you have to pay a 4% sales tax.

Method 2

$$\$399 \cdot 1.04 = \$414.96 \qquad \text{Multiply.}$$

The total cost of the game system is $414.96.

c) Over a 10-year period, the population of one city changed from 3.2 million to 2.8 million. What was the percent change in the city's population?

Solution

Percent change:

$$\frac{(2.8 - 3.2)}{3.2} \cdot 100\% = -\frac{0.4}{3.2} \cdot 100\% \qquad \text{Subtract.}$$
$$= -12.5\% \qquad \text{Simplify.}$$

The percent change in the city's population is −12.5%.

The percent change is negative because there is a drop in the city's population.

Guided Practice

Solve.

10 The temperature in a certain town drops by 1.6°F per hour for 1.2 hours. It then drops by 0.8°F per hour for 2.5 hours. Find the total change in temperature.

You can use a negative number to represent the hourly drop in temperature.

Total change in temperature:

$$-1.6 \cdot \underline{\quad?\quad} + (-0.8) \cdot \underline{\quad?\quad} = \underline{\quad?\quad} + (\underline{\quad?\quad})$$
$$= \underline{\quad?\quad}$$

The total change in temperature is __?__ °F.

11 Mrs. Thompson usually uses 0.5 cup of sugar to bake a raisin cake. To bake a healthier raisin cake using less sugar, she decreases the amount of sugar by 20%. What is the amount of sugar that Mrs. Thompson uses for baking the healthier raisin cake?

$$0.5 - (\underline{\quad?\quad} \cdot \underline{\quad?\quad}) = 0.5 - \underline{\quad?\quad} \qquad \text{Multiply.}$$
$$= \underline{\quad?\quad} \qquad \text{Add.}$$

The amount of sugar that she uses is __?__ cup.

12 Janice buys four boxes of paper clips. She pays with a $10 bill and receives $6.08 in change. What is the price of one box of paper clips?

13 According to the 2000 census and the 2010 census, the population of the United States changed from 281.4 million to 308.7 million. Find the percent change in the population of the United States over the 10-year period. Round your answer to the nearest tenth.

14 Stratosphere Tower in Las Vegas, Nevada, is the tallest freestanding observation tower in United States. Its height is 350.2 meters. The Eiffel Tower in Paris, France, is the country's tallest building. Its height is 324 meters. Find the difference in their heights.

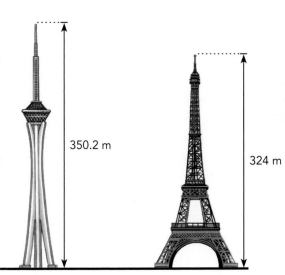

350.2 m

324 m

Practice 2.6

Evaluate each sum or difference.

1 $-6.25 + 3.9$

2 $-2.074 + 1.8$

3 $-11.52 - 6.3$

4 $-29.4 - (-7.21)$

5 $-8.106 - 0.98$

Evaluate each product.

6 $0.3 \cdot (-4.8)$

7 $-1.6 \cdot 2.9$

8 $-3.25 \cdot (-1.7)$

9 $2.03 \cdot (-5.4)$

10 $-0.08 \cdot 3.2$

Evaluate each quotient.

11 $-29.52 \div 3.6$

12 $107.64 \div (-2.3)$

13 $-40.56 \div (-5.2)$

14 $9.758 \div 0.41$

Evaluate each expression.

15 $-0.59 - 1.2 - 3.4$

16 $-2.38 + 15.6 - 140.05$

17 $38.92 - 6.7 - (-12.04)$

18 $712.14 - 356.8 - (-9.03)$

19 $11.3 - 5.1 + 3.1 \cdot 0.2 - 1.1$

20 $(29.3 + 4) \div 3 + 0.5 \cdot 2$

Solve. Show your work.

21 In Arizona, a minimum temperature of −40.0°F was recorded at Hawley Lake in 1971. A maximum recorded temperature of 53.3°F was recorded at Lake Havasu City in 1994. Find the difference between these maximum and minimum temperatures.

22 A shop owner buys 5 handbags to sell in his shop. The owner pays $39.75 for each handbag. Later, the owner has to sell the handbags at a loss. If he charges $27.79 for each handbag, what is his total loss for the 5 handbags?

23 The original price of a football helmet was $78.60. If Peter was given a 15% discount, how much did he pay for the football helmet?

24 The state sales tax in New York is 4.25%. Jean spends $208 at a department store, but only half of the merchandise she purchases is taxed. What is her total bill?

25 Sarah bought some T-shirts and a pair of shorts for $66.30. The pair of shorts costs $15.90 and each T-shirt costs $5.60. How many T-shirts did she buy?

26 Margaret wants to buy 10 books. Six of them cost $12.50 each and the rest cost $26.35 each. If she only has $150, how much is she short?

27 The recommended calcium intake for men and women is about 1.2 grams per day. A glass of milk contains about 0.27 gram of calcium. If a man drinks 3 glasses of milk, how much additional calcium does he need from other food sources?

28 *Math Journal* Susannah evaluated an expression as follows:

$$48 \div 2(0.9 + 0.3) = 48 \div 2 \cdot 1.2$$
$$= 48 \div 2.4$$
$$= 20$$

She made a common mistake when applying the order of operations. Explain her mistake and help her solve the problem correctly.

29 One day in February, the temperature at 9 A.M. is $-6.8°F$. At 3 P.M. on the same day, the temperature is $1.72°F$.

a) Find the change in temperature.

b) Find the average hourly rate of change in temperature.

30 A submarine was cruising at 1,328.4 feet below sea level. It then rose at a rate of 14.76 feet per minute for 15 minutes.

a) Find the submarine's depth after it rose for 15 minutes.

b) If the submarine continued to rise at this same rate, find the time it took to reach the surface from the depth you found in **a)**.

31 James is mountain climbing. Using a rope, James climbs down from the top of a steep cliff for 4 minutes at a rate of 12.2 feet per minute. He then climbs back up for 10 minutes at a rate of 3.6 feet per minute. How far from the top of the cliff is he after 14 minutes?

32 Salina has 120 shares in a shipyard company. On Monday, the value of each share dropped by $0.38. On Tuesday, the value of each share rose by $0.16. Find the total change in the value of Salina's 120 shares.

33 An organization that raises funds for charity raised $2.45 million last year and $1.96 million this year. Find the percent change in the amount raised.

34 A company suffered a loss of $5.4 million in its first year. It lost another $3.1 million in the second year. It made a profit of $4.9 million in the third year.

   a) Find the average profit or loss for the first three years.

   b) After its fourth year of business, the company's combined profit for all four years was $0. Find the company's profit or loss during the fourth year.

Brain @ Work

1 The average of seven rational numbers is −5.16.

   a) Find the sum of the rational numbers.

   b) If six of the numbers each equal −5.48, find the seventh number.

2 The temperature of dry air decreases by about 0.98°F for every 100-meter increase in altitude.

   a) The temperature above a town is 16°F on a dry day. Find the temperature of an aircraft 3.6 kilometers above the town.

   b) The temperature outside an aircraft 1.8 kilometers above the town is −5.64°F. Find the temperature in the town.

3 Julie finds a way to use mental math to find the averages of these numbers:

15, 19, 18, 12, 20

She guesses that the mean is about 17, and uses mental math to find how far above or below this value each data item is:

−2, 2, 1, −5, 3

She uses mental math to add these amounts:

−2 + 2 + 1 + (−5) + 3 = −1

She then divides −1 by 5 to get an average of −0.2. She says this means that the average of the numbers is 0.2 less than 17, the number she estimated. Check that Julie's method gives the correct average. Then use it to find the average of these 4 numbers:

32, 35, 38, 36

Chapter Wrap Up

Concept Map

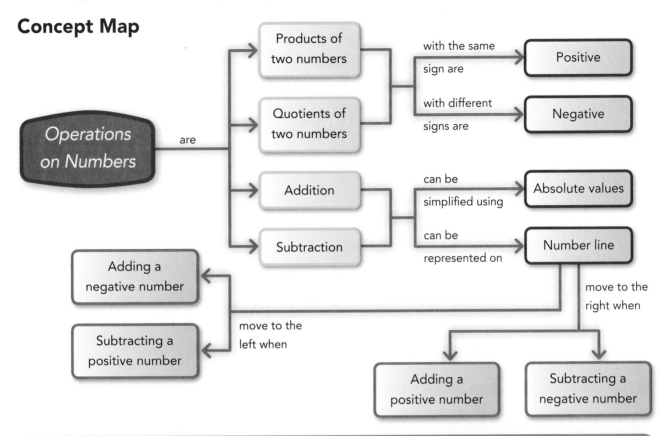

Key Concepts

▶ You can use a number line or absolute values to add or subtract integers, rational numbers, and decimal numbers. The sum of positive numbers is positive. The sum of negative numbers is negative.

▶ Subtracting a number is the same as adding its opposite, or additive inverse.
Example: $3 - (-2) = 3 + 2$.

▶ To evaluate the sum or difference of rational numbers with the same denominators, add or subtract their numerators.
Examples: $\frac{1}{5} + \frac{2}{5} = \frac{1+2}{5} = \frac{3}{5}$ and $\frac{2}{3} - \frac{1}{3} = \frac{2-1}{3} = \frac{1}{3}$.

▶ To evaluate the sum or difference of rational numbers with different denominators, rewrite the rational numbers using a common denominator, and then add or subtract. **Example:** $\frac{1}{2} - \frac{2}{3} = \frac{3}{6} - \frac{4}{6} = \frac{3-4}{6} = -\frac{1}{6}$.

▶ The product or quotient of two numbers with the same sign is positive. The product or quotient of two numbers with different signs is negative.
Examples: $-3(-2) = 6$ and $3(-2) = -6$.

Chapter Review/Test

Concepts and Skills

Evaluate each sum or difference.

1 $-6 + 14$

2 $-25 + (-9)$

3 $52 + (-52)$

4 $46 + (-17) + 38$

5 $-80 + 63 + (-24)$

6 $35 - 140$

7 $-61 - 28$

8 $128 - (-73)$

9 $-8 - (-50)$

10 $\dfrac{1}{4} - \dfrac{7}{8}$

11 $14\dfrac{2}{3} - 8\dfrac{4}{5}$

12 $-6\dfrac{1}{7} + 3\dfrac{5}{14}$

Evaluate each product or quotient.

13 $-5 \cdot 11$

14 $-30 \cdot (-4)$

15 $144 \div (-6)$

16 $-48 \div (-3)$

17 $-126 \div 9$

18 $104 \div (-8)$

19 $\dfrac{-5}{8} \cdot \dfrac{8}{15}$

20 $-\dfrac{3}{4} \cdot \left(-1\dfrac{2}{3}\right)$

21 $5\dfrac{1}{4} \div \left(-\dfrac{7}{12}\right)$

22 $-4\dfrac{4}{5} \div 1\dfrac{1}{3}$

23 $\dfrac{-\left(\frac{2}{5}\right)}{-\left(\frac{8}{15}\right)}$

24 $\dfrac{\left(3\frac{1}{3}\right)}{-\left(2\frac{2}{9}\right)}$

Evaluate each expression.

25 $12.3 - 8.1 + 2\dfrac{1}{10} \cdot 0.4 - 1.6$

26 $(25.7 + 4) \div 3 + 0.8 \cdot 2$

27 $10 - 32.86 \div 5.3 + 7\left(\dfrac{81}{100}\right)$

28 $3.25(0.9 - 0.74) + 6.3$

29 $\dfrac{\frac{1}{3} - \frac{1}{4}}{\frac{1}{8} + \frac{1}{2}}$

30 $8.5 - \dfrac{-\left(\frac{1}{6}\right)}{\left(\frac{5}{18}\right)}$

Problem Solving

Solve. Show your work.

31 When you wake up on Monday, the temperature is $-18°F$. During the day, the temperature rises $13°F$. By the time you wake up on Tuesday, it has dropped $19°F$. What is the temperature when you wake up on Tuesday?

32 Tim dug a hole that was $16\frac{1}{2}$ inches deep. He left a pile of dirt next to the hole that was $8\frac{3}{4}$ inches high. Show how you could use subtraction to find the distance from the top of the pile of dirt to the bottom of the hole.

33 Daniel bought four bags of potatoes. The weight of the first bag was 2.6 pounds. The second bag weighed 0.4 pound less than twice the weight of the first bag. The third bag weighed 0.6 pound more than the first bag. The fourth bag weighed 0.3 pound less than the weight of the second bag. What is the average weight of the bags of potatoes that Daniel bought? Round your answer to the nearest tenth.

34 A hiker descended 320 feet in 40 minutes. Find the hiker's average change in elevation per minute.

35 A hot air balloon descends 305 feet per minute for 4 minutes and then ascends at a rate of 215 feet per minute for another 2 minutes. Find the total change in the balloon's altitude.

36 Suppose you deposit $12.50 into your savings account each week for 4 weeks and then withdraw $4.80 each week for the next two weeks. Find the total change in the amount of money in your account.

37 A game show awards 30 points for each correct answer and deducts 50 points for each incorrect answer. A contestant answers 2 questions incorrectly and 3 questions correctly. What is his final score?

38 The price of a stock falls $1.50 each day for 7 days.

   a) Find the total change in the price of the stock.

   b) If the value of the stock was $36 before the price of the stock started falling for 7 days, find the price of the stock after those 7 days.

39 Martin uses 24 boards that are each $5\frac{3}{4}$ feet long to build a tree house. The wood costs $1.65 per foot. Find the total cost of the wood.

40 James bought 8 baseball caps for $12.99 each before sales tax. The sales tax in his state is 6%. How much must James pay in total?

41 Over a period of 5 years, the enrollment at a college changes from 12,000 students to 14,000 students. Find the percent change in enrollment.

Cumulative Review Chapters 1–2

Concepts and Skills

Write each number as $\frac{m}{n}$ in simplest form, where m and n are integers with $n \neq 0$. (Lesson 1.1)

1 -0.87

2 12.8

3 -1.9

Using long division, write each rational number as a terminating or a repeating decimal. Identify a pattern of repeating digits using bar notation. (Lesson 1.2)

4 $\frac{9}{5}$

5 $\frac{23}{16}$

6 $-\frac{51}{110}$

Use a calculator. Locate each irrational number to 2 decimal places on the number line using rational approximations. (Lesson 1.3)

7 $\sqrt{44}$

8 $\sqrt{132}$

9 $-\sqrt{162}$

10 $-\sqrt[3]{100}$

11 $\frac{\pi}{7}$

12 π^3

Order the real numbers below from greatest to least using the symbol $>$. (Lesson 1.4)

13 $\sqrt{345}$, $\frac{244}{7}$, $\sqrt[3]{675}$, $-\frac{86}{3}$, 33.9

Round each number to the given number of significant digits. (Lesson 1.5)

14 $349{,}950$ (to 4 significant digits)

15 0.09608 (to 3 significant digits)

Evaluate each expression. (Lessons 2.1, 2.2)

16 $7 + (-12)$

17 $-15 + (-20)$

18 $-8 + 6 - 4$

19 $11 - (-14)$

20 $32 - (-17)$

21 $-7 - 5 - (-6)$

22 $-250 + 480$

23 $-109 - (-121)$

24 $43 + (-95) - (-16)$

Evaluate each product or quotient. As needed, give your answer in simplest form. (Lessons 2.3, 2.5)

25 $-12 \cdot 8$

26 $\frac{2}{15} \cdot \left(-\frac{5}{8}\right)$

27 $2\frac{2}{5} \cdot \left(-1\frac{1}{4}\right)$

28 $-9 \div (-7)$

29 $-\frac{7}{16} \div \left(-\frac{21}{6}\right)$

30 $\dfrac{\left(-\frac{3}{4}\right)}{\left(2\frac{1}{4}\right)}$

Evaluate each expression. (Lessons 2.3, 2.4, 2.5, 2.6)

31 $-3 \cdot 12 - (-6) + 2(-7) \div 7$

32 $\frac{2}{3} \cdot \frac{1}{6} + 1\frac{5}{9} + 2\left(-\frac{7}{18}\right)$

33 $-4 \cdot 5.2 - 0.5 \cdot (-7.8) + 2 \cdot 1.3$

34 $-\frac{1}{5}[-20 + 1.2(-3)] + 1\frac{2}{5}$

Problem Solving

Solve. Show your work.

35 An athlete completes a 400-meter dash in 46.3 seconds. What is his speed in meters per second correct to 3 significant digits? (Chapter 1)

36 The greatest and least temperatures ever recorded in Tim's hometown are 101°F and −36°F. Find the difference between these two temperatures. (Chapter 2)

37 On a math quiz consisting of 100 questions, the teacher gives 2 points for a correct answer, −1 point for an incorrect answer, and −2 points for not answering a question at all. (Chapter 2)

   a) Emily answered 75 questions correctly, 18 incorrectly, and did not answer 7 questions. What is her score?

   b) Amy answered 30 questions correctly and 62 incorrectly. What is her score?

38 Justin dug a hole that was $9\frac{1}{2}$ inches deep. His sister Jean built a sand castle next to the hole that was $12\frac{3}{4}$ inches high. Show how you could use subtraction to find the vertical distance from the top of the castle to the bottom of the hole. (Chapter 2)

39 Rick started his hike at an elevation of 8,975 feet. He descended at a constant rate of 8.5 feet per minute for 45 minutes. Find Rick's elevation after 45 minutes. Give your answer to 4 significant digits. (Chapters 1, 2)

40 A car travels at $68\frac{2}{3}$ miles per hour for $2\frac{1}{12}$ hours. Find the distance that the car has traveled correct to 3 significant digits. (Chapters 1, 2)

41 In a particular town, the temperature at midnight is −2°C. It rises at a steady rate for 12 hours to reach a temperature of 22°C at noon. (Chapter 2)

   a) Find the difference between the temperature at noon and at midnight.

   b) Find the temperature at 7 A.M.

   c) Find the time when the temperature is 4°C.

Algebraic Expressions

What are the costs for a field trip?

Your teacher has decided to bring the class on a field trip to the Statue of Liberty National Monument. Each student going on the trip must bring a signed permission form and money to pay for lunch and the bus fare.

Each student has to pay a certain amount for lunch and a certain amount for the bus fare. The teacher can use an algebraic expression to estimate the total cost per student. For a given number of students, the teacher can also write an algebraic expression to find the total amount of money that will be collected for the field trip.

BIG IDEA

▶ Algebraic expressions containing rational numbers and several variables can be simplified, expanded, or factored to write equivalent expressions.

Recall Prior Knowledge

Recognizing parts of an algebraic expression

A variable can be used to represent an unknown value or quantity. An algebraic expression is a mathematical phrase that includes variables, numbers, and operation symbols.

✓ Quick Check

Consider the algebraic expression 3x + 4. State the following.

1 How many terms are there?

2 State the coefficient of the algebraic term.

3 What is the constant term?

4 Write the operation symbol.

Evaluating algebraic expressions

Evaluate an algebraic expression by replacing all its variables with their assigned values.

Given that $a = 5$ in the expression $2a - 3$, find the value of the expression.

$$2a - 3 = (2 \cdot 5) - 3$$
$$= 10 - 3$$
$$= 7$$

✓ Quick Check

5 **Complete the table.**

x	x + 9	7x	5x − 2
0	0 + 9 = 9	?	?
2	?	?	?
−1	?	?	?
7	?	?	?

Simplifying algebraic expressions

Simplify expressions by adding or subtracting the coefficients of like terms (terms with same variable). Algebraic terms cannot be added to or subtracted from constant terms.

Can be Simplified	Cannot be Simplified
• $4a + 3 + 6 = 4a + 9$ • $6x - 2x + 5 = 4x + 5$	• $4x + 3y + 7$ has no like terms. • $2a - b + 3$ has no like terms.

☑ Quick Check

State whether each expression can be simplified. Explain your reasoning.

6 $2k - 3 + k$

7 $7x + 3 - 3y$

8 $6u + 5w - 1$

9 $4g - 3g - g$

Simplify each expression.

10 $4t + 1 + 6$

11 $5p - 5p$

12 $4y + 5y + 3$

13 $4m - 3m - 3$

Expanding algebraic expressions

Expand algebraic expressions by applying the distributive property to remove the parentheses.

$3(p + 2) = 3(p) + 3(2)$
$\qquad = 3p + 6$

$6(w - 4) = 6(w) - 6(4)$
$\qquad = 6w - 24$

☑ Quick Check

Expand each expression.

14 $4(h + 2)$

15 $5(4 + 5c)$

16 $3(4x - 11)$

17 $7(3 - 5p)$

Factoring algebraic expressions

Factoring is the inverse of expansion. Factor an algebraic expression by writing it as a product of its factors. You can use the distributive property to factor expressions whose terms have a common factor.

$2x + 10 = 2(x) + 2(5)$ The common factor of 2x and 10 is 2.

$ = 2(x + 5)$

☑ Quick Check

Factor each expression.

18 $6m + 3$

19 $4v + 14$

20 $10p - 2$

21 $6 - 18c$

Recognizing equivalent expressions

Equivalent expressions are expressions that are equal for any values of the variables. Use an equal sign to relate equivalent expressions.

$4(x + 3)$ and $4x + 12$ are equivalent expressions because they are equal for all values of x. So, you can write $4x + 12 = 4(x + 3)$.

☑ Quick Check

Choose an equivalent expression.

22 $6y - 3$ is equivalent to

   a) $3(3y - 1)$ **b)** $3(2y - 1)$ **c)** $3(2y - 3)$ **d)** $6(3y - 1)$

Writing algebraic expressions to represent unknown quantities

Wesley is 2 years older than his brother Jeremy.
- When Jeremy is 12 years old, Wesley will be $(12 + 2) = 14$ years old.
- When Jeremy is x years old, Wesley will be $(x + 2)$ years old.

☑ Quick Check

x is an unknown number. Write an expression for each of the following.

23 7 more than the number

24 Product of 8 and the number

25 5 less than twice the number

26 3 more than half the number

Adding Algebraic Terms

Lesson Objectives

• Represent algebraic expressions using bar models.
• Simplify algebraic expressions with decimal and fractional coefficients by adding like terms.

Represent Algebraic Expressions Using Bar Models.

You have learned that to simplify an algebraic expression like $2x + x$, where x is a variable, you add the like terms:

$2x + x = 3x$

In the expression $2x + x$, the terms have coefficients that are whole numbers. Algebraic terms can also have fractional or decimal coefficients.

Examples: $\frac{2}{3}x$, $0.5y$, $\frac{3}{2}p$, $1.8q$

You can represent algebraic terms with rational coefficients using bar models as follows:

a) $\frac{2}{3}x$

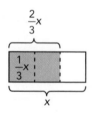

Divide x (the whole) into three $\frac{1}{3}x$ sections.

b) $0.5y$

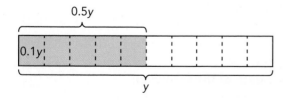

Divide y (the whole) into ten $0.1y$ sections.

> **Think Math**
>
> Give a reason why you write $\frac{1}{2}p$ or $0.5y$ instead of $p\frac{1}{2}$ or $y0.5$.

c) $\frac{3}{2}p$

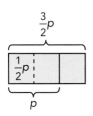

Divide p (the whole) into two $\frac{1}{2}p$ sections. Then add one $\frac{1}{2}p$ section to make a bar that is $\frac{3}{2}p$ sections long.

d) $1.2q$

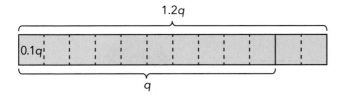

Divide q (the whole) into ten $0.1q$ sections. Then add two $0.1q$ sections to make a bar that is $1.2q$ sections long.

Simplify Algebraic Expressions with Decimal Coefficients by Adding.

You simplify algebraic expressions like $0.7x + 0.3x$ by adding the two like terms.

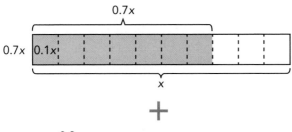

Represent the term $0.7x$ using a bar divided into ten $0.1x$ sections.

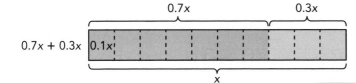

Represent the term $0.3x$ using a bar divided into ten $0.1x$ sections.

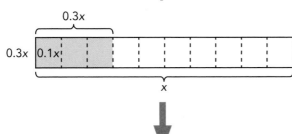

Add the like terms.

When the coefficient of a variable, x, is 1, you can write "x" instead of "$1x$".

From the bar model,
$0.7x + 0.3x = 1x$
$\qquad\qquad\quad\ = x$

You can add two like terms by adding their coefficients. The sum of the coefficients is the coefficient of the term in the simplified expression.

Example 1 **Simplify algebraic expressions with decimal coefficients by adding.**

Simplify the expression $0.9p + 0.7p$.

Solution

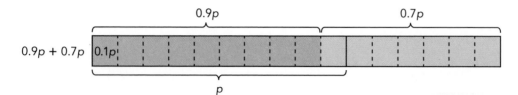

$0.9p$ $0.7p$

$0.9p + 0.7p$ | $0.1p$ |

p

Represent the term $0.9p$ with nine $0.1p$ sections and the term $0.7p$ with seven $0.1p$ sections.

From the bar model,
$0.9p + 0.7p = 1.6p$

The sum is the total number of colored sections in the model.

Guided Practice

Copy and complete to simplify each expression.

1 $0.2y + 0.6y$

?   ?

$0.2y + 0.6y$ | $0.1y$ |

?

$0.2y + 0.6y = \underline{}$

2 $0.8p + 0.5p$

?   ?

$0.8p + 0.5p$ | $0.1p$ |

?

$0.8p + 0.5p = \underline{}$

3 $1.3g + 0.9g$

$1.3g + 0.9g = \underline{}$

Simplify Algebraic Expressions with Fractional Coefficients by Adding.

In the same way, $\frac{1}{2}a + \frac{1}{4}a$ can be simplified as follows:

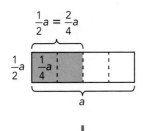

Represent the term $\frac{1}{2}a$ by dividing a bar into two $\frac{1}{2}a$ sections. Then further divide each $\frac{1}{2}a$ section into two equal parts. Each part is now one $\frac{1}{4}a$ section.

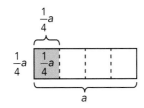

Represent the term $\frac{1}{4}a$ by dividing a bar into four $\frac{1}{4}a$ sections.

Add the like terms.

From the bar model,

$$\frac{1}{2}a + \frac{1}{4}a = \frac{3}{4}a$$

To simplify $\frac{1}{2}a$ and $\frac{1}{4}a$, you can also add the coefficients of the terms $\frac{1}{2}a$ and $\frac{1}{4}a$.

First rewrite the coefficients so that they have the same denominator.

The least common denominator (LCD) of $\frac{1}{2}$ and $\frac{1}{4}$ is 4.

You can rewrite $\frac{1}{2}a$ as an equivalent fraction with denominator 4.

$\frac{1}{2}a = \frac{1 \cdot 2}{2 \cdot 2}a$ Write the products.

    $= \frac{2}{4}a$ Multiply all products.

Then add the fractional terms.

$\frac{1}{2}a + \frac{1}{4}a = \frac{2}{4}a + \frac{1}{4}a$ Rewrite $\frac{1}{2}a$ as $\frac{2}{4}a$.

      $= \frac{3}{4}a$ Simplify.

Simplify each expression.

a) $m + \frac{2}{3}m$

Recall that m is the same as $1m$.
You can rewrite m as $\frac{3}{3}m$.

Solution

Method 1

Use a bar model.

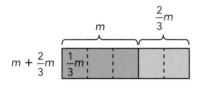

Represent the term m using a bar divided into three $\frac{1}{3}m$ sections.

From the bar model, $m + \frac{2}{3}m = \frac{5}{3}m$

Method 2

Use a common denominator for both coefficients.

$m + \frac{2}{3}m = \frac{3}{3}m + \frac{2}{3}m$ Rewrite m as a fraction with denominator 3.

$\qquad = \frac{5}{3}m$ Simplify.

Math Note

In algebraic expressions, fractional coefficients that are greater than 1 are left as improper fractions.

b) $\frac{1}{4}y + \frac{1}{6}y$

Solution

Method 1

Use a bar model.

$\frac{1}{4}y = \frac{3}{12}y \quad \frac{1}{6}y = \frac{2}{12}y$

The LCD of $\frac{1}{4}$ and $\frac{1}{6}$ is 12.
So, divide y into twelve
$\frac{1}{12}y$ sections.

From the bar model, $\frac{1}{4}y + \frac{1}{6}y = \frac{5}{12}y$

Method 2

Use a common denominator for both coefficients.

$\frac{1}{4}y + \frac{1}{6}y = \frac{3}{12}y + \frac{2}{12}y$ The LCD of $\frac{1}{4}$ and $\frac{1}{6}$ is 12. Rewrite the coefficients as fractions with denominator 12.

$\qquad = \frac{5}{12}y$ Simplify.

Guided Practice

Copy and complete to simplify each expression.

4 $x + \frac{3}{4}x$

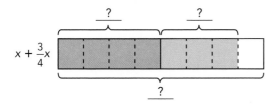

$x + \frac{3}{4}x = \underline{\quad?\quad}$

5 $\frac{1}{2}p + \frac{2}{5}p$

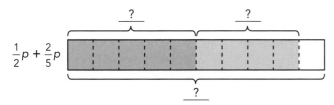

The LCD of $\frac{1}{2}$ and $\frac{2}{5}$ is $\underline{\quad?\quad}$.
So, p is divided into $\underline{\quad?\quad}$ p sections.

$\frac{1}{2}p + \frac{2}{5}p = \underline{\quad?\quad}$

Simplify each expression.

6 $m + \frac{5}{6}m$

7 $\frac{1}{4}x + \frac{2}{3}x$

8 *Math Journal* In questions **5** and **7**, you can multiply the two denominators to get the LCD. Does this always work? Explain.

Simplify each expression with decimal coefficients.

1 $0.5y + 0.2y$

2 $0.2x + 0.8x$

3 $x + 0.6x$

4 $0.4a + 1.2a$

5 $0.7b + 0.9b$

6 $0.6m + 0.8m$

7 $0.5k + 1.6k$

8 $0.8a + 1.8a$

Simplify each expression with fractional coefficients.

9 $\frac{1}{5}x + \frac{2}{5}x$

10 $\frac{3}{7}p + \frac{2}{7}p$

11 $\frac{5}{8}m + \frac{7}{8}m$

12 $\frac{4}{9}n + \frac{7}{9}n$

Simplify each expression with fractional coefficients by rewriting the fractions.

13 $\frac{1}{6}a + \frac{1}{3}a$

14 $\frac{1}{2}k + \frac{3}{8}k$

15 $\frac{2}{5}p + \frac{7}{10}p$

16 $\frac{7}{9}r + \frac{2}{3}r$

17 $\frac{1}{4}a + \frac{1}{3}a$

18 $\frac{1}{2}x + \frac{2}{5}x$

19 $\frac{3}{5}p + \frac{3}{4}p$

20 $\frac{4}{5}y + \frac{1}{3}y$

Solve. Show your work.

21 The figures show rectangle A and rectangle B. Write and simplify an algebraic expression for each of the following.

a)   The perimeter of rectangle A.

b)   The perimeter of rectangle B.

c)   The sum of the perimeters of the two rectangles.

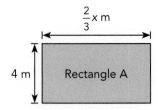

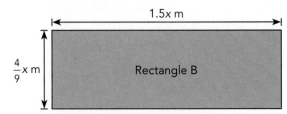

22 The length and width of two rectangular gardens are shown. Find the sum of the areas of the two gardens in simplest form.

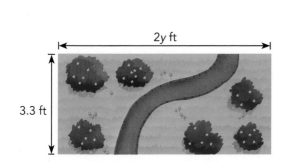

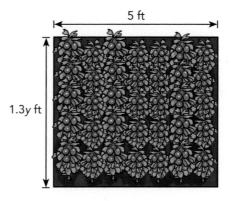

23 ✎ *Math Journal* James and Evan simplified the same algebraic expression. Their work is shown.

James
$\frac{1}{5}x + 0.3x = \frac{1}{2}x$

Evan
$\frac{1}{5}x + 0.3x = 0.5x$

Describe a method each person might have used to get his answer. Which method do you prefer? Why?

24 Which of the following expressions has a greater value if y is a positive number? Explain your reasoning.

$$1.4y + \frac{2}{5}y \quad \text{or} \quad \frac{1}{3}y + \frac{3}{4}y$$

25 A restaurant serves x meals of chicken quarters daily and makes soup each day using $\frac{1}{2}$ of a chicken. The chef expresses the number of chickens she uses each day as $\frac{1}{4}x + \frac{1}{2}$. How many chickens does she use in three days?

26 Mary simplified the algebraic expression $\frac{2}{3}x + \frac{1}{4}x$ as shown below.

$$\frac{2}{3}x + \frac{1}{4}x = \frac{3}{7}x$$

Describe and correct the error Mary made.

Subtracting Algebraic Terms

Lesson Objective

- Simplify algebraic expressions with decimal and fractional coefficients by subtracting like terms.

Simplify Algebraic Expressions with Decimal Coefficients by Subtracting.

You can simplify algebraic expressions like $x - 0.4x$ by subtracting the like terms.

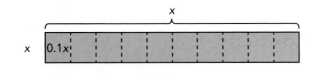

Represent the x term using a bar divided into ten $0.1x$ sections.

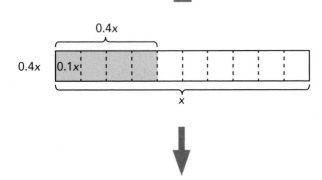

Represent the $0.4x$ term using a bar divided into ten $0.1x$ sections.

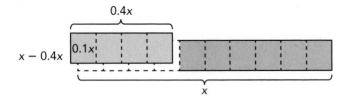

Subtract the like terms.

From the bar model,
$x - 0.4x = 0.6x$

You can subtract one term from another by finding the difference of their coefficients. This difference of the coefficients is the coefficient of the term in the simplified expression.

Simplify the expression $1.8y - 0.9y$.

Solution

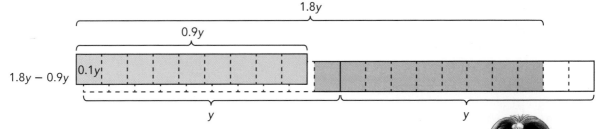

From the bar model,
$1.8y - 0.9y = 0.9y$

The difference is represented by the shaded part that remain.

Guided Practice

Copy and complete to simplify each expression.

1 $0.7y - 0.4y$

$0.7y - 0.4y = \underline{\quad ? \quad}$

2 $1.1a - 0.2a$

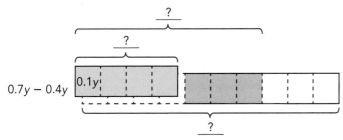

$1.1a - 0.2a = \underline{\quad ? \quad}$

3 $1.2y - y$

$1.2y - y = \underline{\quad ? \quad}$

Simplify Algebraic Expressions with Fractional Coefficients by Subtracting.

An algebraic expression like $\frac{5}{6}a - \frac{1}{3}a$ can be simplified using either a model or the coefficients.

Method 1

Use a bar model.

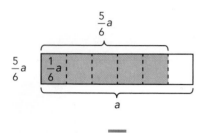

Represent the term $\frac{5}{6}a$ by dividing a bar into six $\frac{1}{6}a$ sections.

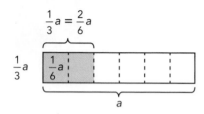

The LCD of $\frac{5}{6}$ and $\frac{1}{3}$ is 6.

So, divide a into six $\frac{1}{6}a$ sections.

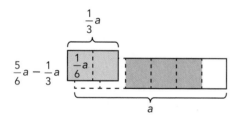

Subtract the like terms.

From the bar model, $\frac{5}{6}a - \frac{1}{3}a = \frac{3}{6}a$

$$= \frac{1}{2}a$$

Remember to express your answers in simplest form.

Method 2

Use a common denominator for both coefficients.

To simplify $\frac{5}{6}a - \frac{1}{3}a$, you can also subtract the coefficient of the term $\frac{1}{3}a$ from the coefficient of the term $\frac{5}{6}a$.

$\frac{5}{6}a - \frac{1}{3}a = \frac{5}{6}a - \frac{2}{6}a$ Rewrite $\frac{1}{3}a$ as $\frac{2}{6}a$.

$\phantom{\frac{5}{6}a - \frac{1}{3}a} = \frac{3}{6}a$ Subtract.

$\phantom{\frac{5}{6}a - \frac{1}{3}a} = \frac{1}{2}a$ Express in simplest form.

Example 4 **Simplify algebraic expressions with fractional coefficients by subtracting.**

Simplify the expression $\frac{2}{3}b - \frac{1}{4}b$.

Solution

Method 1

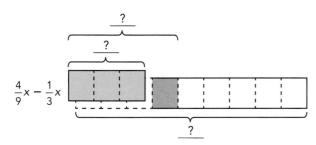

The LCD of $\frac{2}{3}$ and $\frac{1}{4}$ is 12. So, divide b into twelve $\frac{1}{12}b$ sections.

From the bar model,

$$\frac{2}{3}b - \frac{1}{4}b = \frac{5}{12}b$$

Method 2

$$\frac{2}{3}b - \frac{1}{4}b = \frac{8}{12}b - \frac{3}{12}b$$

$$= \frac{5}{12}b$$

The LCD of $\frac{2}{3}$ and $\frac{1}{4}$ is 12. Rewrite the coefficients as fractions with denominator 12. Subtract.

Guided Practice

Copy and complete to simplify each expression.

4 $\frac{4}{9}x - \frac{1}{3}x$

The LCD of $\frac{4}{9}$ and $\frac{1}{3}$ is __?__. So, x is divided into __?__ x sections.

$$\frac{4}{9}x - \frac{1}{3}x = \underline{}$$

5 $\frac{3}{4}p - \frac{1}{6}p$

$$\frac{3}{4}p - \frac{1}{6}p = \underline{}$$

$$= \underline{}$$

Rewrite the coefficients as fractions with denominator __?__.

Simplify each expression with decimal coefficients.

1 $0.8y - 0.7y$

2 $0.9x - 0.6x$

3 $1.7p - 0.4p$

4 $1.9h - 0.9h$

5 $1.3m - 0.5m$

6 $1.6n - 0.8n$

Simplify each expression with fractional coefficients.

7 $\frac{5}{6}x - \frac{1}{6}x$

8 $\frac{7}{8}x - \frac{5}{8}x$

9 $\frac{9}{5}x - \frac{1}{5}x$

10 $\frac{8}{3}p - \frac{1}{3}p$

Simplify each expression with fractional coefficients by rewriting the fractions.

11 $\frac{1}{4}a - \frac{1}{8}a$

12 $\frac{5}{6}m - \frac{2}{3}m$

13 $\frac{5}{3}b - \frac{1}{6}b$

14 $\frac{7}{4}x - \frac{1}{8}x$

15 $\frac{4}{5}p - \frac{1}{3}p$

16 $\frac{3}{4}r - \frac{2}{3}r$

17 $\frac{11}{7}k - \frac{1}{2}k$

18 $\frac{7}{4}d - \frac{3}{5}d$

Solve. Show your work.

19 ✏️ *Math Journal* Matthew simplified the algebraic expression $\frac{3}{2}x - \frac{1}{3}x$ as shown below.

$$\frac{3}{2}x - \frac{1}{3}x = \frac{18}{12}x - \frac{4}{12}x$$
$$= \frac{14}{12}x$$

Is Matthew's simplification correct? Why or why not?

20 Rectangle A, shown below, is larger than rectangle B. Write and simplify an algebraic expression that represents the difference in the areas of the two rectangles.

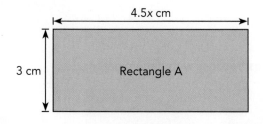

3.3 Simplifying Algebraic Expressions

Lesson Objectives

- Simplify algebraic expressions with more than two terms.
- Simplify algebraic expressions by using the commutative property of addition.
- Simplify algebraic expressions with two variables.

Simplify Algebraic Expressions with More Than Two Terms and Involving Decimal Coefficients.

Algebraic expressions may contain more than two terms. Not all the terms may be like terms. To simplify such expressions, first identify the like terms. Then add or subtract the like terms.

A bar model can help you simplify expressions such as $0.2x + 0.5x + 2$.

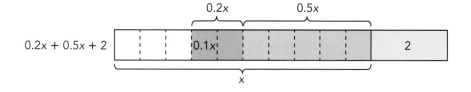

$0.2x + 0.5x + 2$ Add like terms.

The like terms are $0.2x$ and $0.5x$.

From the bar model,

$0.2x + 0.5x + 2 = 0.7x + 2$

$0.7x$ and 2 are not like terms, so $0.7x + 2$ cannot be simplified further.

Example 5 **Simplify algebraic expressions with more than two terms and involving decimal coefficients.**

Simplify the expression $1.2p + 0.1p + 4$.

Solution

From the bar model,
$1.2p + 0.1p + 4 = 1.3p + 4$

Guided Practice

Complete.

1 $1.5t + 4t + 3$

$\quad\quad \underbrace{1.5t + 4t} + 3$

$= \quad\underline{\ ?\ } \quad + \quad\underline{\ ?\ }$

2 $1.8m - 0.9m + 2$

$\quad\quad \underbrace{1.8m - 0.9m} + 2$

$= \quad\underline{\ ?\ } \quad + \quad\underline{\ ?\ }$

Simplify Algebraic Expressions with More Than Two Terms and Involving Fractional Coefficients.

You can simplify algebraic expressions such as $\frac{1}{2}x - \frac{1}{4}x + 5 + 2$ by writing like terms with a common denominator.

Rewrite $\frac{1}{2}x$ as $\frac{2}{4}x$.

Then subtract like terms.

From the bar model,
$\frac{1}{2}x - \frac{1}{4}x + 5 + 2 = \frac{1}{4}x + 7$

Example 6 **Simplify algebraic expressions with more than two terms and involving fractional coefficients.**

Simplify the expression $\frac{2}{5}x + \frac{3}{10}x - 1 - 2$.

Solution

$$\frac{2}{5}x + \frac{3}{10}x - 1 - 2 = \frac{4}{10}x + \frac{3}{10}x - 1 - 2$$

$$= \frac{7}{10}x - 3$$

Rewrite the coefficients as fractions with denominator 10. Two like terms are $\frac{4}{10}x$ and $\frac{3}{10}x$. Two other like terms are -1 and -2. Simplify.

Remember that
$-1 - 2 = -1 + (-2)$
$= -3$

Guided Practice

Copy and complete to simplify each expression.

3 $\frac{2}{3}x - \frac{1}{6}x + 1 + 6$

$$\frac{2}{3}x - \frac{1}{6}x + 1 + 6 = \frac{?}{6}x - \frac{1}{6}x + 1 + 6$$

$$= \frac{\underline{?}}{}x + \frac{\underline{?}}{}$$
$$= \underline{?}x + \underline{?}$$

4 $\frac{1}{3}d + \frac{7}{12}d - 5 - 1$

$$\frac{1}{3}d + \frac{7}{12}d - 5 - 1 = \frac{?}{}d + \frac{7}{12}d - 5 - 1$$

$$= \underline{?}d - \underline{?}$$

5 $\frac{1}{2}k - \frac{2}{5}k + 8 - 3$

$$\frac{1}{2}k - \frac{2}{5}k + 8 - 3 = \frac{?}{}k - \frac{?}{}k + 8 - 3$$

$$= \underline{?}k + \underline{?}$$

Simplify Algebraic Expressions with Three Like Terms.

When you add or subtract more than two numbers, work from left to right. In the same way, when simplifying algebraic expressions with more than two like terms, you work from left to right.

Example 7 Simplify algebraic expressions with three like terms.

Simplify each expression.

a) $0.8x + 0.4x + 0.1x$

Solution

$0.8x + 0.4x + 0.1x = 1.2x + 0.1x$ Add the first two like terms.

$ = 1.3x$ Simplify.

b) $\dfrac{3}{5}a + \dfrac{1}{5}a - \dfrac{1}{10}a$

Solution

$\dfrac{3}{5}a + \dfrac{1}{5}a - \dfrac{1}{10}a = \dfrac{4}{5}a - \dfrac{1}{10}a$ Add the first two like terms.

$\phantom{\dfrac{3}{5}a + \dfrac{1}{5}a - \dfrac{1}{10}a} = \dfrac{8}{10}a - \dfrac{1}{10}a$ Rewrite the coefficients to have a common denominator 10.

$\phantom{\dfrac{3}{5}a + \dfrac{1}{5}a - \dfrac{1}{10}a} = \dfrac{7}{10}a$ Subtract the two like terms.

Guided Practice

Copy and complete to simplify each expression.

6 $0.5k + 0.3k + 1.2k$

$0.5k + 0.3k + 1.2k = \underbrace{\underline{\ \ ?\ \ }k + 1.2k}$

$ = \quad \underline{\ \ ?\ \ }$

7 $\dfrac{4}{9}p + \dfrac{1}{9}p - \dfrac{1}{3}p$

$\dfrac{4}{9}p + \dfrac{1}{9}p - \dfrac{1}{3}p = \underline{\ \ ?\ \ }p - \dfrac{1}{3}p$

$\phantom{\dfrac{4}{9}p + \dfrac{1}{9}p - \dfrac{1}{3}p} = \underbrace{\underline{\ \ ?\ \ }p - \underline{\ \ ?\ \ }p}$

$\phantom{\dfrac{4}{9}p + \dfrac{1}{9}p - \dfrac{1}{3}p} = \quad \underline{\ \ ?\ \ }$

Simplify Algebraic Expressions by Grouping Like Terms.

You may need to change the order of the terms in an expression before you simplify it. To reorder the terms, you can use the commutative property of addition, just as you do to make mental addition easier.

$$4 + 9 + 6 = 4 + 6 + 9$$
$$= 10 + 9$$
$$= 19$$

You can use the same property to simplify an algebraic expression.

$$4t + 9 + 6t = 4t + 6t + 9 \qquad \text{Use commutative property to group like terms.}$$
$$= 10t + 9 \qquad \text{Simplify.}$$

You can group like terms when simplifying expressions involving subtraction, like $2t + 4 - 12t$.

$$2t + 4 - 12t = 2t + 4 + (-12t) \qquad \text{Rewrite subtraction as adding the opposite.}$$
$$= 2t + (-12t) + 4 \qquad \text{Group like terms.}$$
$$= 2t - 12t + 4 \qquad \text{Rewrite the expression.}$$
$$= -10t + 4 \qquad \text{Simplify.}$$

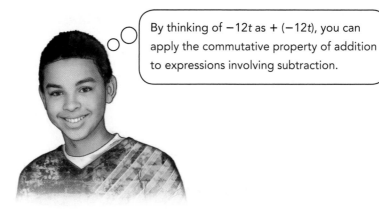

By thinking of $-12t$ as $+ (-12t)$, you can apply the commutative property of addition to expressions involving subtraction.

Example 8 **Simplify algebraic expressions by grouping like terms.**

Simplify each expression.

a) $5m + 7 + 3m + 2$

Solution

$$5m + 7 + 3m + 2 = 5m + 3m + 7 + 2 \qquad \text{Group like terms.}$$
$$= 8m + 9 \qquad \text{Simplify.}$$

Continue on next page

b) $\frac{3}{8}b + \frac{2}{3} - \frac{1}{8}b - \frac{1}{3}$

Solution

$$\frac{3}{8}b + \frac{2}{3} - \frac{1}{8}b - \frac{1}{3} = \frac{3}{8}b - \frac{1}{8}b + \frac{2}{3} - \frac{1}{3}$$ Group like terms.

$$= \frac{2}{8}b + \frac{1}{3}$$ Simplify.

$$= \frac{1}{4}b + \frac{1}{3}$$ Write fractions in simplest form.

Guided Practice

Complete to simplify each expression.

8 $4a + 5 + a + 7$

$4a + 5 + a + 7$

$= \underbrace{\underline{} + \underline{}}_{} + \underbrace{5 + 7}_{}$

$= \underline{} + \underline{}$

9 $\frac{3}{7}x + \frac{3}{5} - \frac{2}{7}x - \frac{2}{5}$

$\frac{3}{7}x + \frac{3}{5} - \frac{2}{7}x - \frac{2}{5}$

$= \underbrace{\underline{} - \underline{}}_{} + \underbrace{\underline{} - \underline{}}_{}$

$= \underline{} + \underline{}$

Simplify Algebraic Expressions with Two Variables.

You have learned how to simplify expressions with one variable. Some expressions like $x + y + 2x$ contain two variables, each representing a different unknown quantity.

Method 1

To simplify $x + y + 2x$, you can add the like terms using a model.

$x + y + 2x$ | x | y | x | x |

$x + 2x + y$ | x | x | x | y | Group like terms.

From the bar model,
$x + y + 2x = 3x + y$

Like terms have the same variable part, so you cannot add an x term to a y term.

Method 2

You can also simplify the expression $x + y + 2x$ by first adding the coefficients of the terms x and $2x$.

$$x + y + 2x = (x + 2x) + y \qquad \text{Group like terms.}$$
$$= 3x + y \qquad \text{Simplify.}$$

You can simplify algebraic expressions such as $4x + 3y - x - 2y$ by first grouping the like terms. Then add or subtract the like tems.

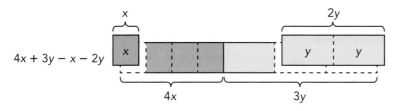

$4x + 3y - x - 2y$

$$4x + 3y - x - 2y = (4x - x) + (3y - 2y) \qquad \text{Group like terms.}$$
$$= 3x + y \qquad \text{Simplify.}$$

Example 9 **Simplify algebraic expressions with two variables.**

Simplify each expression.

a) $5y + 3x + 2y + 2x$

Solution

$$5y + 3x + 2y + 2x = (5y + 2y) + (3x + 2x) \qquad \text{Group like terms.}$$
$$= 7y + 5x \qquad \text{Add like terms.}$$

> **Caution** ///////
> $7y + 5x \neq 12xy$

b) $6c + 5d - c - 8d$

Solution

$$6c + 5d - c - 8d = (6c - c) + (5d - 8d) \qquad \text{Group like terms.}$$
$$= 5c - 3d \qquad \text{Simplify.}$$

Guided Practice

Copy and complete to simplify each expression.

10 $6a + 9b + a + b$

$$6a + 9b + a + b$$
$$= \underline{\ ?\ } + \underline{\ ?\ } + 9b + b$$
$$= \underline{\ ?\ } + \underline{\ ?\ }$$

11 $3x + 2y - 2x - 3y$

$$3x + 2y - 2x - 3y$$
$$= \underline{\ ?\ } - \underline{\ ?\ } + \underline{\ ?\ } - \underline{\ ?\ }$$
$$= \underline{\ ?\ } - \underline{\ ?\ }$$

Simplify each expression with one variable.

1 $0.3x + 0.6x + 3$

2 $\frac{2}{7}x + \frac{3}{7}x + 4$

3 $0.8x - 0.2x - 5$

4 $\frac{7}{8}x - \frac{1}{8}x - 5$

Simplify each expression with three algebraic terms.

5 $0.3p + 0.2p + 0.4p$

6 $0.2p + 0.8p - 0.6p$

7 $\frac{1}{3}y + \frac{1}{6}y + \frac{5}{12}y$

8 $\frac{1}{2}a + \frac{2}{3}a - \frac{1}{6}a$

Simplify each expression with one variable.

9 $7x + 6 + 4x$

10 $8y + 4 - 6y$

11 $1.8x - 0.6 - 0.7x$

12 $\frac{4}{7}x + \frac{1}{5} + \frac{2}{7}x$

Simplify each expression with two variables.

13 $2x + 4x + 7y$

14 $5x + x + 3y$

15 $9x - 7x + 3y$

16 $8m - 7m - 6n$

17 $2.3a - 1.8a + 3.5b - 2.7b$

18 $2.5x + 1.8z + 1.6x - 0.9z$

19 $\frac{3}{5}a + \frac{2}{5}a + \frac{1}{6}b + \frac{1}{6}b$

20 $\frac{2}{3}a - \frac{1}{6}a + \frac{3}{5}b - \frac{3}{10}b$

Find the perimeter of each figure.

21

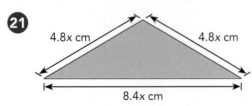

4.8x cm   4.8x cm

8.4x cm

22

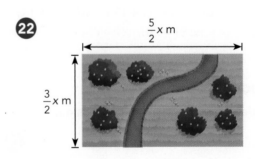

$\frac{5}{2}$x m

$\frac{3}{2}$x m

23 *Math Journal* When adding or subtracting algebraic expressions, how do you identify the like terms?

Lesson Objective

- Expand algebraic expressions with fractional, decimal, and negative factors.

Expand Algebraic Expressions with Fractional Factors.

You have learned how to expand algebraic expressions involving integers, like $3(2x + 4)$ and $2(5x - 1)$. You use the distributive property to expand such expressions.

$3(2x + 4) = 3(2x) + 3(4)$ Use the distributive property.

        $= 6x + 12$ Multiply.

$2(5x - 1) = 2(5x) - 2(1)$ Use the distributive property.

        $= 10x - 2$ Multiply.

You obtain an expression equivalent to the original expression after expanding.

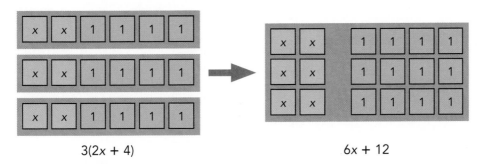

        $3(2x + 4)$ $6x + 12$

$3(2x + 4)$ and $6x + 12$ are equivalent expressions because the value of both expressions remains the same for all values of x. In the same way, $2(5x - 1)$ and $10x - 2$ are also equivalent expressions.

You can expand algebraic expressions like $\frac{1}{2}(2x + 4)$ using either bar models or the distributive property. This will produce an equivalent expression, just as expanding an expression with a whole number factor did.

Continue on next page

Method 1

You can rearrange the bar model into 2 equal groups.

From the bar model,

$\frac{1}{2}(2x + 4) = x + 2$

> You can rearrange the bar model into 2 equal groups to find one half of (2x + 4).

Method 2

You can also use the distributive property to expand $\frac{1}{2}(2x + 4)$.

$\frac{1}{2}(2x + 4) = \frac{1}{2}(2x) + \frac{1}{2}(4)$ Use the distributive property.

$= x + 2$ Multiply.

$\frac{1}{2}(2x + 4)$ and $x + 2$ are equivalent expressions.

Example 10   **Expand algebraic expressions with fractional factors.**

Expand the expression $\frac{1}{3}(3x + 15)$.

Solution

Method 1

Use a bar model.

> You can arrange the bar model for 3x + 15 into 3 equal groups to find one third of (3x + 15).

From the bar model, $\frac{1}{3}(3x + 15) = x + 5$

Method 2

Use the distributive property.

$\frac{1}{3}(3x + 15) = \frac{1}{3}(3x) + \frac{1}{3}(15)$ Use the distributive property.

$= x + 5$ Multiply.

Guided Practice

Copy and complete to expand the expression.

1 $\frac{1}{4}(8x + 12)$

Method 1

Use a bar model.

$8x + 12$ | 2x | 3 | ? | ? | ? | ? | ? | ? |

$\frac{1}{4}(8x + 12)$

From the bar model, $\frac{1}{4}(8x + 12) = \underline{\ ?\ }$

Method 2

Use the distributive property.

$\frac{1}{4}(8x + 12) = \frac{1}{4}(\underline{\ ?\ }) + \frac{1}{4}(\underline{\ ?\ })$

$= \underline{\ ?\ }$

Expand each expression.

2 $\frac{1}{3}(9x + 6)$

3 $\frac{1}{5}(25x + 15)$

Expand Algebraic Expressions with Decimal Factors.

You can also use the distributive property to expand expressions involving decimals, such as $0.2(4x + 3)$.

$0.2(4x + 3) = 0.2(4x) + 0.2(3)$ Use the distributive property.

$= 0.8x + 0.6$ Multiply.

Example 11 Expand algebraic expressions with decimal factors.

Expand the expression $0.7(0.2t - 3)$.

Solution

$0.7(0.2t - 3) = 0.7[0.2t + (-3)]$ Rewrite subtraction as adding the opposite.

$= 0.7(0.2t) + 0.7(-3)$ Use the distributive property.

$= 0.14t + (-2.1)$ Multiply.

$= 0.14t - 2.1$ Rewrite the expression.

> **Caution** ///////
>
> Writing subtraction as adding the opposite of a number will help you work more carefully and not lose track of negative signs.

Guided Practice

Copy and complete to expand each expression. Write + or − in each ? .

4 0.3(2x + 5)

0.3(2x + 5) = 0.3(__?__) + 0.3(__?__)

= __?__ + __?__

5 0.5(1.4y − 2.1)

0.5(1.4y − 2.1) = 0.5 (__?__) ? 0.5(− __?__)

= __?__ ? (− __?__)

= __?__ ? __?__

Expand each expression.

6 0.4(3y + 2)

7 0.2(4x − 3.1)

Expand Algebraic Expressions with Negative Factors.

When expanding algebraic expressions with negative factors, such as −3(x + 2) and −2(5x − 1), you use the distributive property and apply the rules for multiplying integers.

−3(x + 2) = −3(x) + (−3)(2)   Use the distributive property.

= −3x + (−6)   Multiply.

= −3x − 6   Rewrite the expression.

−5(y − 2) = −5[y + (−2)]   Rewrite subtraction as adding the opposite.

= −5(y) + (−5)(−2)   Use the distributive property.

= −5y + 10   Multiply.

> **Math Note**
>
> You have learned that:
>
> −1 · 2 = −(1 · 2) = −2
>
> 1 · (−2) = −(1 · 2) = −2
>
> −1 · (−2) = 1 · 2 = 2

Example 12   Expand algebraic expressions with negative factors.

Expand each expression.

a) $-3\left(-\dfrac{2}{3}a + \dfrac{1}{5}\right)$

Solution

$-3\left(-\dfrac{2}{3}a + \dfrac{1}{5}\right) = -3\left(-\dfrac{2}{3}a\right) + (-3)\left(\dfrac{1}{5}\right)$ Use the distributive property.

$= 2a - \dfrac{3}{5}$ Multiply.

b) $-(-0.4k - 2.5)$

Solution

$$-(-0.4k - 2.5) = -1[-0.4k + (-2.5)] \qquad \text{Rewrite the expression.}$$
$$= -1(-0.4k) + (-1)(-2.5) \qquad \text{Use the distributive property.}$$
$$= 0.4k + 2.5 \qquad \text{Multiply.}$$

c) $-\dfrac{1}{3}(p + 2q)$

Solution

$$-\frac{1}{3}(p + 2q) = -\frac{1}{3}(p) + \left(-\frac{1}{3}\right)(2q) \qquad \text{Use the distributive property.}$$
$$= -\frac{1}{3}p - \frac{2}{3}q \qquad \text{Multiply.}$$

Guided Practice

Expand each expression.

8 $-4(3d - 2)$

9 $-7(5k + e)$

10 $-4(0.6x - 4)$

11 $-\dfrac{1}{4}\left(-3y + \dfrac{1}{2}\right)$

Expand and Simplify Algebraic Expressions.

When you simplify an algebraic expression, you may need to expand it first before you add or subtract the like terms.

To simplify an expression like $4(2x + 1) + 3x$, you first need to expand $4(2x + 1)$.

$$4(2x + 1) + 3x = 4(2x) + 4(1) + 3x \qquad \text{Use the distributive property.}$$
$$= 8x + 4 + 3x \qquad \text{Multiply.}$$
$$= 8x + 3x + 4 \qquad \text{Group like terms.}$$
$$= 11x + 4 \qquad \text{Simplify by combining like terms.}$$

To simplify an expression like $7 - 2(x + 2)$, you first need to rewrite the expression.

$$7 - 2(x + 2) = 7 + (-2)(x + 2) \qquad \text{Rewrite the expression.}$$
$$= 7 + (-2)(x) + (-2)(2) \qquad \text{Use the distributive property.}$$
$$= 7 + (-2x) + (-4) \qquad \text{Multiply.}$$
$$= 7 + (-4) + (-2x) \qquad \text{Group like terms.}$$
$$= 7 - 4 - 2x \qquad \text{Rewrite the expression.}$$
$$= 3 - 2x \qquad \text{Subtract.}$$

Example 13 Expand and simplify algebraic expressions.

Expand and simplify each expression.

a) $4(p + 5q) - 3q$

Solution

$$
\begin{aligned}
4(p + 5q) - 3q &= 4(p) + 4(5q) - 3q && \text{Use the distributive property.} \\
&= 4p + 20q - 3q && \text{Multiply.} \\
&= 4p + 17q && \text{Simplify.}
\end{aligned}
$$

b) $-2(0.5y - 3) + y$

Solution

$$
\begin{aligned}
-2(0.5y - 3) + y &= -2[0.5y + (-3)] + y && \text{Rewrite the expression.} \\
&= (-2)(0.5y) + (-2)(-3) + y && \text{Use the distributive property.} \\
&= -y + 6 + y && \text{Multiply.} \\
&= -y + y + 6 && \text{Group like terms.} \\
&= 6 && \text{Simplify.}
\end{aligned}
$$

c) $4(2n + 5) - (m - 1)$

Solution

$$
\begin{aligned}
4(2n + 5) - (m - 1) &= 4(2n + 5) + (-1)[m + (-1)] && \text{Rewrite the expression.} \\
&= 4(2n) + 4(5) + (-1)(m) + (-1)(-1) && \text{Use the distributive property.} \\
&= 8n + 20 + (-m) + 1 && \text{Multiply.} \\
&= 8n + (-m) + 20 + 1 && \text{Group like terms.} \\
&= 8n - m + 21 && \text{Remove parentheses and simplify.}
\end{aligned}
$$

> **Caution** ////////////
> $8n - m \neq 7nm$

Guided Practice

Copy and complete to expand and simplify the expression.

12 $2(2a + 3b) + 5b$

$$
\begin{aligned}
2(2a + 3b) + 5b &= 2(2a) + 2(\underline{\,?\,}) + \underline{\,?\,} \\
&= \underline{\,?\,} + \underline{\,?\,} + \underline{\,?\,} \\
&= \underline{\,?\,}
\end{aligned}
$$

Expand and simplify each expression.

13 $-3\left(\dfrac{1}{2}k - 4\right) - 2k$

14 $5(2h - 3) - (2k - 1)$

Expand each expression.

1 $\frac{1}{4}(4x + 8)$

2 $\frac{1}{3}(6b + 9)$

3 $\frac{1}{2}(p + 2)$

4 $\frac{1}{5}(4a + 3)$

5 $\frac{1}{2}(4k - 6)$

6 $\frac{1}{3}(16a - 8)$

7 $\frac{1}{3}(5b - 1)$

8 $\frac{2}{5}(k - 10)$

9 $3(4x + 0.2)$

10 $4(0.1y + 5)$

11 $0.2(3x + 4)$

12 $0.6(3h + 5)$

13 $0.2(m - 3)$

14 $0.3(p - 3)$

15 $0.4(1.5d + 0.5)$

16 $1.2(0.3x - 1.4)$

Expand each expression with a negative factor.

17 $-2(x + 1)$

18 $-3(2x + 5)$

19 $-3(4a + 9b)$

20 $-7(2k - h)$

21 $-4\left(p + \frac{1}{2}\right)$

22 $-\frac{1}{2}\left(6x - \frac{1}{3}\right)$

23 $-2(5k + 1.7)$

24 $-3(0.2m + 5)$

25 $-5(q - 0.3)$

26 $-0.6(0.4y - 1)$

Expand and simplify each expression.

27 $3(2y + 1) + 4$

28 $3(2a + 5) - 8$

29 $2(x + 2) + 3x$

30 $6(b + 3) - 2b$

31 $5\left(\frac{1}{6}a + 1\right) + 3$

32 $4\left(\frac{1}{8}a - 3\right) - \frac{1}{2}a$

Expand and simplify each expression.

33 $0.2(x + 1) + 0.7x$

34 $0.5(y + 2) - 0.3y$

35 $-2(4m + 1) - m$

36 $10 - 3(2n - 1)$

37 $-0.8(r + 3) + 2.2r$

38 $-(1.2x + 7) + 1.5x$

Expand and simplify each expression with two variables.

39 $4x + 6(3y + x)$

40 $7a + 5(3a - b)$

41 $8g + 5(v - g)$

42 $4q + 6(p - 2q)$

43 $2(a + 2b) + (a + 3b)$

44 $3(m - 2n) + 6(n - 2m)$

45 $4(d + e) - 3(d - 2e)$

46 $3(3q - p) - (q - 6p)$

47 $-4(x + 3y) + 3(2x - 5y)$

48 $-7(y + 2t) - 3(y - t)$

Write an expression for the missing dimension of each shaded figure and a multiplication expression for its area. Then expand and simplify the multiplication expression.

49
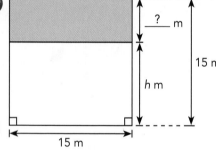

50
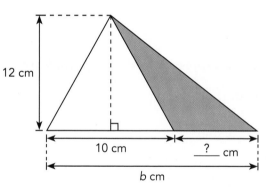

Write an expression for the area of the figure. Expand and simplify.

51
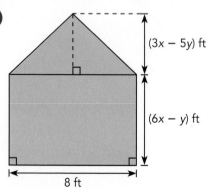

Factoring Algebraic Expressions

Lesson Objectives

- Factor algebraic expressions with two variables.
- Factor algebraic expressions with negative terms.

Factor Algebraic Expressions with Two Variables.

You have learned how to factor an algebraic expression, such as $2a - 4$. You can factor the expression by using the bar models or greatest common factor (GCF).

Method 1

Factoring $2a - 4$ results in an equivalent expression $2(a - 2)$.

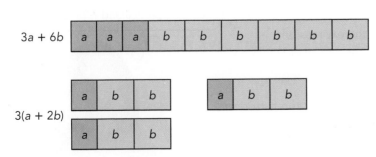

$2a - 4$　　　　　　　　$2(a - 2)$

You can check that you have factored correctly by expanding $2(a - 2)$.

From the bar model, $2a - 4 = 2(a - 2)$

Method 2

$$2a - 4 = 2a + (-4) \quad \text{Rewrite the expression.}$$
$$ = 2(a) + 2(-2) \quad \text{The GCF of } 2a \text{ and } -4 \text{ is } 2.$$
$$ = 2(a - 2) \quad \text{Use the distributive property to factor 2 from each term.}$$

You can also factor expressions with two variables, like $3a + 6b$, using models or the GCF.

Method 1

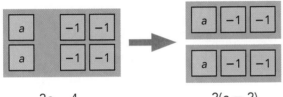

$3a + 6b$

Draw a group of three a sections and six b sections.

Rearrange into three identical groups. Each group has one a section and two b sections to represent $(a + 2b)$.

$3(a + 2b)$

From the bar model, $3a + 6b = 3(a + 2b)$

Continue on next page

Method 2

$$3a + 6b = 3(a) + 3(2b)$$ The GCF of $3a$ and $6b$ is 3.
$$= 3(a + 2b)$$ Factor 3 from each term.

Check: Expand the expression $3(a + 2b)$ to check the factoring.

$$3(a + 2b) = 3(a) + 3(2b)$$
$$= 3a + 6b$$

$3a + 6b$ is factored correctly.

Example 14 **Factor algebraic expressions with two variables.**

Factor the expression $3x - 9y$.

Solution

Method 1

Use a bar model.

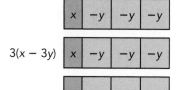

$3x - 9y$ | x | x | x | −y | −y | −y | −y | −y | −y | −y | −y | −y

Draw a group of three x sections and nine $-y$ sections.

$3(x − 3y)$

| x | −y | −y | −y |

Rearrange into three identical groups. Each group has one x section and three $-y$ sections to represent $(x − 3y)$.

From the bar model,
$$3x − 9y = 3(x − 3y)$$

Method 2

Use the distributive property.

$$3x − 9y = 3x + (−9y)$$ Rewrite the expression.
$$= 3(x) + 3(−3y)$$ The GCF of $3x$ and $−9y$ is 3.
$$= 3(x − 3y)$$ Factor 3 from each term.

> The factors of 3 are 3 and 1.
> 3 is also a factor of −9 because $3(−3) = −9$.
>
> So, the GCF of 3 and −9 is 3.

Check: Expand the expression $3(x − 3y)$ to check the factoring.

$$3(x − 3y) = 3(x) + 3(−3y)$$
$$= 3x − 9y$$

$3x − 9y$ is factored correctly.

Guided Practice

Copy and complete to factor the expression.

1 $2j - 10k$

$$2j - 10k = \underline{\ ?\ } + (\underline{\ ?\ })$$
$$= \underline{\ ?\ } (\underline{\ ?\ }) + \underline{\ ?\ } (\underline{\ ?\ })$$
$$= \underline{\ ?\ }$$

Rewrite the expression.
The GCF of $2j$ and $-10k$ is 2.
Factor 2 from each term.

Factor each expression.

2 $6a - 18b$

3 $8p - 12q$

Factor Algebraic Expressions with Negative Terms.

An expression such as $-x - 2$ is not factored completely because you can factor out -1 from the expression.

$$-x - 2 = -x + (-2) \qquad \text{Rewrite the expression.}$$
$$= (-1)(x) + (-1)(2) \qquad \text{The GCF of } -x \text{ and } -2 \text{ is } (-1).$$
$$= (-1)(x + 2) \qquad \text{Factor } (-1) \text{ from each term.}$$
$$= -(x + 2) \qquad \text{Simplify.}$$

Check: Expand the expression $-(x + 2)$ to check the factoring.

$$-(x + 2) = (-1)(x + 2)$$
$$= (-1)(x) + (-1)(2)$$
$$= -x - 2$$

$-(x + 2)$ is factored correctly.

> The expression $-(x + 2)$ is factored completely because the terms inside the parentheses have no common factors.

Example 15 **Factor algebraic expressions with negative terms.**

Factor each expression.

a)   −2x − 3

Solution

$$-2x - 3 = -2x + (-3)$$ Rewrite the expression.
$$= (-1)(2x) + (-1)(3)$$ The GCF of −2x and −3 is (−1).
$$= -1(2x + 3)$$ Factor (−1) from each term.
$$= -(2x + 3)$$ Simplify.

The expression −(2x + 3) is factored completely because the terms inside the parentheses have no common factors.

Check: Expand the expression −(2x + 3) to check the factoring.

$$-(2x + 3) = (-1)(2x + 3)$$
$$= (-1)(2x) + (-1)(3)$$
$$= -2x - 3$$

−2x − 3 is factored correctly.

b)   −4a − 8

Solution

$$-4a - 8 = -4a + (-8)$$ Rewrite the expression.
$$= (-4)(a) + (-4)(2)$$ The GCF of −4a and −8 is (−4).
$$= -4(a + 2)$$ Factor (−4) from each term and simplify.

Check: Expand the expression −4(a + 2) to check the factoring.

$$-4(a + 2) = (-4)(a) + (-4)(2)$$
$$= -4a - 8$$

−4a − 8 is factored correctly.

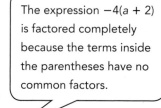

The expression −4(a + 2) is factored completely because the terms inside the parentheses have no common factors.

Guided Practice

Factor each expression.

4 −5x − 3

5 −3f − 6

6 −8p − 10q

Factor each expression with two terms.

1 $2x + 8$

2 $5a + 5$

3 $3x - 12$

4 $4x - 16$

5 $2x + 8y$

6 $7a + 7b$

7 $5p + 15q$

8 $14w + 49m$

9 $4j - 16k$

10 $8t - 32u$

11 $2a - 10p$

12 $9h - 45f$

Factor each expression with negative terms.

13 $-p - 2$

14 $-x - 5$

15 $-2d - 7$

16 $-4y - 11$

17 $-3a - 6$

18 $-4x - 20$

19 $-5k - 25$

20 $-7u - 49$

21 $-1 - 4n$

22 $-3 - 6a$

23 $-12x - 16y$

24 $-25m - 10n$

Factor each expression with three terms.

25 $4x + 4y + 8$

26 $2a + 6b + 4$

27 $5p + 10q + 10$

28 $12d + 6e + 18$

29 $3s - 9t - 15$

30 $4a - 6b - 12$

31 $12a - 9b - 6$

32 $24g - 12h - 36$

Solve. Show your work.

33 A rectangle has an area of $(12m - 30n)$ square units. Its width is 6 units. Factor the expression for the area to find an expression for the length of the rectangle.

$\underline{\quad ? \quad}$ units

6 units | Area = $(12m - 30n)$ units^2

3.6 Writing Algebraic Expressions

Lesson Objectives

- Translate verbal descriptions into algebraic expressions with one or more variables.
- Translate verbal descriptions into algebraic expressions with parentheses.

Translate Verbal Descriptions into Algebraic Expressions with One Variable.

You have learned to translate verbal descriptions into algebraic expressions.

You can translate verbal descriptions with variable terms that have decimal, fractional, and negative coefficients as in the following problem.

Amy used two-thirds of a ribbon that is y-inches long to tie her hair. Write an algebraic expression for the length of the ribbon she used.

Two-thirds	of	y	
$\frac{2}{3}$	$\cdot$	y	Translate by parts.
	$\frac{2}{3}y$		Combine.

The length of the ribbon is $\frac{2}{3}y$ inches.

A retailer doubles the value of a coupon worth t dollars on a purchase of $15. Write an algebraic expression for the final cost of the purchase.

> **Math Note**
>
> $\frac{2}{3}y$ can also be expressed as $\frac{2y}{3}$.

$-2t$	plus	15	
$-2t$	$+$	15	Translate by parts. Combine.

The final cost of purchase is $(-2t + 15)$ dollars.

You can translate verbal descriptions into algebraic expressions using more than one operation. Simplify algebraic expressions when you can.

Seven sticks of clay are shared equally among 28 students. Each stick of clay weighs *c* grams. Write an algebraic expression for the weight of the clay that each student receives.

You can translate verbal descriptions into algebraic expressions by parts before you combine them into an expression.

Simplify when you can.

Product of 7 and *c*   divided by   28

$7 \cdot c$ $\div$ 28 Translate by parts.

$$\frac{7c}{28}$$ Combine and simplify.

$$= \frac{c}{4}$$

Each student receives $\frac{c}{4}$ grams of clay.

Example 16 **Translate verbal descriptions into algebraic expressions.**

a) A fruit punch makes seven quarts when made with *r* quarts of orange juice. This time it is being made with 30% less orange juice. Write an expression for the number of quarts of the fruit punch made this time.

Solution

7   adds to   −0.3   times   *r*

        −0.3   ·   *r*   Translate by parts.

7   +   −0.3*r*   Combine.

$7 + (-0.3r) = 7 - 0.3r$

$(7 - 0.3r)$ quarts of fruit punch is made.

> **Math Note**
>
> Percent is written as %, which means *out of 100*. It can be written as a decimal.
>
> $30\% = \frac{30}{100}$
>
> $= 0.3$

Continue on next page

b) James paid x dollars plus 3% sales tax for a pen. Write an algebraic expression for the amount of money he paid for the pen.

Solution

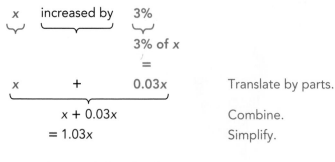

x increased by 3%

3% of x
=

x + 0.03x Translate by parts.

$x + 0.03x$ Combine.

$= 1.03x$ Simplify.

> **Math Note**
>
> A sales tax is a state or local tax on purchases. It ranges from 2% to 9% of the purchase price.

He paid 1.03x dollars for the pen.

c) Seven watermelons each weighs w pounds. A basket can hold 11 pounds less than two-fifths of the weight of the watermelons. What weight can the basket hold?

Solution

Because w represents the weight of one watermelon, $7 \cdot w$ represents the weight of seven watermelons.

Two-fifths   of the   product of 7 and w less   11

$\dfrac{2}{5}$ $\cdot$ $7w$

$\dfrac{14}{5}w$ $-$ 11   Translate by parts.

$\dfrac{14}{5}w - 11$ Combine.

The basket can hold $\left(\dfrac{14}{5}w - 11 \right)$ pounds.

Keep the meaning of the phrase and consider the order of operations when translating.

Guided Practice

Complete.

1 The price of a ring was w dollars. Wendy bought it at a discount of 25%. Write an algebraic expression for the discounted price of the ring.

w reduced by   25%

           $\underline{\quad ? \quad}$ % of w

           =

w − $\underline{\quad ? \quad} w$ Translate by parts.

     $\underline{\quad ? \quad} - \underline{\quad ? \quad}$ Combine.

     = $\underline{\quad ? \quad}$ Simplify.

The discounted price of the ring is $\underline{\quad ? \quad}$ dollars.

2 $6n$ blocks of clay are shared among 14 students. Write an algebraic expression for the number of blocks of clay that each student will get.

$6n$ shared among   14

$\underline{\quad ? \quad}$ ÷ $\underline{\quad ? \quad}$ Translate by parts.

     = $\dfrac{?}{?}$ Combine.

     = $\dfrac{?}{?}$ Simplify.

Each student gets $\underline{\quad ? \quad}$ blocks of clay.

3 Desmond has w marbles and Mandy has $\dfrac{1}{2}w$ marbles. Desmond gives one-tenth of his marbles and Mandy gives two-fifth of her marbles to their cousin Joel. Write an expression for the number of marbles Joel receives.

$\underline{\quad ? \quad} + \underline{\quad ? \quad} = \underline{\quad ? \quad}$

Joel receives $\underline{\quad ? \quad}$ marbles.

4 After baking some bread, Janis has $\dfrac{2}{3}b$ pounds of butter left. Then she uses $\dfrac{3}{4}$ pound for a white sauce. Write an algebraic expression for the amount of butter left.

$\underline{\quad ? \quad} - \underline{\quad ? \quad}$ Subtract $\dfrac{3}{4}$ from $\dfrac{2}{3}b$.

> **Caution** /////////
> a subtracted from b is not $a - b$.

There are $\underline{\quad ? \quad}$ pounds of butter left.

Translate Verbal Descriptions into Algebraic Expressions with One Variable Using Diagrams.

You can use diagrams, models, or tables to visualize the information in a real-world problem. These visual aids help you to solve problems involving algebraic expressions.

Example 17 Translate a real-world problem into an algebraic expression using a diagram.

John's farm has a rectangular shape. Its width is x yards. Its length is 6 yards more than one-third of the width. Write an algebraic expression for the perimeter of John's farm.

Solution

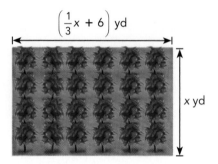

$\left(\frac{1}{3}x + 6\right)$ yd

x yd

Draw a diagram to visualize the problem.

Perimeter of John's farm:

$$x + \left(\frac{1}{3}x + 6\right) + x + \left(\frac{1}{3}x + 6\right) = \frac{8}{3}x + 12 \qquad \text{Add the like terms.}$$

The perimeter of John's farm is $\left(\frac{8}{3}x + 12\right)$ yards.

Guided Practice

Complete.

5 Anne's garden has a shape of an isosceles triangle with a base of length $2y$ feet and sides of length $\left(\frac{2}{5}y + 3\right)$ feet each. Write an algebraic expression for the perimeter of Anne's garden.

Perimeter of Anne's garden:

$\underline{\quad?\quad} + \underline{\quad?\quad} + \underline{\quad?\quad} = \underline{\quad?\quad}$ \qquad Add the like terms.

The perimeter of Anne's garden is $\underline{\quad?\quad}$ feet.

$\underline{\quad?\quad}$ ft $\qquad$ $\underline{\quad?\quad}$ ft

$\underline{\quad?\quad}$ ft

Translate Verbal Descriptions into Algebraic Expressions with More Than One Variable.

Some situations may require you to use more than one variable.

Andrew has m coins. Katherine has $\frac{1}{2}r$ coins. How many more coins does Andrew have than Katherine?

$$m \quad \text{minus} \quad \frac{1}{2}r$$

$$m \quad - \quad \frac{1}{2}r \qquad \text{Translate by parts. Combine.}$$

Andrew has $\left(m - \frac{1}{2}r\right)$ coins more than Katherine.

Tom made t dollars and his sister Sandra made u dollars while working at a restaurant for their summer vacation. They gave 12% of their earnings to charity. Find the total amount they gave to the charity.

$$12\% \quad \text{of the} \quad \text{sum of } t \text{ and } u$$

$$0.12 \quad \cdot \quad t + u \qquad \text{Translate by parts.}$$

$$0.12(t + u) \qquad \text{Combine.}$$

Tom and Sandra gave $[0.12(t + u)]$ dollars to the charity.

Example 18 **Translate a real-world problem into an algebraic expression using a table.**

Grapes, papayas, and strawberries are sold in a supermarket at the following prices:

x dollars Per lb   *y dollars Per lb*   *⅗ x dollars Per lb*

Daniele bought 4.5 pounds of grapes, 2.65 pounds of papayas, and 6 pounds of strawberries. What is the total cost of the fruits she bought?

Continue on next page

Solution

Use a table to organize the information.

Fruits	Price Per Pound	Total Weight	Cost
Grapes	x dollars	4.5	4.5x dollars
Papayas	y dollars	2.65	2.65y dollars
Strawberries	$\frac{3}{5}x$ dollars	6	3.6x dollars

Total cost of fruits:

$$4.5x + 2.65y + 3.6x = 4.5x + 3.6x + 2.65y \quad \text{Group the like terms.}$$
$$= 8.1x + 2.65y \quad \text{Add the like terms.}$$

The total cost of the fruits that she bought is (8.1x + 2.65y) dollars.

Guided Practice

Complete.

6 The price of a buffet lunch is $14.80 per adult and $12 per child. For a group of m adults and n children, how much does the lunch cost before tax and tips?

Diners	Price Per Person	Number of Diners	Cost
Adult	$14.80	_?_	_?_
Child	_?_	n	_?_

Total cost of lunch before tax and tips:

_?_ + _?_

The total cost of lunch before tax and tips is _?_ dollars.

7 Joshua had m quarters in his pocket. He also had one dime and n nickels. What was the total value of his coins?

Translate Verbal Descriptions into Algebraic Expressions with Parentheses.

You can use parentheses when you translate more complicated verbal descriptions into algebraic expressions.

You should expand and simplify the algebraic expressions when you can.

Example 19 **Translate a real-world problem into an algebraic expression with parentheses.**

Nancy had *n* baseball cards that she wanted to give away. She gave 12 baseball cards to her brother and divided the rest of them equally among 4 friends. How many baseball cards did each friend receive?

Solution

Before
Baseball cards

n

After
Baseball cards

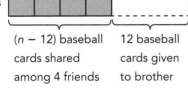

(*n* − 12) baseball cards shared among 4 friends

12 baseball cards given to brother

4 units represent (*n* − 12) baseball cards.

From the bar model, the number of baseball cards each friend received is:

$\frac{1}{4}(n - 12) = \frac{1}{4}n - 3$ Use the distributive property.

Each friend received $\left(\frac{1}{4}n - 3\right)$ baseball cards.

Guided Practice

Complete.

8 Anderson had *b* tennis balls. He gave 30 to his sister and divided the rest of the tennis balls equally among 5 friends. How many tennis balls did each friend receive?

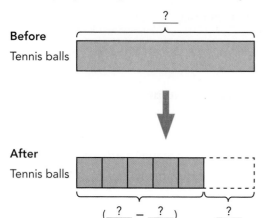

Before
Tennis balls

?

After
Tennis balls

(__?__ − __?__)   __?__

From the bar model, the number of tennis balls each friend received is:

__?__ (__?__ − __?__) = __?__   Use the distributive property.

Each friend received __?__ tennis balls.

Technology Activity

Materials:
- spreadsheet software

USE ALGEBRAIC EXPRESSIONS IN REAL-WORLD SITUATIONS

Work in groups of three or four.

Translate verbal descriptions into algebraic expressions.

Maria used her smartphone for 4 days. Her average calling time was 130 minutes each day. Suppose that Maria used the phone for *m* minutes on the fifth day. Write an algebraic expression for the average number of minutes she spent on the phone over 5 days.

 1 Complete.

Total number of minutes spent over five days:

Total number of minutes spent over four days + Number of minutes spent on the fifth day

= __?__ + *m*

Average minutes over five days:

$$\frac{\text{Total number of minutes spent over five days}}{\text{Five days}} = \underline{\quad ? \quad}$$

> **Math Note**
>
> Average number of minutes spent over four days
>
> $$= \frac{\text{Total number of minutes spent over four days}}{\text{Four days}}$$

Use a spreadsheet to solve real-world problem involving algebraic expressions.

2 Label your spreadsheet and enter the values in column A as shown.

Number of Minutes Spent on Fifth Day (*m*)	Total Number of Minutes Spent over Five Days	Average Number of Minutes Spent over Five Days
0		
50		
100		
150		
200		

3 Enter the formula =130*4+A2 in cell B2 to find the total number of minutes she spent on her phone over five days. What is the value in cell B2 after you have entered the formula?

Number of Minutes Spent on Fifth Day (*m*)	Total Number of Minutes Spent over Five Days	Average Number of Minutes Spent over Five Days
0	=130*4+A2	
50	570	
100	620	
150	670	
200	720	

4 Complete cell C2 with a formula to find the average number of minutes she spent on her phone over five days.

Number of Minutes Spent on Fifth Day (*m*)	Total Number of Minutes Spent over Five Days	Average Number of Minutes Spent over Five Days
0	520	?
50	570	114
100	620	124
150	670	134
200	720	144

5 Maria would like to have an average number of minutes she spent on her phone over five days to be 150 minutes. Determine the number of minutes she can spend on the fifth day by repeating **3** and **4** with different values in column A.

Math Journal Based on your activity, what is the relationship between the algebraic expressions of **1** and the formula used in the spreadsheet cell of **3** and **4** ? Explain how you can use technology to solve real-world problems.

Practice 3.6

Translate each verbal description into an algebraic expression. Simplify the expression when you can.

1 Sum of one-sixth of x and 2.8

2 One-half u subtracted from 3 times u

3 4.5 times q divided by 9

4 60% of one-half x

5 5x increased by 120%

6 7 times z reduced by a third of the product

7 24% of w plus 50% of y

8 Three-fourths of v subtracted from 6 times two-ninths y

9 One-fourth of the sum of 2p and 11

10 Sum of 2x, $\left(\frac{2}{3}x + 5\right)$, and $(11 - x)$

Solve. You may use a diagram, model, or table.

11 The length of $\frac{2}{3}$ of a rope is $(4u - 5)$ inches. Express the total length of the rope in terms of u.

12 If 50 lb = 22.68 kg, what is $\frac{15}{8}y$ pounds in kilograms?

13 The minute hand of a clock makes one complete round every 60 minutes. How many rounds does the minute hand make in 650x minutes?

14 Fifteen cards are added to n cards. 6 people then share the cards equally. Express the number of cards for each person in terms of n.

15 The pump price was g dollars per gallon of gasoline yesterday. The price increases by 10 cents per gallon today. If a driver pumps 12.4 gallons of gasoline today, how much does he have to pay?

16 ✏️ *Math Journal* Each algebraic expression contains an error. Copy and complete the table.

Verbal Description	Expression with Error	Description of Error	Correct Expression
35% of s plus 65% of t	$s + t$	?	?
$\frac{1}{6}x$ subtracted from $\frac{1}{6}y$	$\frac{1}{6}x - \frac{1}{6}y$	?	?
One more than half of n	$1\frac{1}{2}n$	?	?
$\frac{2}{3}x$ divided by $\frac{1}{5}$	$\frac{2}{15}x$	?	?

17 The ratio of red counters to blue counters is 9 : 11. There are y blue counters. Express the number of red counters in terms of y.

18 When 18 boys joined a group of y students, the ratio of boys to girls in the group became 4 : 5. Write an algebraic expression for the number of girls in terms of y.

19 Adrian is x years old. Benny is 7 years younger than Adrian. In 5 years' time, Benny will be twice the age of Celine. How old is Celine now in terms of x?

20 A group has an equal number of adults and children. When n oranges are given to the group, each adult gets two oranges while each child gets one orange and there are still 5 oranges left. Write an algebraic expression for the number of oranges given to the adults.

21 The list price of a camera was w dollars. Paul bought the camera for $35 less than the list price. If the sales tax was 8%, how much did Paul pay for the camera including the sales tax?

22 There were m visitors in an exhibition on the first day and 1,200 fewer visitors on the second day. On the third day, the number of visitors was 30% greater than the number of visitors on the second day. What was the average number of visitors over the three days?

23 A man drove x miles per hour for 3 hours and $(2x - 60)$ miles per hour for the next 4.75 hours.

a) Express the total distance he traveled in terms of x.

b) If $x = 64$, what is the total distance he traveled?

Real-World Problems: Algebraic Reasoning

Lesson Objective

- Solve real-world problems using algebraic reasoning.

Solve Real-World Problems Using Algebraic Reasoning.

You have used models, diagrams, and tables to translate verbal descriptions into algebraic expressions. When solving problems algebraically, you can use these mental pictures to guide you.

After Donavan gives Mabel 6 pears, she has $(x + 6)$ pears. If Mabel gives one-third of her pears to Nelson, how many pears, in terms of x, does Nelson have?

Number of pears that Nelson has:

$\frac{1}{3}(x + 6)$ Translate verbal descriptions into algebraic expression.

$= \frac{1}{3} \cdot x + \frac{1}{3} \cdot 6$ Use the distributive property.

$= \frac{1}{3}x + 2$ Simplify.

Nelson has $\left(\frac{1}{3}x + 2 \right)$ pears.

Simplifying is a logical step after expanding.

There are n apples in a box but 5 apples are too green to eat. Aaron and Barry share the ripe apples in the ratio 2 : 3. How many ripe apples does Barry get?

Solution

Method 1

Use a bar model.

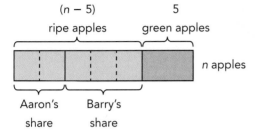

From the bar model, the number of ripe apples Barry gets is:

$$\frac{3}{5}(n - 5) = \frac{3}{5}(n) - \frac{3}{5}(5) \qquad \text{Use the distributive property.}$$

$$= \frac{3}{5}n - 3$$

Barry gets $\left(\frac{3}{5}n - 3\right)$ ripe apples.

Method 2

Use algebraic reasoning.

Only ripe apples are shared. So, subtract 5 green apples from n apples.

Aaron's apples : Barry's apples
            2 : 3

So, Barry gets 3 out of every 5 of the ripe apples.

Number of ripe apples:
$n - 5$

Number of ripe apples Barry gets:

$$\frac{3}{5}(n - 5) = \frac{3}{5}(n) - \frac{3}{5}(5) \qquad \text{Use the distributive property.}$$

$$= \frac{3}{5}n - 3$$

Barry gets $\left(\frac{3}{5}n - 3\right)$ ripe apples.

Guided Practice

Complete.

1 The area of a triangle is (u + 10) square centimeters. The ratio of the area of the unshaded region to the area of the shaded region is 1 : 3. Using algebraic reasoning, express the area of the shaded region in terms of u.

3 out of 4 units are shaded.

Area of shaded region:

$\frac{?}{?}$ (__?__) = __?__   Use the distributive property. Simplify.

The area of the shaded region of the triangle is __?__ square centimeters.

2 There are 25 nickels and quarters. w coins are nickels and the rest are quarters.

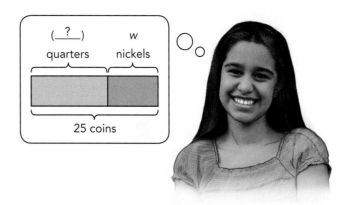

(__?__) quarters w nickels

25 coins

a) Write an algebraic expression for the number of coins that are quarters.

Number of quarters:
__?__ − __?__ .

There are __?__ quarters.

b) Find the total value of the quarters.

Total value of quarters:
__?__ · __?__ = __?__

The total value of the quarters is __?__ dollars.

Example 21 **Solve a word problem involving algebraic expressions.**

One number is n and a second number is $\left(\dfrac{2n}{3} + 2\right)$. A third number is $\dfrac{n}{6}$ less than the second number. Express the sum of the three numbers in terms of n.

Solution

First number   Second number   Third number

Sum of three numbers: $n + \left(\dfrac{2n}{3} + 2\right) + \left(\dfrac{2n}{3} + 2 - \dfrac{n}{6}\right)$ Write the addition expression.

$= n + \dfrac{2}{3}n + 2 + \dfrac{2}{3}n + 2 - \dfrac{1}{6}n$ Rewrite the expression.

$= n + \dfrac{2}{3}n + \dfrac{2}{3}n - \dfrac{1}{6}n + 2 + 2$ Group like terms.

$= \dfrac{6}{6}n + \dfrac{4}{6}n + \dfrac{4}{6}n - \dfrac{1}{6}n + 2 + 2$ LCM of 3 and 6 is 6.

$= \dfrac{13}{6}n + 4$ Simplify.

The sum of the three numbers is $\left(\dfrac{13}{6}n + 4\right)$.

Guided Practice

Complete each ⬤? with + or −, and __?__ with the correct value.

3 Amy has x comic books, Melvin has $\left(\dfrac{2x}{5} + 1\right)$ comic books, and Joel has $\dfrac{x}{10}$ fewer comic books than Melvin. Express the total number of comic books that Amy, Melvin, and Joel have in terms of x.

Amy's books   Melvin's books   Joel's books

Total number of comic books: $x + \left(\dfrac{2x}{5} + 1\right) + (\underline{\;?\;} \; ⬤? \; \underline{\;?\;})$ Write the addition expression.

$= x + \dfrac{2}{5}x + 1 + \underline{\;?\;} \; ⬤? \; \underline{\;?\;}$ Rewrite the expressions.

$= x + \dfrac{2}{5}x + \underline{\;?\;}$ Group like terms.

$= \underline{\;?\;}$ LCD of $\dfrac{2}{5}$ and $\dfrac{1}{10}$ is $\underline{\;?\;}$.

$= \underline{\;?\;}$ Simplify.

The total number of comic books is $\underline{\;?\;}$.

Example 22 **Solve a percent problem involving algebraic expressions using algebraic reasoning.**

There are an equal number of boys and girls in a group of 80 children. Within the group, *p* percent of the boys and *q* percent of the girls wear glasses. Write an algebraic expression for the number of children who do not wear glasses. Factor any terms with a common factor.

Solution

Number of boys = Number of girls:

$\frac{80}{2} = 40$

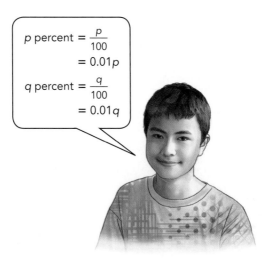

p percent = $\frac{p}{100}$
     = $0.01p$
q percent = $\frac{q}{100}$
     = $0.01q$

Number of boys who wear glasses:
$0.01p \cdot 40 = 0.4p$

Number of girls who wear glasses:
$0.01q \cdot 40 = 0.4q$

Number of children who do not wear glasses:

$80 - 0.4p - 0.4q$	Write the subtraction expression.
$= 80 + (-0.4)(p) + (-0.4)(q)$	Rewrite the expression.
$= 80 + (-0.4)(p + q)$	Factor.
$= 80 - 0.4(p + q)$	Simplify.

The number of children who do not wear glasses is $[80 - 0.4(p + q)]$.

Guided Practice

Solve.

 4 A shoe store stocks *x* pairs of sneakers and *y* pairs of sandals. During a promotion, a pair of sneakers is priced at $50 and a pair of sandals at $36. The shop manages to sell half the sneakers and 80% of the sandals. Write an expression for the total amount of sales the store makes.

Solve each question using algebraic reasoning.

1. 40% of *k* liters of acid are added to 60% of *w* liters of water. Write an algebraic expression for the total volume of the solution.

2. Write an algebraic expression for the perimeter of the quadrilateral shown.

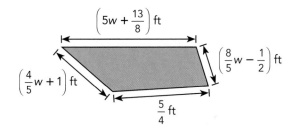

$\left(5w + \frac{13}{8}\right)$ ft

$\left(\frac{8}{5}w - \frac{1}{2}\right)$ ft

$\left(\frac{4}{5}w + 1\right)$ ft

$\frac{5}{4}$ ft

3. If the average daily sales amount for the past 5 days was $(2.3q + 1.4)$ dollars, write an algebraic expression for the total sales amount for the past 5 days.

4. The weight of 2 science fiction books and 1 autobiography is $\frac{5}{6}w$ pounds. What is the total weight of 4 of these science fiction books and 2 of these autobiographies?

5. On her way to work, Ms. Bowman waited 20 minutes at a subway station. The train ride took her $(x + 30)$ minutes to reach Grand Central Station. Then, she walked for another $\frac{1}{3}x$ minutes before reaching her office. How much time, in minutes, did Ms. Bowman take to travel to her office?

6. A ribbon measuring $(v + 4)$ feet in length was cut into two pieces in the ratio 3 : 7. What was the length of the longer piece?

7. When one-fifth of the boys left, there were still *b* boys and *g* girls who stayed to see a program. What was the total number of boys and girls at the beginning of the program?

8. John is paid at an hourly-rate of $15 an hour and overtime time rate of 1.5 times his hourly-rate for his work. If John puts in *w* regular hours and *y* overtime hours in a week, what is his total wage for the week?

9. Nathan is *p* years old now. In 10 years' time, he will be 3 times as old as Martin. Express Martin's age 10 years from now in terms of *p*.

10. Tom bought a computer for 15% off from the list price of *p* dollars. If the sales tax was 8%, how much did he pay for the computer including sales tax?

11 A farmer collected some eggs from his farm and found *b* eggs broken. He packed the remaining eggs in *c* egg cartons. Each egg carton can hold a dozen eggs and no eggs were leftover. Write an algebraic expression for the number of eggs he collected initially in terms of *b* and *c*.

12 A teacher from Anderson Middle School printed *k* nametags in preparation for the science fair. Half of the nametags were given out to students and 100 nametags were given out to parents. Three-fifths of the remaining nametags were given out to teachers and contest judges. How many nametags were not given out?

13 At the beginning of a journey, the fuel tank of a car was $\frac{3}{4}$-full. When the car reached its destination, it had consumed 60% of the gasoline in the tank. The full capacity of the fuel tank is *w* gallons.

a) Write an algebraic expression for the amount of gasoline left in the fuel tank.

b) If *w* = 15.5, how much gasoline was left at the end of the journey?

Brain @ Work

Bryan and his father are from Singapore, where the temperature is measured in degrees Celsius. While visiting downtown Los Angeles, Bryan saw a temperature sign that read 72°F. He asked his father what the equivalent temperature was in °C.

His father could not recall the Fahrenheit-to-Celsius conversion formula, $C = \frac{5}{9}(F - 32)$. However, he remembered that water freezes at 0°C or 32°F and boils at 100°C or 212°F.

Using these two pieces of information, would you be able to help Bryan figure out the above conversion formula? Explain.

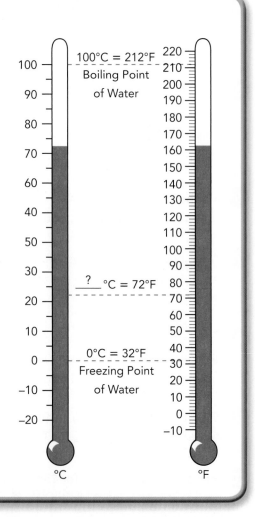

Chapter Wrap Up

Concept Map

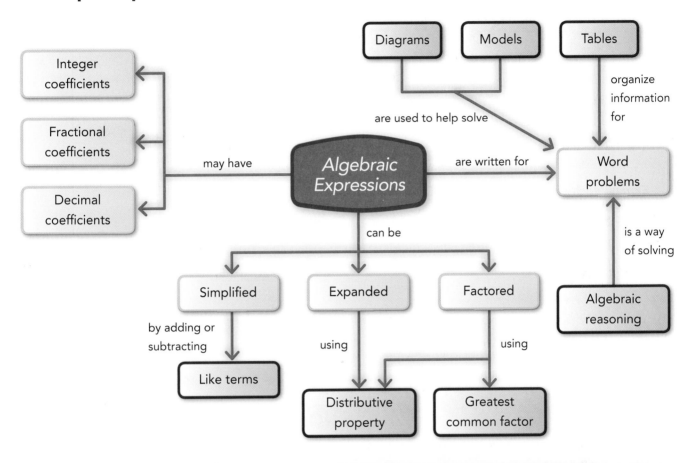

Key Concepts

▶ Algebraic expressions may contain more than one variable with rational coefficients and rational constants. **Example:** $\frac{1}{2}x + 1.2u - 3$.

▶ Algebraic expressions are written in simplest form by adding and subtracting the coefficients of the like terms.

▶ Algebraic expressions may be simplified using the commutative property of addition.

▶ Algebraic expressions are expanded using the distributive property.

▶ Algebraic expressions are factored using the greatest common factor (GCF) of the terms and the distributive property.

▶ You can use diagrams, models, or tables to help solve real-world problems algebraically.

Chapter Review/Test

Concepts and Skills

Simplify each expression.

1 $1.4w - 0.6w$

2 $\frac{3}{4}m + \frac{4}{5}m$

3 $\frac{1}{6}y + \frac{1}{2}y + \frac{1}{3}y$

4 $1.8m - 0.2m - 7m$

5 $1.3a - 0.8b + 2.2b - a$

6 $1 + \frac{1}{5}a + \frac{3}{5}b + \frac{4}{5}a$

Expand each expression. Then simplify when you can.

7 $1.2(2p - 3)$

8 $\frac{1}{3}(12p + 9q)$

9 $\frac{1}{5}\left(\frac{t}{3} + \frac{1}{2}\right)$

10 $-4(-2q + 2.5)$

11 $-\frac{2}{3}(6x + 3)$

12 $-0.5(2m - 4n)$

13 $3(a + 3) + 2a$

14 $4(2p - 3) - 3(p + 2)$

15 $2.5(m - 2) + 5.6m$

16 $4(0.6n - 3) - 0.2(2n - 3)$

Factor each expression.

17 $4t - 20s$

18 $-6p - 21q$

19 $8i + 12 + 4j$

20 $6a + 10b - 20$

21 $-9m - 3n - 6$

22 $-15x - 6 - 12y$

Translate each verbal description into an algebraic expression. Then simplify when you can.

23 One-fourth x less than the sum of 7 and 2x.

24 4 times 5y divided by 18.

25 Five-ninths of $(3p + 1)$ subtracted from one-third of $(q + p)$.

Problem Solving

Solve. Show your work.

26 After 14 boys leave a concert, the ratio of boys to girls is 3 : 10. If there are p girls at the concert, write an algebraic expression for the number of boys at the beginning of the concert in terms of p.

27 40 percent of the fish in a pond are goldfish and the rest are Koi. The number of goldfish is g. The farmer then increases the number of Koi by 10 percent. How many Koi are there in the pond, in terms of g, now?

28 Three-fourths of the weight of a bunch of grapes is equivalent to three-fifths of the weight of a papaya. If the grapes weigh $(x + 28)$ pounds, what is the weight of a papaya in terms of x?

29 Sally ordered some pizzas to be delivered. The bill for the pizza was m dollars. Sally tipped the deliverer 15% of the bill.

   a) Write an expression for the total amount of money Sally paid.

   b) The bill for the pizza was $30. Find the amount of money Sally paid.

30 A box contains n quarters and some dimes. The ratio of quarters to dimes is $1 : 2$.

   a) Write an expression for the total amount of money in the box.

   b) If there are 12 quarters, find the total amount of money in the box.

31 Rai is considering two mobile phone plans that charge for each call made. The charges are shown below.

Mobile Plan	Monthly Subscription	Cost Per Minute
A	$10	21.4¢/min
B	$14	18.5¢/min

On average, Rai uses n minutes of calling time each month.

   a) Write an expression for the total charges for Rai's usage based on each mobile plan.

   b) If $n = 100$, find the total cost for each mobile plan. Which mobile plan should Rai choose? Justify your choice.

32 The admission fee to a museum is $12.50 per nonsenior adult, $8 per child, and $6.50 per senior citizen. A tour group consists of m nonsenior adults, $\left(\frac{5}{4}m + 6\right)$ children, and $8n$ senior citizens.

   a) What is the total admission fee of the group?

   b) Write an expression for the admission fees of the children in the group subtracted from the combined admission fees of the nonsenior adults and senior citizens in the group.

   c) Evaluate your expression from **b)**, when $m = 24$ and $n = 4$.

Algebraic Equations and Inequalities

Going to the amusement park?

You and your friends are headed to an amusement park. It costs $12 to get into the park, and you also want to have $15 for lunch. You can also buy tickets to go on rides. If each ride ticket costs $2, how many rides can you go on? The answer to this question depends on how much money you take along.

In this chapter, you will learn how to use algebraic equations and inequalities to represent and solve problems.

BIG IDEA

▶ Algebraic equations and inequalities can be used to model mathematical or real-world situations and to find values of variables.

Recall Prior Knowledge

Solving algebraic equations by balancing

You can use inverse operations to solve an equation. When you do, keep the equation balanced by performing addition, subtraction, multiplication, or division by the same nonzero number on both sides.

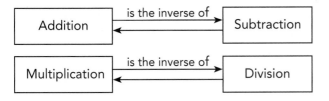

Solve each equation.

a) $x + 2 = 9$

b) $\frac{2}{3}x = 2$

....

a)
$$x + 2 = 9$$
$$x + 2 - 2 = 9 - 2 \qquad \text{Subtract 2 from both sides.}$$
$$x = 7 \qquad \text{Simplify.}$$

b)
$$\frac{2}{3}x = 2$$
$$\frac{2}{3}x \div \frac{2}{3} = 2 \div \frac{2}{3} \qquad \text{Divide both sides by } \frac{2}{3}.$$
$$\frac{2}{3}x \cdot \frac{3}{2} = 2 \cdot \frac{3}{2} \qquad \text{Rewrite division as multiplication by the reciprocal of } \frac{2}{3}.$$
$$x = 3 \qquad \text{Simplify.}$$

✓ Quick Check

Solve each equation.

1 $x + 4 = 10$

2 $x - \frac{1}{2} = 2$

3 $\frac{1}{5}x = 3$

4 $1.2x = 2.4$

Solving algebraic equations by substitution

You can use substitution to solve an algebraic equation.

Solve $x + 6 = 8$.

If $x = 1$, $x + 6 = 1 + 6$ Substitute 1 for x.

                    $= 7$ $(\neq 8)$ 1 is not the solution.

If $x = 2$, $x + 6 = 2 + 6$ Substitute 2 for x.

                    $= 8$ 2 is the solution.

The equation $x + 6 = 8$ is true when $x = 2$.
$x = 2$ gives the solution of the equation $x + 6 = 8$.

✔ Quick Check

State whether each statement is True or False.

5 $x = 1$ gives the solution of the algebraic equation $3x + 5 = 8$.

6 $y = 2$ gives the solution of the algebraic equation $6y - 3 = 8$.

7 $z = 6$ gives the solution of the algebraic equation $\dfrac{z}{3} = 3$.

8 $w = 3$ gives the solution of the algebraic equation $2w = 6$.

Graphing inequalities on a number line

You can represent an inequality on a number line using circles and arrows.

$p > 5.5$

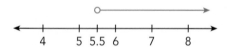

Use an empty circle to show that
5.5 is not a solution of the inequality.

$q \leq 11$

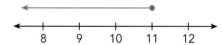

Use a shaded circle to show that
11 is a solution of the inequality.

✔ Quick Check

Draw a number line to represent each inequality.

9 $x \geq 3.5$

10 $y < \dfrac{1}{2}$

Writing algebraic inequalities

Use $>$, $<$, $\geq$, $\leq$, or $\neq$ to compare unequal quantities or quantities that may not be equal.

Verbal Descriptions	Algebraic Inequality
The cost of an apple, a, is **not** $3.	$a \neq 3$
The cost of a greeting card, c, is **less than** $6.	$c < 6$
The width of the pond, w, is **at most** 5 meters. OR The width of the pond, w, is **no more than** 5 meters. OR The width of the pond, w, is **less than or equal to** 5 meters.	$w \leq 5$
The mass of the strawberries, s, is **more than** 500 grams.	$s > 500$
The length of the ribbon, r, is **at least** 10 inches. OR The length of the ribbon, r, is **no less than** 10 inches. OR The length of the ribbon, r, is **greater than or equal to** 10 inches.	$r \geq 10$

✔ Quick Check

Complete each ? with $=$, $>$, or $<$.

11 11 ? -12

12 -9 ? -7

13 $25 \cdot (-1)$? $(-1) \cdot 25$

14 $3 \div (-1)$? $(-1) \div 3$

Use x to represent the unknown quantity. Write an algebraic inequality for each statement.

15 The box can hold less than 70 pounds.

16 You have to be at least 17 years old to qualify for the contest.

17 The width of luggage that you can carry onto the plane is at most 17 inches.

18 There are more than 120 people standing in line for the roller coaster.

Understanding Equivalent Equations

Lesson Objective

- Identify equivalent equations.

Vocabulary

equivalent equations

Identify Equivalent Equations.

You have learned that factoring, simplifying, or expanding an expression produces an equivalent expression. Equivalent expressions have the same value for any given value of the variable.

Examples of equivalent expressions:

$4x + 3 + 3x = 7x + 3$ Group like terms.

$4x + 6 = 2(2x + 3)$ Factor. The common factor of $4x$ and 6 is 2.

$2(x - 5) = 2x - 10$ Use the distributive property to expand.

Equivalent equations are equations that have the same solution. Given an equation, you can use the operations of addition, subtraction, multiplication, or division to produce an equivalent equation. For example, you can subtract 2 from both sides of the equation $x - 1 = 7$ as shown.

Balance	Algebraic Equation
■ represents 1 counter. represents x counters.	

 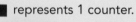

Left side = Right side

$x - 1 = 7$

Subtract 2 counters from both sides.

$x - 1 - 2 = 7 - 2$ Subtract both sides by 2.

$x - 3 = 5$ Simplify.

Compare the solutions of the original equation and the new equation:

$x = 8$ gives the solution of the equation $x - 1 = 7$.

$x = 8$ gives the solution of the equation $x - 3 = 5$.

Now suppose you add 3 to both sides of the equation $x - 3 = 5$.

Balance	Algebraic Equation
Add 3 counters to both sides.	$x - 3 + 3 = 5 + 3$ Add 3 to both sides. $x = 8$ Simplify.

Compare the solutions of the original equation and the new equation:

$x = 8$ gives the solution of the equation $x - 3 = 5$.

$x = 8$ gives the solution of the equation $x = 8$.

Then suppose you multiply both sides of the equation $x = 8$ by 2.

Balance	Algebraic Equation
Multiply both sides by 2.	$x \cdot 2 = 8 \cdot 2$ Multiply both sides by 2. $2x = 16$ Simplify.

Compare the solutions of the original equation and the new equation:

$x = 8$ gives the solution of the equation $x = 8$.

$x = 8$ gives the solution of the equation $2x = 16$.

Finally, suppose you divide both sides of the equation $2x = 16$ by 4.

Balance	Algebraic Equation
Divide into four equal groups.	$2x \div 4 = 16 \div 4$ Divide both sides by 4. $\frac{1}{2}x = 4$ Simplify.

Compare the solutions of the original equation and the new equation:

$x = 8$ gives the solution of the equation $2x = 16$.

$x = 8$ gives the solution of the equation $\frac{1}{2}x = 4$.

So, you can see that performing the same operation on both sides of an equation may produce an equivalent equation with the same solution. You can use the fact that equivalent equations have the same solution to decide whether two equations are equivalent.

Example 1 **Identify equivalent equations.**

State whether each pair of equations are equivalent equations. Give a reason for your answer.

a) $x + 3 + 6x = 13$ and $7x + 3 = 13$

Solution

$x + 3 + 6x = 13$

$x + 6x + 3 = 13$ Use commutative property to group like terms.

$7x + 3 = 13$ Add like terms.

$x + 3 + 6x = 13$ can be rewritten as $7x + 3 = 13$ using familiar number properties. So, the equations have the same solution and are equivalent.

b) $5x - 4 = 6$ and $5x = 20$

Solution

You can check to see if both equations have the same solution.

First solve $5x = 20$.

$5x \div 5 = 20 \div 5$ Divide both sides by 5.

$x = 4$ Simplify.

Then check to see if 4 is the solution of the equation $5x - 4 = 6$.

If $x = 4$, $5x - 4 = 5 \cdot 4 - 4$ Substitute 4 for x.

$= 16$ $(\neq 6)$ 4 is not a solution.

Because the equations have different solutions, they are not equivalent equations. So, $5x - 4 = 6$ and $5x = 20$ are not equivalent equations.

c) $\frac{2}{3}x = 4$ and $x = 6$

Solution

You can check to see if both equations have the same solution.

If $x = 6$, $\frac{2}{3}x = \frac{2}{3} \cdot 6$ Substitute 6 for x.

$= 4$ 6 is a solution.

Because the equations have the same solution, 6, they are equivalent equations.

So, $\frac{2}{3}x = 4$ and $x = 6$ are equivalent equations.

Guided Practice

Copy and complete to state whether each pair of equations are equivalent equations. Give a reason for your answer.

1 $x - 3 + 4x = 5$ and $5x = 2$

Check to see if $x - 3 + 4x = 5$ can be rewritten as $5x = 2$.

$x - 3 + 4x = 5$

$5x - 3 = 5$ Group like terms.

$5x - 3 + \underline{\ ?\ } = 5 + \underline{\ ?\ }$ Add $\underline{\ ?\ }$ to both sides.

$5x = \underline{\ ?\ }$ Simplify.

$x - 3 + 4x = 5 \underline{\ ?\ }$ be rewritten as $5x = 2$.

So, the equations have $\underline{\ ?\ }$ solutions and are $\underline{\ ?\ }$.

2 $x + 7 = 12$ and $2x = 10$

First solve $x + 7 = 12$.

For questions **2** to **4**, check to see if both equations have the same solution.

$x + 7 = 12$

$x + 7 - \underline{\ ?\ } = 12 - \underline{\ ?\ }$ Subtract $\underline{\ ?\ }$ from both sides.

$x = \underline{\ ?\ }$ Simplify.

Then check to see if $\underline{\ ?\ }$ is the solution of the equation $2x = 10$.

If $x = \underline{\ ?\ }$, $2x = 2 \cdot \underline{\ ?\ }$ Substitute $\underline{\ ?\ }$ for x.

$= \underline{\ ?\ }$ $\underline{\ ?\ }$ a solution.

Because the equations have the $\underline{\ ?\ }$ solution, they are $\underline{\ ?\ }$ equations.

3 $1.2x = 2.4$ and $x - 6 = 8$

First solve $x - 6 = 8$.

$x - 6 = 8$

$x - 6 + \underline{\ ?\ } = 8 + \underline{\ ?\ }$ Add $\underline{\ ?\ }$ to both sides.

$x = \underline{\ ?\ }$ Simplify.

Then check to see if $\underline{\ ?\ }$ is the solution of the equation $1.2x = 2.4$.

If $x = \underline{\ ?\ }$, $1.2x = 1.2 \cdot \underline{\ ?\ }$ Substitute $\underline{\ ?\ }$ for x.

$= \underline{\ ?\ }$ $\underline{\ ?\ }$ a solution.

Because the equations have $\underline{\ ?\ }$ solutions, they are $\underline{\ ?\ }$ equations.

4 $\frac{2}{5}x = 4$ and $x = 10$.

If $x = 10$, $\frac{2}{5}x = \frac{2}{5} \cdot 10$ Substitute 10 for x.

$= \underline{\ ?\ }$ $\underline{\ ?\ }$ a solution.

Because the equations have the $\underline{\ ?\ }$ solution, they are $\underline{\ ?\ }$ equations.

Think Math

When Judy multiplies both sides of the equation $\frac{1}{4}y - 1 = 2$ by 4, she gets $y - 1 = 8$. What mistake did she make? What is the equation she should have written?

Practice 4.1

Tell whether each pair of equations are equivalent. Give a reason for your answer.

1 $2x = 4$ and $4x + 5 = 13$

2 $-2x + 9 = 7$ and $-2x = 2$

3 $5x - 4 + 3x = 8$ and $8x = 12$

4 $\frac{3}{4}x - 7 = 2$ and $x = 12$

Match each equation with an equivalent equation.

5 $0.5x + 1 = 1.5$

    a) $6x = 9$

6 $9 + 3.5x = 16$

    b) $\frac{3}{5}x = \frac{1}{15}$

7 $\frac{4}{5}x = 4$

    c) $\frac{3}{2}x = 3$

8 $2x + \frac{1}{2} = \frac{7}{2}$

    d) $\frac{2}{3}x = \frac{2}{3}$

9 $x - 8.3 = 1.3$

    e) $2x = 10$

10 $13.9 = 2.5x$

    f) $1.2 + x = 6.76$

11 $4x = \frac{4}{9}$

    g) $\frac{1}{2}x = 4.8$

Solve.

12 ✏️ *Math Journal* Max was asked to write an equation equivalent to $\frac{2}{3}x = 3 - x$. He wrote the following:

$$\frac{2}{3}x = 3 - x$$

$$\frac{2}{3}x \cdot 3 = 3 \cdot 3 - x$$

$$2x = 9 - x$$

He concluded that $\frac{2}{3}x = 3 - x$ and $2x = 9 - x$ are equivalent equations.

Do you agree with his conclusion? Give a reason for your answer.

Solving Algebraic Equations

Lesson Objectives

- Solve algebraic equations with variables on the same side of the equation.
- Solve algebraic equations with with variables on both sides of the equation.
- Solve algebraic equations in factored form.

Solve Algebraic Equations with Variables on the Same Side of the Equation.

To solve an equation means to find the value of the variable that makes the equation a true statement. Sometimes, you have to define the variable when you translate a verbal description into an equation.

For example, the weight of a bowling ball is 6 kilograms. Two bowling pins and a bowling ball weighed 9 kilograms. What is the weight of a bowling pin?

First you define the variable. In this case, let x be the weight of one bowling pin.

Then you translate the verbal description into an algebraic equation: $2x + 6 = 9$.

Total weight of two bowling pins and a bowling ball is 9 kg.

$$2x \qquad + \qquad 6 \qquad = \qquad 9$$

Finally, you solve the equation.

Method 1

Solve an algebraic equation by substitution.

If $x = 1$, $\quad 2x + 6 = 2 \cdot 1 + 6$ Try substituting 1 for x.
$\qquad\qquad\qquad\quad = 8 \quad (\neq 9)$ 1 is not the solution.

If $x = 2$, $\quad 2x + 6 = 2 \cdot 2 + 6$ Try substituting 2 for x.
$\qquad\qquad\qquad\quad = 10 \quad (\neq 9)$ 2 is not the solution.

The solution lies between $x = 1$ and $x = 2$.

If $x = 1.1$, $2x + 6 = 2 \cdot 1.1 + 6$ Try substituting 1.1 for x.
$\qquad\qquad\qquad\quad = 8.2 \quad (\neq 9)$ 1.1 is not the solution.

If $x = 1.5$, $2x + 6 = 2 \cdot 1.5 + 6$ Try substituting 1.5 for x.
$\qquad\qquad\qquad\quad = 9$ 1.5 is the solution.

$x = 1.5$ gives the solution of the equation $2x + 6 = 9$.
The weight of one bowling pin is 1.5 kilograms.

Continue on next page

Method 2

Solve an algebraic equation by balancing.

To solve an equation, you can add, subtract, multiply, or divide both sides of the equation by the same nonzero number. Your goal is to produce an equivalent equation in which the variable is alone, or "isolated" on one side of the equation.

Remember to keep an equation "balanced" by performing the same operation on both sides.

The diagrams below show how to solve the equation $2x + 6 = 9$.

Balance	Algebraic Equation
■ represents 1 counter. x represents x counters. 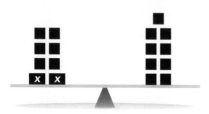	You can solve the equation by isolating the variable, x. Left side Equals Right side $2x + 6 \quad = \quad 9$
Remove 6 counters from both sides. 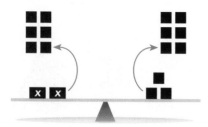	First isolate the algebraic term, $2x$, on one side of the equation. Decide which operation to use. Subtraction is the inverse of addition. To undo the addition of 6 to $2x$, subtract 6 from both sides of the equation. $2x + 6 - 6 = 9 - 6$ Subtract 6 from both sides. $2x = 3$ Simplify.

Math Note

An inverse operation is an operation that will "undo" another operation.

In this case, use subtraction of 6 to "undo" the addition of 6 because subtraction is the inverse operation of addition.

Divide each side into two equal groups.

The counters on both sides are equal.

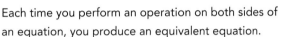

Then isolate the variable, x. In other words, x will have a coefficient of 1.

Decide which operation to use. Division is the inverse of multiplication. To undo the multiplication of 2 and x, divide both sides of the equation by 2.

$2x \div 2 = 3 \div 2$ Divide both sides by 2.
$x = 1.5$ Simplify.

$x = 1.5$ gives the solution of the equation $2x + 6 = 9$.

Each time you perform an operation on both sides of an equation, you produce an equivalent equation.

In this example, $2x + 6 = 9$, $2x = 3$, and $x = 1.5$ are equivalent equations.

Check: Substitute the value of $x = 1.5$ into the original equation.

$2x + 6 = 2 \cdot (1.5) + 6$
$\qquad = 9$

When $x = 1.5$, the equation $2x + 6 = 9$ is true. $x = 1.5$ gives the solution.

The weight of one bowling pin is 1.5 kilograms.

To avoid errors, always check your solution.

When an expression in an algebraic equation involves more than one operation, you can use the order of operations "in reverse" to undo the operations and isolate the variable.

Steps for solving an equation:

STEP 1   "Undo" addition or subtraction using inverse operations.
STEP 2   "Undo" multiplication or division using inverse operations.

Solve each equation.

a) $3 - 7x = 10$

Solution

$$3 - 7x = 10$$

$3 - 7x - 3 = 10 - 3$ Subtract 3 from both sides to undo addition.

$-7x = 7$ Simplify.

$-7x \div -7 = 7 \div -7$ Divide both sides by -7 to undo multiplication.

$x = -1$ Simplify.

$x = -1$ gives the solution of the equation $3 - 7x = 10$.

Check: Substitute the value of $x = -1$ into the original equation.

$$3 - 7x = 3 - 7 \cdot (-1)$$
$$= 10$$

When $x = -1$, the equation $3 - 7x = 10$ is true. $x = -1$ gives the solution.

Math Note

Multiplying and Dividing Rational Numbers:

Two signs are the same:

Multiplication	Division
$(+) \cdot (+) = (+)$	$(+) \div (+) = (+)$
$(-) \cdot (-) = (+)$	$(-) \div (-) = (+)$

For example, $(-1) \cdot (-2) = 2$ and $1 \cdot 2 = 2$.

Two signs are different:

Multiplication	Division
$(+) \cdot (-) = (-)$	$(+) \div (-) = (-)$
$(-) \cdot (+) = (-)$	$(-) \div (+) = (-)$

For example, $(-1) \cdot 2 = -2$, and $1 \cdot (-2) = -2$.

b) $\frac{1}{6}y - \frac{1}{3} = 2$

Solution

In this equation, the term $\frac{1}{6}y$ can be written as $\frac{y}{6}$. Then you can see that there are two operations to undo: The subtraction of $\frac{1}{3}$ and the division by 6.

Method 1

Solve by balancing the equation.

$$\frac{y}{6} - \frac{1}{3} = 2$$

$\frac{y}{6} - \frac{1}{3} + \frac{1}{3} = 2 + \frac{1}{3}$ Add $\frac{1}{3}$ to both sides.

$\frac{y}{6} = \frac{7}{3}$ Simplify.

$6 \cdot \left(\frac{y}{6}\right) = 6 \cdot \left(\frac{7}{3}\right)$ Multiply both sides by 6, which is the reciprocal of the coefficient, $\frac{1}{6}$.

$y = 14$ Simplify.

Method 2

Solve by multiplying the equation by the least common denominator (LCD).

$$6 \cdot \left(\frac{y}{6} - \frac{1}{3} \right) = 6 \cdot 2$$

Multiply both sides by 6, the LCD of $\frac{1}{6}$ and $\frac{1}{3}$.

$$6 \cdot \frac{y}{6} - 6 \cdot \frac{1}{3} = 6 \cdot 2$$

Use the distributive property.

$$y - 2 = 12$$ Simplify.

$$y - 2 + 2 = 12 + 2$$ Add 2 to both sides.

$$y = 14$$ Simplify.

$y = 14$ gives the solution of the equation $\frac{1}{6}y - \frac{1}{3} = 2$.

> **Math Note**
>
> When you multiply equations involving fractional coefficients by the LCD, the two sides of the equation will remain equal.
>
> This will result in equivalent equations that do not contain fractions.

Check: Substitute the value of $y = 14$ into the original equation.

$$\frac{1}{6}y - \frac{1}{3} = \frac{14}{6} - \frac{1}{3}$$

$$= \frac{7}{3} - \frac{1}{3}$$

$$= \frac{6}{3}$$

$$= 2$$

When $y = 14$, the equation $\frac{1}{6}y - \frac{1}{3} = 2$ is true.

$y = 14$ gives the solution.

c) $x + 1.5 - 0.5x = 4.5$

Solution

$$x + 1.5 - 0.5x = 4.5$$

$$0.5x + 1.5 = 4.5$$ Subtract the like terms.

$$0.5x + 1.5 - 1.5 = 4.5 - 1.5$$ Subtract 1.5 from both sides.

$$0.5x = 3$$ Simplify.

$$0.5x \div 0.5 = 3 \div 0.5$$ Divide both sides by 0.5.

$$x = 6$$ Simplify.

$x = 6$ gives the solution of $x + 1.5 - 0.5x = 4.5$.

Check: Substitute the value of $x = 6$ into the original equation.

$$x + 1.5 - 0.5x = 6 + 1.5 - 0.5 \cdot 6$$

$$= 4.5$$

When $x = 6$, the equation $x + 1.5 - 0.5x = 4.5$ is true.

$x = 6$ gives the solution.

Guided Practice

Solve.

1 $6x + 2 = 8$

$$6x + 2 = 8$$
$$6x + 2 - \underline{\ ?\ } = 8 - \underline{\ ?\ } \qquad \text{Subtract } \underline{\ ?\ } \text{ from both sides.}$$
$$\underline{\ ?\ } = \underline{\ ?\ } \qquad \text{Simplify.}$$
$$\frac{?}{?}x = \frac{?}{?} \qquad \text{Divide both sides by } \underline{\ ?\ }.$$
$$x = \underline{\ ?\ } \qquad \text{Simplify.}$$

2 $5 - 3x = 20$

3 $4x - 3 + 0.5x = 1.5$

4 $\frac{9}{10}x - \frac{4}{5} = 1$

Solve Algebraic Equations with Variables on Both Sides of the Equation.

The idea of balancing can also be used to solve an equation with variables on both sides. You can solve the equation by isolating the variable on one side of the equation.

Paul and Rachel are asked to solve $4x + 7 = x + 10$. As shown, they isolate the variable on different sides of the equation.

Paul's Method:

First he isolates the algebraic term on the left side of the equation.

$$4x + 7 = x + 10$$
$$4x + 7 - x = x + 10 - x \qquad \text{Subtract } x \text{ from both sides.}$$
$$3x + 7 = 10 \qquad \text{Simplify.}$$
$$3x + 7 - 7 = 10 - 7 \qquad \text{Subtract 7 from both sides.}$$
$$3x = 3 \qquad \text{Simplify.}$$

Then he isolates the variable.

$$\frac{3x}{3} = \frac{3}{3} \qquad \text{Divide both sides by 3.}$$
$$x = 1 \qquad \text{Simplify.}$$

Rachel's Method:

First she isolates the algebraic term on the right side of the equation.

$$4x + 7 = x + 10$$
$$4x + 7 - 4x = x + 10 - 4x \qquad \text{Subtract } 4x \text{ from both sides.}$$
$$7 = 10 - 3x \qquad \text{Simplify.}$$
$$7 - 10 = 10 - 3x - 10 \qquad \text{Subtract 10 from both sides.}$$
$$-3 = -3x \qquad \text{Simplify.}$$

Then she isolates the variable.

$$\frac{-3}{-3} = \frac{-3x}{-3}$$ Divide both sides by -3.

$$1 = x$$ Simplify.

$$x = 1$$ Write an equivalent equation.

You can see that isolating the variable on either side of the equation will still give you the same solution.

Example 3   **Solve algebraic equations with variables on both sides of the equation.**

Solve each equation.

a) $8 - 5x = 2x + 22$

Solution

Method 1

$$8 - 5x = 2x + 22$$

$$8 - 5x - 2x = 2x + 22 - 2x$$ Subtract $2x$ from both sides.

$$8 - 7x = 22$$ Simplify.

$$8 - 7x - 8 = 22 - 8$$ Subtract 8 from both sides.

$$-7x = 14$$ Simplify.

$$\frac{-7x}{-7} = \frac{14}{-7}$$ Divide both sides by -7.

$$x = -2$$ Simplify.

Method 2

$$8 - 5x = 2x + 22$$

$$8 - 5x + 5x = 2x + 22 + 5x$$ Add $5x$ to both sides.

$$8 = 22 + 7x$$ Simplify.

$$8 - 22 = 22 + 7x - 22$$ Subtract 22 from both sides.

$$-14 = 7x$$ Simplify.

$$\frac{-14}{7} = \frac{7x}{7}$$ Divide both sides by 7.

$$-2 = x$$ Simplify.

Remember to check your solution by substituting the solution $x = -2$ into the original equation.

Continue on next page

b) $2.9y + 2.7 = 1.1y - 9.9$

Solution

$2.9y + 2.7 - 1.1y = 1.1y - 9.9 - 1.1y$	Subtract 1.1y from both sides.
$1.8y + 2.7 = -9.9$	Simplify.
$1.8y + 2.7 - 2.7 = -9.9 - 2.7$	Subtract 2.7 from both sides.
$1.8y = -12.6$	Simplify.
$\dfrac{1.8y}{1.8} = \dfrac{-12.6}{1.8}$	Divide both sides by 1.8.
$y = -7$	Simplify.

Another way to solve the equation is to first multiply both sides by 10 to rewrite decimal coefficients as integer coefficients.

$$2.9y + 2.7 = 1.1y - 9.9$$
$$10(2.9y) + 10(2.7) = 10(1.1y) - 10(9.9)$$
$$29y + 27 = 11y - 99$$

Then you solve the equation $29y + 27 = 11y - 99$ by isolating the variable on either side of the equation. Remember to check your solution.

c) $\dfrac{3}{4}x - \dfrac{1}{2} = \dfrac{3}{8}x + 4$

Solution

Method 1

Solve by balancing the equation.

$\dfrac{3}{4}x - \dfrac{1}{2} = \dfrac{3}{8}x + 4$	
$\dfrac{3}{4}x - \dfrac{1}{2} - \dfrac{3}{8}x = \dfrac{3}{8}x + 4 - \dfrac{3}{8}x$	Subtract $\dfrac{3}{8}x$ from both sides.
$\dfrac{6}{8}x - \dfrac{1}{2} - \dfrac{3}{8}x = 4$	The LCD of $\dfrac{3}{4}$ and $\dfrac{3}{8}$ is 8. $\dfrac{3}{4}x = \dfrac{6}{8}x$.
$\dfrac{3}{8}x - \dfrac{1}{2} = 4$	Subtract the like terms.
$\dfrac{3}{8}x - \dfrac{1}{2} + \dfrac{1}{2} = 4 + \dfrac{1}{2}$	Add $\dfrac{1}{2}$ to both sides.
$\dfrac{3}{8}x = \dfrac{9}{2}$	Simplify.
$\dfrac{8}{3} \cdot \dfrac{3}{8}x = \dfrac{8}{3} \cdot \dfrac{9}{2}$	Multiply both sides by the reciprocal of $\dfrac{3}{8}$, $\dfrac{8}{3}$.
$x = \dfrac{72}{6}$	Divide.
$x = 12$	Simplify.

Method 2

Solve by multiplying both sides of the equation by the LCD.

$$8 \cdot \left(\frac{3}{4}x - \frac{1}{2}\right) = 8 \cdot \left(\frac{3}{8}x + 4\right)$$ Multiply both sides by 8, the LCD of $\frac{3}{4}$, $\frac{1}{2}$, and $\frac{3}{8}$.

$$8 \cdot \frac{3}{4}x - 8 \cdot \frac{1}{2} = 8 \cdot \frac{3}{8}x + 8 \cdot 4$$ Use the distributive property.

$$6x - 4 = 3x + 32$$ Simplify.

$$6x - 4 - 3x = 3x + 32 - 3x$$ Subtract 3x from both sides.

$$3x - 4 = 32$$ Simplify.

$$3x - 4 + 4 = 32 + 4$$ Add 4 to both sides.

$$3x = 36$$ Simplify.

$$\frac{3x}{3} = \frac{36}{3}$$ Divide both sides by 3.

$$x = 12$$ Simplify.

In **Method 1** and **Method 2**, the variable is isolated on the left side of the equation.

You can also isolate the variable on the right side of the equation. Remember to check your solution.

Guided Practice

Solve each equation. Check your solution.

5 $11 - 4x = x + 16$

$$11 - 4x = x + 16$$

$$11 - 4x - x = x + 16 - x$$ Subtract x from both sides.

$$11 + \underline{\quad?\quad} = 16$$ Simplify.

$$11 + \underline{\quad?\quad} - 11 = 16 - 11$$ Subtract 11 from both sides.

$$\underline{\quad?\quad} = 5$$ Simplify.

$$\frac{?}{?}x = \frac{?}{?}$$ Divide both sides by $\underline{\quad?\quad}$.

$$x = \underline{\quad?\quad}$$ Simplify.

6 $3.4y - 5.2 = 3y + 2$

7 $\frac{5}{9}y - \frac{1}{3} = \frac{2}{3}y + \frac{1}{3}$

Solve Algebraic Equations in Factored Form.

Sometimes an equation includes an expression with parentheses. You can solve these equations in more than one way.

Solve $2(3x + 1) = 11$.

Method 1

Use the distributive property and inverse operations.

First use the distributive property to expand the expression.

$$2(3x + 1) = 11$$
$$2 \cdot 3x + 2 \cdot 1 = 11 \qquad \text{Use the distributive property.}$$
$$6x + 2 = 11 \qquad \text{Simplify.}$$

Then isolate the algebraic term.

$$6x + 2 - 2 = 11 - 2 \qquad \text{Subtract 2 from both sides.}$$
$$6x = 9 \qquad \text{Simplify.}$$

Finally, isolate the variable.

$$6x \div 6 = 9 \div 6 \qquad \text{Divide both sides by 6.}$$
$$x = 1.5 \qquad \text{Simplify. Express in simplest form.}$$

Method 2

Use inverse operations.

First divide both sides by 2 to "undo" the multiplication.

$$2(3x + 1) = 11$$
$$\frac{2(3x + 1)}{2} = \frac{11}{2} \qquad \text{Divide both sides by 2.}$$
$$3x + 1 = 5.5 \qquad \text{Simplify.}$$

Then isolate the algebraic term.

$$3x + 1 - 1 = 5.5 - 1 \qquad \text{Subtract 1 from both sides.}$$
$$3x = 4.5 \qquad \text{Simplify.}$$

Finally, isolate the variable.

$$3x \div 3 = 4.5 \div 3 \qquad \text{Divide both sides by 3.}$$
$$x = 1.5 \qquad \text{Simplify. Express in simplest form.}$$

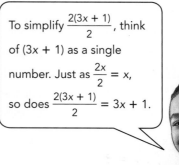

To simplify $\frac{2(3x + 1)}{2}$, think of $(3x + 1)$ as a single number. Just as $\frac{2x}{2} = x$, so does $\frac{2(3x + 1)}{2} = 3x + 1$.

The answer is still the same, even if you use a different method to solve the equation.

Example 4 **Solve algebraic equations in factored form.**

Solve each equation.

a) $\frac{1}{6}(z + 1) = 6$

Solution

Method 1

Use the distributive property and inverse operations.

$\frac{1}{6}(z + 1) = 6$

$\frac{1}{6} \cdot z + \frac{1}{6} \cdot 1 = 6$ Use the distributive property.

$\frac{1}{6}z + \frac{1}{6} = 6$ Simplify.

$\frac{1}{6}z + \frac{1}{6} - \frac{1}{6} = \frac{36}{6} - \frac{1}{6}$ Subtract $\frac{1}{6}$ from both sides. Rewrite 6 as $\frac{36}{6}$.

$\frac{1}{6}z = \frac{35}{6}$ Simplify.

$6 \cdot \frac{1}{6}z = 6 \cdot \frac{35}{6}$ Multiply both sides by 6.

$z = 35$ Simplify.

Method 2

Use inverse operations.

$\frac{1}{6}(z + 1) = 6$

$6 \cdot \frac{1}{6}(z + 1) = 6 \cdot 6$ Multiply both sides by 6.

$z + 1 = 36$ Simplify.

$z + 1 - 1 = 36 - 1$ Subtract 1 from both sides.

$z = 35$ Simplify.

b) $1.5(w + 2) + 2 = 8$

Solution

$1.5(w + 2) + 2 = 8$

$1.5 \cdot w + 1.5 \cdot 2 + 2 = 8$ Use the distributive property.

$1.5w + 5 = 8$ Simplify.

$1.5w + 5 - 5 = 8 - 5$ Subtract 5 from both sides.

$1.5w = 3$ Simplify.

$1.5w \div 1.5 = 3 \div 1.5$ Divide both sides by 1.5.

$w = 2$ Simplify.

Think Math

Allison wants to solve $1.5(w + 2) + 2 = 8$ by "undoing" the addition of **2** first before using the distributive property. Will she get the same solution? Explain your reasoning.

Continue on next page

c) $2x + 5(2 - x) = 40$

There is more than one way to solve this equation.
Suppose you first divide each term by 5:

$$2x + 5(2 - x) = 40$$
$$2x \div 5 + 5(2 - x) \div 5 = 40 \div 5$$
$$\frac{2}{5}x + (2 - x) = 8$$
$$\frac{2}{5}x + 2 - x = 8$$
$$-\frac{3}{5}x + 2 = 8$$

Then you have to solve an equation involving a variable
with a negative fractional coefficient. A better method
is to use the distributive property first.

Solution

$2x + 5(2 - x) = 40$	
$2x + 5 \cdot 2 - 5 \cdot x = 40$	Use the distributive property.
$2x + 10 - 5x = 40$	Simplify.
$10 - 3x = 40$	Subtract the like terms.
$10 - 3x - 10 = 40 - 10$	Subtract 10 from both sides.
$-3x = 30$	Simplify.
$\dfrac{-3x}{-3} = \dfrac{30}{-3}$	Divide both sides by -3.
$x = -10$	Simplify.

Guided Practice

Solve each equation. Check your solutions.

8 $1.5(p + 3) = 18$

9 $\frac{1}{4}(q + 1) = 9$

10 $2(x - 3) + 2 = 14$

11 $3(y - 1) + y = 1$

Practice 4.2

Solve each equation with variables on the same side.

1 $4b - 2 = 6$

2 $5x + 4 = 24$

3 $7c - 11 = 17$

4 $18 = 3k - 3$

5 $\frac{a}{4} - 1 = 3$

6 $\frac{2}{3}v = 2 - \frac{4}{3}$

7 $\frac{5}{2}y + 8 = 18$

8 $\frac{3}{5}f - \frac{4}{5} = \frac{2}{5}$

9 $4.5 + 0.2p = 6.1$

10 $1.5d + 3.2 = 9.2$

11 $0.8w - 4 = 4$

12 $1.4z - 0.5 = 3.7$

13 *Math Journal* Priscilla was asked to solve the equation $-4p + 5 = 7$. Her solution is shown.

$$-4p + 5 = 7$$
$$-4p + 5 - 5 = 7 - 5$$
$$-4p = 2$$
$$p = \frac{1}{2}$$

Priscilla concluded that $p = \frac{1}{2}$ is the solution of the equation $-4p + 5 = 7$.

Describe and correct the error Priscilla made.

Solve each equation with variables on both sides.

14 $6a + 7 = 4a + 7$

15 $17g + 3 = 11g + 39$

16 $8h - 5 = 11h - 14$

17 $9j + 4 = 13j - 6$

18 $\frac{1}{2}f - 2 = \frac{1}{6}f$

19 $25 + q = \frac{1}{2}q - 3$

20 $\frac{5}{9}v - \frac{1}{3} = \frac{2}{3}v + \frac{1}{3}$

21 $\frac{5}{4}e + \frac{1}{2} = 2e - \frac{1}{2}$

22 $7.5x - 4.1 = 6.7 - 4.5x$

23 $3.4y - 5.2 = 3y + 2$

24 $b - 2.8 = 0.8b + 1.2$

25 $3.2s - 5 = 5 - 1.8s$

Give your reasoning.

26 ✏️ *Math Journal* How is the process of solving the equation $\frac{3}{5}x - 1 = \frac{3}{10}x + \frac{1}{5}$ different from simplifying the expression $\frac{3}{5}x - 1 + \frac{3}{10}x + \frac{1}{5}$?

Solve each equation involving parentheses.

27 $7(2z + 1) = 35$

28 $18 = 6(5 - g)$

29 $\frac{1}{5}(3r - 4) = \frac{2}{5}$

30 $\frac{1}{8}(5x + 4) = \frac{3}{4}$

31 $0.6(d + 3) = 3d$

32 $0.3(k - 0.2) = 0.6$

33 $3(1.2b - 1) + 3.6 = 4.2$

34 $0.7(h + 2) + 1.6 = 17$

35 $2(a - 1) - 5a = 7$

36 $3(6 - 4x) - 27x = 10x - 31$

37 $\frac{1}{4}(w - 4) - \frac{3}{4}w = 3$

38 $\frac{1}{6}s - \frac{1}{2}(s - 2) = \frac{45}{2}$

39 $5(y + 1) = 3(3y + 4)$

40 $2(b + 5) = 3(4 - b)$

41 ✏️ *Math Journal* Nelson solved the algebraic equation $3(2x + 5) = 17$ as shown below:

$$3(2x + 5) = 17$$
$$3(2x + 5) - 5 = 17 - 5$$
$$3(2x) = 12$$
$$6x = 12$$
$$6x \div 6 = 12 \div 6$$
$$x = 2$$

Describe and correct the error Nelson made.

42 ✏️ *Math Journal* Describe the steps you could use to solve $2(b - 5) + 3(b - 2) = 8 + 7(b - 4)$. Solve and show your work.

4.3 Real-World Problems: Algebraic Equations

Lesson Objective

- Solve real-world problems algebraically.

Solve Real-World Problems Algebraically.

Algebraic equations can be used to model real-world problems. You can use variables to represent unknown quantities in the problem.

For example, Shirley wants to frame a drawing in the frame shown below. The border of the frame is x inches wide. The dimensions of the drawing are 12 inches by 5 inches. If the outer perimeter of the frame is 58 inches, find the width of the frame border.

First you can use models to visualise the problem and use algebraic reasoning to translate the problem into algebraic expressions.

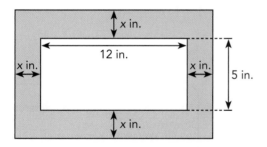

You can use the diagram to write algebraic expressions for the dimension of the frame:

Length of the frame: $12 + 2x$
Width of the frame: $5 + 2x$

Then write an algebraic equation.

$2(\ell + w) = \text{Perimeter}$	Write a perimeter formula.
$2(12 + 2x + 5 + 2x) = 58$	Substitute.
$2(17 + 4x) = 58$	Add like terms.

Finally, solve the equation.

$2 \cdot 17 + 2 \cdot 4x = 58$	Use the distributive property.
$34 + 8x = 58$	Simplify.
$34 + 8x - 34 = 58 - 34$	Subtract 34 from both sides.
$8x = 24$	Simplify.
$\dfrac{8x}{8} = \dfrac{24}{8}$	Divide both sides by 8.
$x = 3$	Simplify.

The border of the frame is 3 inches wide.

You should check your answer by substituting $x = 3$ into the original equation.

Lisa wrote a riddle: A positive number is $\frac{1}{3}$ of another positive number. If their difference is 48, find the two positive numbers.

Solution

Method 1

Use bar models.

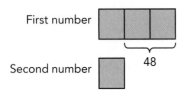

First number

Second number   48

From the bar models,

2 units $\longrightarrow$ 48

1 unit $\longrightarrow \dfrac{48}{2} = 24$

3 units $\longrightarrow 24 \cdot 3 = 72$

The two positive numbers are 72 and 24.

Method 2

Use algebraic reasoning.

Let one of the numbers be x.   Define the variable.

Then the other number is $\frac{1}{3}x$.   Write the other number in terms of the variable.

Because $x > \frac{1}{3}x$ and their difference is 48, you write $x - \frac{1}{3}x = 48$.

Find one of the numbers, x:

$x - \dfrac{1}{3}x = 48$ Write an equation.

$\dfrac{3}{3}x - \dfrac{1}{3}x = 48$ Rewrite x as $\dfrac{3}{3}x$.

$\dfrac{2}{3}x = 48$ Simplify.

$\dfrac{2}{3}x \cdot \dfrac{3}{2} = 48 \cdot \dfrac{3}{2}$ Multiply both sides by the reciprocal of $\dfrac{2}{3}$.

$x = 72$ Simplify.

Find the other number: $\dfrac{1}{3}x = \dfrac{1}{3} \cdot 72$ Evaluate $\dfrac{1}{3}x$ when $x = 72$.

$= 24$

The two positive numbers are 72 and 24.

Guided Practice

Solve. Copy and complete.

1 Mark wrote a riddle: A negative number is $\frac{2}{5}$ of another negative number. If the sum of the two negative numbers is −35, find the two negative numbers.

Method 1

Use bar models.

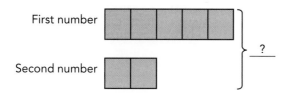

First number

Second number

?

From the bar model,

7 units ⟶ ___?___

1 unit ⟶ ___?___

2 units ⟶ ___?___

5 units ⟶ ___?___

The two negative numbers are __?__ and __?__ .

Method 2

Use algebraic reasoning.

Let one of the numbers be x.

Then the other number is $\frac{2}{5}x$.

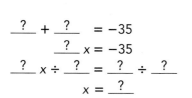

Because the sum of the numbers is −35, you write __?__ + __?__ = −35. Then, solve the equation.

$$\underline{\;?\;} + \underline{\;?\;} = -35 \qquad \text{Write an equation.}$$
$$\underline{\;?\;}\,x = -35 \qquad \text{Add the like terms.}$$
$$\underline{\;?\;}\,x \div \underline{\;?\;} = \underline{\;?\;} \div \underline{\;?\;} \qquad \text{Divide both sides by } \underline{\;?\;}.$$
$$x = \underline{\;?\;} \qquad \text{Simplify.}$$

The other number: $\frac{2}{5}x = \frac{2}{5} \cdot \underline{\;?\;}$ Evaluate $\frac{2}{5}x$ when $x = \underline{\;?\;}$.

$$= \underline{\;?\;}$$

The two negative numbers are __?__ and __?__ .

A theater is divided into a red section and a blue section. The red section has 350 seats, and the rest of the seats are in the blue section. A ticket for a red section seat costs $75, and a ticket for a blue section seat costs $50.

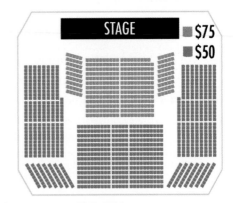

STAGE ■$75 ■$50

a) Write an expression for the total amount collected from the sale of tickets for all the seats in the two sections.

Solution

Let x represent the number of blue section tickets.　　Define the variable.

Method 1

Organize the information into a table.

Type of Ticket	Ticket Price ($)	Number of Tickets	Ticket Sales ($)
Red	75	350	$75 \cdot 350 = 26{,}250$
Blue	50	x	$50 \cdot x = 50x$

From the table, the total sales are $(26{,}250 + 50x)$ dollars.

Method 2

Use algebraic reasoning.

Total sales from 350 red section tickets: $75 \cdot 350 = 26{,}250$
Total sales from x blue section tickets: $50 \cdot x = 50x$

Total sales equal sales of red section tickets plus sales of blue section tickets.

The total sales are $(26{,}250 + 50x)$ dollars.

b) The total sales when all the tickets are sold are $68,750. How many seats are in the blue section?

Solution

$$26{,}250 + 50x = 68{,}750$$　　Write an equation.
$$26{,}250 + 50x - 26{,}250 = 68{,}750 - 26{,}250$$　　Subtract 26,250 from both sides.
$$50x = 42{,}500$$　　Simplify.
$$\frac{50x}{50} = \frac{42{,}500}{50}$$　　Divide both sides by 50.
$$x = 850$$　　Simplify.

There are 850 seats in the blue section.

Guided Practice

Solve.

2 At an auditorium, tickets are sold for "circle seats" and "row seats." There are 220 circle seats, and the rest of the seats are row seats. Each circle seat ticket costs $100 and each row seat ticket costs $60.

a) Write an expression for the total amount collected from the sale of all the seats at the auditorium.

b) The total amount collected when all the tickets are sold is $68,800. How many row seat tickets are sold?

Example 7 **Solve a real-world problem algebraically.**

Jared has 12 more comic books than Zoe. If they have 28 comic books altogether, find the number of comic books Jared has.

Zoe has **some** comic books. Jared has **12 more than** Zoe.

?   (? + 12)

They have **28 books altogether.**

? + (? + 12) = 28

Solution

Let the number of comic books that Zoe has be x.   Define the variable.
Then the number of comic books that Jared has is $x + 12$.

Because they have 28 comic books altogether,

$x + (x + 12) = 28$ Write an equation.
$2x + 12 = 28$ Simplify.
$2x + 12 - 12 = 28 - 12$ Subtract 12 from both sides.
$2x = 16$ Simplify.
$\dfrac{2x}{2} = \dfrac{16}{2}$ Divide both sides by 2.
$x = 8$ Simplify.

Number of books that Jared has: $x + 12 = 8 + 12$
$= 20$ Evaluate $x + 12$ when $x = 8$.

Jared has 20 comic books.

Guided Practice

Copy and complete each __?__ with a value and each ⓘ with +, −, ×, or ÷.

3 James has 16 more game cards than Fay. If they have 48 game cards altogether, find the number of game cards James has.

Let the number of cards that Fay has be x.

Then the number of cards that James has is x ⓘ 16.

Because they have 48 cards altogether,

$$x \text{ ⓘ } (x \text{ ⓘ } 16) = \underline{\quad?\quad}$$
$$\underline{\quad?\quad} x \text{ ⓘ } 16 = \underline{\quad?\quad}$$
$$\underline{\quad?\quad} x \text{ ⓘ } 16 \text{ ⓘ } \underline{\quad?\quad} = \underline{\quad?\quad} \text{ ⓘ } \underline{\quad?\quad}$$
$$\underline{\quad?\quad} x = \underline{\quad?\quad}$$
$$\underline{\quad?\quad} x \text{ ⓘ } \underline{\quad?\quad} = \underline{\quad?\quad} \text{ ⓘ } \underline{\quad?\quad}$$
$$x = \underline{\quad?\quad}$$

Number of cards that James has:

$$x \text{ ⓘ } 16 = \underline{\quad?\quad} \text{ ⓘ } 16$$
$$= \underline{\quad?\quad}$$

James has __?__ game cards.

> ### Think Math
>
> You can also solve this problem by letting x represent the number of cards that James has. What is the number of cards that Fay has now? How does this change the equation and the solution?

Solve. Show your work.

① Two sections of a garden are shaped like identical isosceles triangles. The base of each triangle is 50 feet, and the other two sides are each x feet long. If the combined perimeter of both gardens is 242 feet, find the value of x.

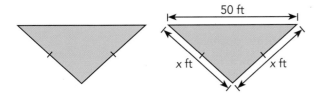

② Richard has a rectangular plot of land that is 525 feet long and y feet wide. He decides to build a fence around the plot. If the perimeter of the plot is 1,504 feet, find the value of y.

③ The diagram shows an artificial lake. When Amanda jogged twice around the lake, she jogged a distance of 2,700 meters. Find the value of x.

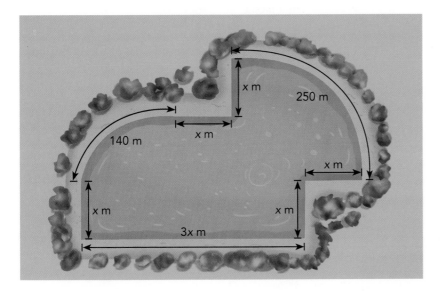

④ Olivia wants to trim a lampshade with braid. The lampshade is shaped like a rectangular prism. The length of the base of the lampshade is 4 inches greater than its width. If the perimeter of the base is 54 inches, find the length of the base.

5 Daphne was given a riddle to solve: The sum of two consecutive positive integers is 71. Find the two positive integers.

6 The sum of a negative number, $\frac{1}{4}$ of the negative number, and $\frac{7}{16}$ of the negative number is $-13\frac{1}{2}$. What is the negative number?

7 3.5 times a positive number is equal to the sum of the positive number and 0.5. What is the positive number?

8 Eugene wrote a riddle: A positive number is 5 less than another positive number. Six times the lesser number minus 3 times the greater number is 3. Find the two positive numbers.

9 At a charity basketball game, 450 tickets were sold to students at a school. The remaining x tickets were sold to the public. The prices of the two types of tickets are shown. When all the tickets were sold, $10,500 was collected. How many tickets were sold to the public?

10 Henry ordered pizzas for a party and organized the information into a table. If Henry paid a total of $93.65, how many large cheese pizzas did he order?

Type of Pizza	Number of Pizzas	Price of One Pizza
Large cheese	x	$13.95
Medium pepperoni	2	$11.95

11 Marvin saved dimes and quarters in his piggy bank to buy a gift for his mother. He counted his savings and organized the information in a table.

Type of Coins	Number of Coins	Value of One Coin
Dime	x	$0.10
Quarter	$x - 12$	$0.25

If he saved $11, how many dimes and quarters did Marvin have?

12 A bike shop charges *x* dollars to rent a bike for half a day. It charges (*x* + 40) dollars to rent a bike for a full day. The table shows the shop's bike rentals for one day. On that day, the shop made a total of $600 from bike rentals.

Time Period	Amount ($)	Number of Bikes
Half day	*x*	5
Full day	*x* + 40	3

How much does it cost to rent a bike for a full day?

13 An artist is weaving a rectangular wall hanging. The wall hanging is already 18 inches long, and the artist plans to weave an additional 2 inches each day. The finished wall hanging will be 60 inches long. How many days will it take the artist to finish the wall hanging?

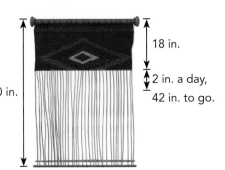

18 in.

2 in. a day, 42 in. to go.

60 in.

14 Ms. Kendrick plans to buy a laptop for $1,345 in 12 weeks. She has already saved $145. How much should she save each week so she can buy the laptop?

15 A plant grows at a rate of 4.5 centimeters per week. It is now 12 centimeters tall. Suppose that the plant continues to grow at the same rate. In how many weeks will it reach a height of 48 centimeters?

16 Mr. Johnson is currently four times as old as his son, David. If Mr. Johnson was 46 years old two years ago, how old is David now?

17 Mr. Warren drove from Townsville to Villaville and back again at the speeds shown. His total driving time was 12 hours. How far apart are the two towns?

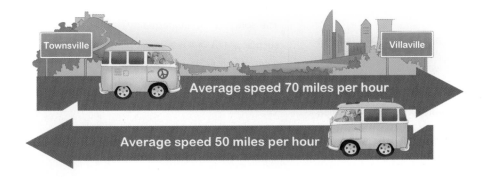

Townsville

Villaville

Average speed 70 miles per hour

Average speed 50 miles per hour

18 A factory made 845 pairs of shoes in January. These shoes were sent to three shoe stores and one outlet mall. The number of pairs of shoes sent to each store was four times the number sent to the outlet mall. How many pairs of shoes were sent to the outlet mall in January?

19 The cost of seeing a weekday show is $\frac{2}{3}$ the cost of a weekend show. In one month, Andy spent $42.50 for 4 weekday shows and 3 weekend shows. Find the price of a weekday show and the price of a weekend show.

Solving Algebraic Inequalities

Lesson Objectives

- Solve algebraic inequalities.
- Graph the solution set of an inequality on a number line.
- Solve multi-step algebraic inequalities.

Solve Algebraic Inequalities Using Addition and Subtraction.

An inequality is a mathematical statement that compares two numbers or expressions that are not equal or may not be equal. An inequality symbol such as $>$, $<$, $\geq$, $\leq$, or $\neq$ is used to make the comparison.

Examples: $-3 < 5$, $-0.5 > -2$, $x < 6$, $3x \geq 12$, $x \neq 0$

The solutions of an inequality are all the of values of the variable that make the inequality true. These values are also called the **solution set** of an inequality.

Consider the inequality $x + 3 > 4$, where x is a positive integer.

Method 1

Solve by substitution.

When $x = 0$, $x + 3 = 0 + 3$
                        $= 3$
                  The inequality $x + 3 > 4$ is false.

When $x = 1$, $x + 3 = 1 + 3$
                        $= 4$
                  The inequality $x + 3 > 4$ is false.

When $x = 1.1$, $x + 3 = 1.1 + 3$
                        $= 4.1$
                  $x + 3 > 4$ is true.

When $x = 2$, $x + 3 = 2 + 3$
                        $= 5$
                  $x + 3 > 4$ is true.

When $x = 3$, $x + 3 = 3 + 3$
                        $= 6$
                  $x + 3 > 4$ is true, and so on.

The solutions of an inequality such as $x + 3 > 4$ is always a set of values. It is not just one value, unlike most equations.

So when $x > 1$, the inequality $x + 3 > 4$ is true. The solution set is $x > 1$.

Method 2

Solve by using inverse operations.

When you perform addition or subtraction on both sides of an inequality, the solution set of the inequality is still the same. You can use inverse operations to solve inequalities.

Solve the inequality $x + 3 > 4$.

Balance	Algebraic Inequality
■ represents 1 counter. $\boxed{x}$ represents x counters.	

<table>
<tr><td>

■ represents 1 counter.

$\boxed{x}$ represents x counters.

</td><td>

$x + 3 > 4$

You can solve an inequality by using inverse operations to isolate the variable.

Decide which operation to use. To undo the addition of 3 to x, you subtract 3 from both sides.

$x + 3 - 3 > 4 - 3$ Subtract 3 from both sides.

$x > 1$ Simplify.

</td></tr>
</table>

The solution set is $x > 1$. The inequalities $x + 3 > 4$ and $x > 1$ are **equivalent inequalities** because the same set of values make both inequalities true.

Graph the Solution Set of an Inequality on a Number Line.

When you solve an inequality such as $0 \geq y - 3$, you are finding the solution set that makes the inequality true. You can graph the solution set of the inequality on a number line after you have solved it.

$0 \geq y - 3$

$0 + 3 \geq y - 3 + 3$ Add 3 to both sides.

$3 \geq y$ Solution set.

The solution set $3 \geq y$ means that the value of y is less than or equal to 3. You can rewrite $3 \geq y$ as $y \leq 3$. The inequality symbol still opens towards 3 and points to y. So, $y \leq 3$ and $3 \geq y$ are equivalent inequalities.

Math Note

An inequality symbol opens towards the greater value and points towards the lesser value.

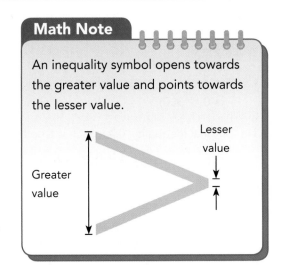

Greater value

Lesser value

Continue on next page

You can change the direction of the inequality symbol in the solution set $3 \geq y$ to help you graph the solution of the original inequality $0 \geq y - 3$.

$y \leq 3$ Switch sides and change direction.

The solution set is $y \leq 3$ and it can be represented on a number line as follows:

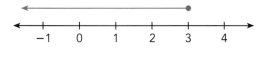

You use a shaded circle above 3 to indicate that 3 is a solution of the inequality, $0 \geq y - 3$.

To check the solution of an equation, you can substitute one value into the original equation to see if it is true. But you cannot check all the solutions of an inequality.

Instead, you can check the solution set by choosing some convenient values from the solution set, $y \geq 3$. You can substitute these values into the original inequality, $0 \geq y - 3$.

The value you choose can be a decimal, a fraction, mixed number, or a whole number. For example, substitute $y = 2.8$ and $y = 3$ into the original inequality, $0 \geq y - 3$.

Check:
When $y = 2.8$,

$y - 3 = 2.8 - 3$ Evaluate $y - 3$ when $y = 2.8$.
$\quad\quad = -0.2$ (≤ 0) 2.8 is in the solution set.

When $y = 3$,

$y - 3 = 3 - 3$ Evaluate $y - 3$ when $y = 3$.
$\quad\quad = 0$ (≤ 0) 3 is also in the solution set.

The original inequality, $0 \geq y - 3$, is true for any value of $y \leq 3$.

$y \leq 3$ is the correct solution set.

If you substitute a value greater than 3, then the inequality $y - 3 \leq 0$ is not true. For example, if $y = 4$, then $4 - 3 = 1$. Because 1 is not less than or equal to 0, $y = 4$ is not in the solution set.

Example 8 **Solve and graph the solution sets of algebraic inequalities with variables on the same side using addition and subtraction.**

Solve each inequality and graph the solution set on a number line.

a) $0.1y + 7 + 0.9y < 9$

Solution

$$0.1y + 7 + 0.9y < 9$$

$y + 7 < 9$	Add the like terms.
$y + 7 - 7 < 9 - 7$	Subtract 7 from both sides.
$y < 2$	Simplify.

The solution set is $y < 2$ and it can be represented on a number line as follows:

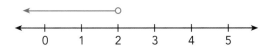

Because $y < 2$, you use an empty circle above 2 to indicate that 2 is not a solution of the inequality.

To check your solution set, substitute any value less than 2 into the original inequality. For example, you might choose $y = 0$, the most convenient number.

Check: Substitute the value of $y = 0$ into the original inequality.

$0.1y + 7 + 0.9y = 0.1 \cdot 0 + 7 + 0.9 \cdot 0$	Evaluate $0.1y + 7 + 0.9y$ when $y = 0$.
$= 7$ (< 9)	0 is in the solution set.

The original inequality, $0.1y + 7 + 0.9y < 9$, is true for any value of $y < 2$.

$y < 2$ is the solution set.

Continue on next page

b) $\frac{1}{2}y - 4 + \frac{1}{2}y \geq 8$

Solution

$$\frac{1}{2}y - 4 + \frac{1}{2}y \geq 8$$

$y - 4 \geq 8$ Add the like terms.

$y - 4 + 4 \geq 8 + 4$ Add 4 to both sides.

$y \geq 12$ Simplify.

The solution set is $y \geq 12$ and it can be represented on a number line as follows:

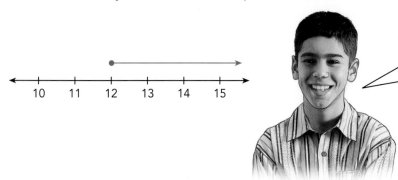

To check your solution set, substitute any value greater than or equal to 12 into the original inequality. For example, you can substitute $y = 14$.

Check: Substitute the value of $y = 14$ into the original inequality $\frac{1}{2}y - 4 + \frac{1}{2}y \geq 8$.

$$\frac{1}{2}y - 4 + \frac{1}{2}y = \frac{1}{2} \cdot 14 - 4 + \frac{1}{2} \cdot 14$$ Evaluate $\frac{1}{2}y - 4 + \frac{1}{2}y$ when $y = 14$.

$$= 7 - 4 + 7$$ Simplify.

$$= 10 \quad (\geq 8)$$ 10 is in the solution set.

The original inequality, $\frac{1}{2}y - 4 + \frac{1}{2}y \geq 8$, is true for any value of $y \geq 12$.

$y \geq 12$ is the solution set.

Guided Practice

Copy and complete. Solve each inequality and graph the solution set on a number line.

1 $0.2x + 3 + 0.8x \leq 4$

$$0.2x + 3 + 0.8x \leq 4$$

$\underline{\quad?\quad} + 3 \leq 4$ Add the like terms.

$\underline{\quad?\quad} + 3 - \underline{\quad?\quad} \leq 4 - \underline{\quad?\quad}$ Subtract $\underline{\quad?\quad}$ from both sides.

$\underline{\quad?\quad} \leq \underline{\quad?\quad}$ Simplify.

2 $\frac{1}{4}x - 1 + \frac{3}{4}x > 0$

$$\frac{1}{4}x - 1 + \frac{3}{4}x > 0$$

$\underline{\quad?\quad} - 1 > 0$ Add the like terms.

$\underline{\quad?\quad} - 1 + \underline{\quad?\quad} > 0 + \underline{\quad?\quad}$ Add $\underline{\quad?\quad}$ to both sides.

$\underline{\quad?\quad} > \underline{\quad?\quad}$ Simplify.

Example 9 **Solve and graph the solution sets of algebraic inequalities with variables on both sides using addition and subtraction.**

Solve each inequality and graph the solution set on a number line.

a) $1.3x - 7.2 \leq 11.8 + 0.3x$

Solution

$$1.3x - 7.2 \leq 11.8 + 0.3x$$

$1.3x - 7.2 - \mathbf{0.3x} \leq 11.8 + 0.3x - \mathbf{0.3x}$ Subtract 0.3x, the variable term with the lesser coefficient.

$x - 7.2 \leq 11.8$ Simplify.

$x - 7.2 + \mathbf{7.2} \leq 11.8 + \mathbf{7.2}$ Add 7.2 to both sides.

$x \leq 19$ Simplify.

The solution set can be represented on a number line as shown:

Think Math

Suppose that your first step in solving the inequality in **a)** is to subtract 1.3x from both sides. Will you still get the same solution set for the inequality? Solve and show your work.

Remember to check your solution set. You can substitute any value within the solution set into the original inequality.

b) $11 - \frac{1}{2}x < 7 + \frac{1}{2}x$

Solution

$$11 - \frac{1}{2}x < 7 + \frac{1}{2}x$$

$11 - \frac{1}{2}x + \frac{1}{2}x < 7 + \frac{1}{2}x + \frac{1}{2}x$ Add $\frac{1}{2}$x to both sides.

$11 < 7 + x$ Simplify.

$11 - 7 < 7 + x - 7$ Subtract 7 from both sides.

$4 < x$ Simplify.

$x > 4$ Switch sides and change the direction of the inequality symbol.

The solution set can be represented on a number line as shown:

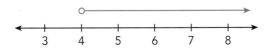

Guided Practice

Solve each inequality and graph the solution set on a number line.

3 $2x + 3 < 13 + x$

4 $1.5x - 3 \geq 4 + 0.5x$

5 $4 + \dfrac{1}{3}x > 8 + \dfrac{4}{3}x$

 # Hands-On Activity

EXPLORE DIVISION AND MULTIPLICATIVE PROPERTIES OF AN INEQUALITY

Work individually.

STEP 1 Use a copy of this table. Complete each ? using the symbols $>$ or $<$.

Mathematical Operation	Number	Inequality Symbol	Number
You know that	16	>	8
Divide by -2	$\dfrac{16}{-2} = -8$	?	$\dfrac{8}{-2} = -4$
Divide by 2	$\dfrac{16}{2} = 8$	?	$\dfrac{8}{2} = 4$
Divide by -4	$\dfrac{16}{-4} = -4$	?	$\dfrac{8}{-4} = -2$
Divide by 4	$\dfrac{16}{4} = 4$	?	$\dfrac{8}{4} = 2$
Divide by -8	$\dfrac{16}{-8} = -2$	?	$\dfrac{8}{-8} = -1$
Divide by 8	$\dfrac{16}{8} = 2$	?	$\dfrac{8}{8} = 1$

 Math Journal What happens to the direction of the inequality symbol when you divide by a positive number? Based on your observation, write a rule for dividing both sides of an inequality by a positive number.

 Math Journal What happens to the direction of the inequality symbol when you divide by a negative number? Based on your observation, write a rule for dividing both sides of an inequality by a negative number.

2 Use a copy of this table. Complete each [?] using the symbols > or <.

Mathematical Operation	Number	Inequality Symbol	Number
You know that	4	<	7
Multiply by −2	$4 \cdot (-2) = -8$	?	$7 \cdot (-2) = -14$
Multiply by 2	$4 \cdot 2 = 8$	?	$7 \cdot 2 = 14$
Multiply by −3	$4 \cdot (-3) = -12$	?	$7 \cdot (-3) = -21$
Multiply by 3	$4 \cdot 3 = 12$	?	$7 \cdot 3 = 21$
Multiply by −5	$4 \cdot (-5) = -20$	?	$7 \cdot (-5) = -35$
Multiply by 5	$4 \cdot 5 = 20$	?	$7 \cdot 5 = 35$

 Math Journal What happens to the direction of the inequality symbol when you multiply by a positive number? Based on your observation, write a rule for multiplying both sides of an inequality by a positive number.

 Math Journal What happens to the direction of the inequality symbol when you multiply by a negative number? Based on your observation, write a rule for multiplying both sides of an inequality by a negative number.

Solve Algebraic Inequalities Using Multiplication and Division.

When you multiply or divide both sides of an inequality by the same positive number, the inequality symbol remains in the same direction for the inequality to be true.

When you multiply or divide both sides of an inequality by the same negative number, you reverse the direction of the inequality symbol for the inequality to be true.

You can apply these rules when you solve an algebraic inequality such as $-5y \le -10$.

$-5y \le -10$

$\dfrac{-5y}{-5} \ge \dfrac{-10}{-5}$ Divide both sides by −5 and **reverse the inequality symbol**.

$y \ge 2$ Simplify.

Continue on next page

The solution set of the inequality $-5y \leq -10$ can be represented on a number line as follows:

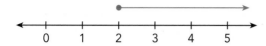

You can check that $y \geq 2$ is the solution by checking to see if values greater than and equal to 2 make the original inequality $-5y \leq -10$ true:

If $y = 2$, then $-5 \cdot 2 \leq -10$ (true)
If $y = 3$, then $-5 \cdot 3 \leq -10$ (true)

If you substitute a value less than 2, then the original inequality $-5y \leq -10$ is not true.

For example, if $y = 1$, then $-5 \cdot 1 = -5$. -5 is greater than -10, not less than -10.

Example 10 **Solve and graph the solution sets of algebraic inequalities using multiplication and division.**

Solve each inequality and graph the solution set on a number line.

a) $-\dfrac{1}{2}p \geq 3$

Solution

$$-\dfrac{1}{2}p \geq 3$$

$-\dfrac{1}{2}p \cdot (-2) \leq 3 \cdot (-2)$ Multiply both sides by -2 and **reverse the inequality symbol.**

$p \leq -6$ Simplify.

The solution set can be represented on a number line as shown:

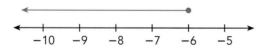

> **Math Note**
>
> The reciprocal of a negative number $-\dfrac{a}{b}$ is the negative number $-\dfrac{b}{a}$, because $\left(-\dfrac{a}{b}\right) \cdot \left(-\dfrac{b}{a}\right) = 1$. So, the reciprocal of $-\dfrac{1}{2}$ is $-\dfrac{2}{1}$, or simply -2.

b) $-0.4x > 1.6$

Solution

$-0.4x > 1.6$

$\dfrac{-0.4x}{-0.4} < \dfrac{1.6}{-0.4}$ Divide both sides by -0.4 and **reverse the inequality symbol**.

$x < -4$ Simplify.

The solution set can be represented on a number line as shown:

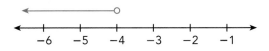

Guided Practice

Solve each inequality and graph the solution set on a number line.

6 $-\dfrac{1}{5}w \le 2$

7 $-7m > 21$

8 $6 > -0.3y$

Solve Multi-Step Algebraic Inequalities.

You can use the same methods you use to solve multi-step equations to solve and then graph multi-step inequalities. Your goal is to isolate the variable on one side of the inequality.

Solve $3a - 7 > 26$ by using inverse operations.

First isolate the algebraic term.

$3a - 7 > 26$

$3a - 7 + 7 > 26 + 7$ Add 7 to both sides.

$3a > 33$ Simplify.

Then isolate the variable.

$\dfrac{3a}{3} > \dfrac{33}{3}$ Divide both sides by 3.

$a > 11$ Simplify.

The solution set is $a > 11$.

The solution set can be represented on a number line as follows:

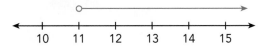

Example 11 **Solve and graph the solution sets of multi-step algebraic inequalities.**

Solve each inequality and graph the solution set on a number line.

a) $\frac{4}{5}x + 1 > 1\frac{3}{5}$

Solution

$$\frac{4}{5}x + 1 > 1\frac{3}{5}$$

$\frac{4}{5}x + 1 - 1 > 1\frac{3}{5} - 1$ Subtract 1 from both sides.

$\frac{4}{5}x > \frac{3}{5}$ Simplify.

$\left(\frac{4}{5}x\right) \cdot \left(\frac{5}{4}\right) > \left(\frac{3}{5}\right) \cdot \left(\frac{5}{4}\right)$ Multiply both sides by $\frac{5}{4}$, which is the reciprocal of $\frac{4}{5}$.

$x > \frac{3}{4}$ Simplify.

The solution set can be represented on a number line as shown:

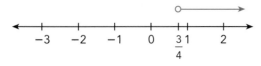

Remember to check your solution set. You can substitute any value within the solution set into the original inequality.

b) $9 - 0.2a \geq 21$

Solution

$9 - 0.2a \geq 21$

$9 - 0.2a - 9 \geq 21 - 9$ Subtract 9 from both sides.

$-0.2a \geq 12$ Simplify.

$\frac{-0.2a}{-0.2} \leq \frac{12}{-0.2}$ Divide both sides by -0.2 and **reverse the inequality symbol**.

$a \leq -60$ Simplify.

Reverse the direction of the inequality symbol when you multiply or divide both sides of the inequality by the **same negative number**.

The solution set can be represented on a number line as shown:

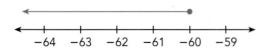

c) $-2a + 3 < -7 - a$

Solution

Method 1

$$-2a + 3 < -7 - a$$

$-2a + 3 + a < -7 - a + a$	Add a to both sides.
$-a + 3 < -7$	Simplify.
$-a + 3 - 3 < -7 - 3$	Subtract 3 from both sides.
$-a < -10$	Simplify.
$-1 \cdot (-a) > -1 \cdot (-10)$	Multiply both sides by -1 and **reverse the inequality symbol**.
$a > 10$	Simplify.

> **Caution** /////////
>
> The solution set of the inequality in **c)** is not $-a < -10$. For an inequality to be solved, the coefficient of the variable has to be $+1$. Remember to reverse the inequality symbol when you multiply both sides of the inequality $-a < -10$ by -1.

Method 2

$$-2a + 3 < -7 - a$$

$-2a + 3 + 2a < -7 - a + 2a$	Add $2a$ to both sides.
$3 < -7 + a$	Simplify.
$3 + 7 < -7 + 7 + a$	Add 7 to both sides.
$10 < a$	Simplify.
$a > 10$	Switch sides and change the direction of the inequality symbol.

The solution set can be represented on a number line as shown:

d) $2(3 - x) \leq 8$

Solution

Method 1

Use the distributive property and inverse operations.

$$2(3 - x) \leq 8$$

$2 \cdot 3 - 2 \cdot x \leq 8$	Use the distributive property.
$6 - 2x \leq 8$	Simplify.
$6 - 2x - 6 \leq 8 - 6$	Subtract 6 from both sides.
$-2x \leq 2$	Simplify.
$\dfrac{-2x}{-2} \geq \dfrac{2}{-2}$	Divide both sides by -2 and **reverse the inequality symbol**.
$x \geq -1$	Simplify.

Continue on next page

Method 2

Use inverse operations.

$$2(3 - x) \le 8$$
$$2(3 - x) \div 2 \le 8 \div 2 \qquad \text{Divide both sides by 2.}$$
$$3 - x \le 4 \qquad \text{Simplify.}$$
$$3 - x - 3 \le 4 - 3 \qquad \text{Subtract 3 from both sides.}$$
$$-x \le 1 \qquad \text{Simplify.}$$
$$\frac{-x}{-1} \ge \frac{1}{-1} \qquad \text{Divide both sides by } -1 \text{ and \textbf{reverse the}}$$
$$\qquad\qquad\qquad \textbf{inequality symbol.}$$
$$x \ge -1 \qquad \text{Simplify.}$$

The solution set can be represented on a number line as shown:

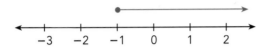

Guided Practice

Solve each inequality and graph the solution set on a number line.

9 $4y + 7 < 27$

$$4y + 7 < 27$$
$$4y + 7 - \underline{\ ?\ } < 27 - \underline{\ ?\ } \qquad \text{Subtract } \underline{\ ?\ } \text{ from both sides.}$$
$$4y < \underline{\ ?\ } \qquad \text{Simplify.}$$
$$4y \div \underline{\ ?\ } < \underline{\ ?\ } \div \underline{\ ?\ } \qquad \text{Divide both sides by } \underline{\ ?\ }.$$
$$y < \underline{\ ?\ } \qquad \text{Simplify.}$$

10 $-5y - 9 \ge 21$

$$-5y - 9 \ge 21$$
$$-5y - 9 + \underline{\ ?\ } \ge 21 + \underline{\ ?\ } \qquad \text{Add } \underline{\ ?\ } \text{ to both sides.}$$
$$-5y \ge \underline{\ ?\ } \qquad \text{Simplify.}$$
$$-5y \div \underline{\ ?\ } \le \underline{\ ?\ } \div \underline{\ ?\ } \qquad \text{Divide both sides by } \underline{\ ?\ } \text{ and reverse the}$$
$$\qquad\qquad\qquad \text{inequality symbol.}$$
$$y \le \underline{\ ?\ } \qquad \text{Simplify.}$$

11 $\frac{1}{2}x + \frac{3}{4} \ge 5$

12 $1.5 - 0.3y > 3.6$

13 $-8y + 32 \le -17 - y$

14 $4(2 - y) \ge 20$

Solve each inequality using addition and subtraction. Then graph each solution set on a number line.

1 $x + 8 > 14$

2 $2 \geq x - 12$

3 $-7x + 5 + 8x > 3$

4 $-2x - 3 + 3x \geq 12$

5 $29 < \frac{2}{3}x + 14 + \frac{1}{3}x$

6 $\frac{1}{5}x + 9 + \frac{4}{5}x > -11$

7 $0.7x + 4 + 0.3x \leq 10$

8 $0.4x - 6 + 0.6x \geq 19$

9 $3x + 4 < 2x + 9$

10 $8 - 4x > 12 - 3x$

11 $\frac{2}{3}x + 2 \geq 9 - \frac{1}{3}x$

12 $13 + 1\frac{3}{5}x \geq 18 + \frac{3}{5}x$

13 $1.7x + 5 < 16 + 0.7x$

14 $8.5 - 0.9x > 9.8 - 1.9x$

15 *Math Journal* Solve the inequality $8 + 2x \geq 12$ and show your work. What value is a solution of $8 + 2x \geq 12$ but is not a solution of $8 + 2x > 12$?

16 *Math Journal* Eric solved the inequality $6y \leq -18$ as shown below:

$6y \leq -18$
$6y \div 6 \geq -18 \div 6$
$y \geq -3$

Describe and correct the error that Eric made.

Solve each inequality using division and multiplication. Then graph the solution set on a number line.

17 $3 \geq -3x$

18 $-4x > 12$

19 $-\frac{x}{5} \leq 2$

20 $-\frac{2}{3}x > 8$

21 $-0.2x \geq 6$

22 $9 > -0.5x$

Solve each inequality using the four operations. Then graph each solution set on a number line.

23 $7y - 3 > 11$

24 $-3a + 5 < -7$

25 $\dfrac{x}{4} + \dfrac{3}{16} \geq 1$

26 $\dfrac{3}{5}a - \dfrac{4}{5} < \dfrac{7}{10}$

27 $7 - 0.3x > 4$

28 $2.4y + 5 < 29$

29 $5x + 3 < 7 + 7x$

30 $11 - 7x \leq 20 - 8x$

31 $\dfrac{4}{3} - \dfrac{5}{6}x \geq -\dfrac{1}{6} - \dfrac{2}{3}x$

32 $\dfrac{2}{5}x + 4 \leq \dfrac{7}{10}x - 8$

33 $5.4x + 4.2 - 3.8x > 9$

34 $6.6 + 1.3x - 5.2x \leq 14.4$

Solve each inequality with parentheses using the four operations.

35 $3(y + 2) \leq 18$

36 $8(y - 1) > 24$

37 $\dfrac{1}{2}(a + 1) \leq 4$

38 $\dfrac{2}{3}(3 - a) < 3$

39 $1.3(2 - x) > 3.9$

40 $3.6(5x - 1) < 5.4$

41 $4 + 2(1 - 3y) < 36$

42 $2(3 - x) > 5x - 1$

43 $\dfrac{5}{9}(x + 1) \geq \dfrac{2}{3}$

44 $\dfrac{2}{3}(1 - 3x) > \dfrac{1}{6}$

45 $1.7 + 0.2(1 - x) \geq 2.7$

46 $2.5(3 - 2x) + 1 \geq 29$

47 *Math Journal* Compare solving the inequality $-5(x + 6) < 10$ with solving the equation $-5(x + 6) = 10$. Describe the similarities and differences between solving the inequality and solving the equation. Explain how the solution set of the inequality $-5(x + 6) < 10$ is different from the solution of the equation $-5(x + 6) = 10$.

Solve each inequality using the four operations.

48 $10 - 3(4a - 3) < 2(3a - 4) - 9$

49 $7(2a - 3) \leq 5 - 2(3a - 1)$

4.5 Real-World Problems: Algebraic Inequalities

Lesson Objective

- Solve real-world problems involving algebraic inequalities.

Solve Real-World Problems Involving Algebraic Inequalities.

In English, certain phrases suggest inequalities. For example, the temperature today is greater than the temperature yesterday.

You use inequalities to compare amounts that may not be equal. You can apply the equation solving techniques you have learned to solve inequalities. The table shows some commonly used phrases and their corresponding inequalities symbols.

Equivalent Verbal Phrases	Inequality Symbol
at least; no less than; greater than or equal to	$\geq$
at most; no more than; less than or equal to	$\leq$
more than; greater than	$>$
less than; lesser than	$<$

Example 12 **Solve a word problem involving algebraic inequalities.**

The average of 70, 75, 83, 80, and a fifth number is at least 80. Describe the value of the fifth number.

Solution

Let x be the fifth number.   Define the variable.

$$\text{Average} \geq 80$$

$$\frac{70 + 75 + 83 + 80 + x}{5} \geq 80 \qquad \text{Write an inequality.}$$

$$\frac{308 + x}{5} \geq 80 \qquad \text{Simplify.}$$

$$5 \cdot \left(\frac{308 + x}{5} \right) \geq 5 \cdot 80 \qquad \text{Multiply both sides by 5.}$$

$$308 + x \geq 400 \qquad \text{Simplify.}$$

$$308 + x - 308 \geq 400 - 308 \qquad \text{Subtract 308 from both sides.}$$

$$x \geq 92 \qquad \text{Simplify.}$$

The fifth number is at least 92.

Guided Practice

Solve.

1 The average of 87, 90, 89, and a fourth number is at least 90. Describe the value of the fourth number.

Example 13 | **Solve a real-world problem involving algebraic inequalities.**

Kelly goes to an amusement park with her friends. The admission fee to the amusement park is $4 and each ride costs $0.80. If Kelly has only $25 to spend, how many rides can she go on?

Solution

Let x be the number of rides that Kelly can go on.   Define the variable.

Admission fee	plus	cost of x rides	is at most	$25.
4	+	$0.8 \cdot x$	≤	25

$$4 + 0.8x \leq 25$$

$4 + 0.8x \leq 25$	Write an inequality.
$4 + 0.8x - 4 \leq 25 - 4$	Subtract 4 from both sides.
$0.8x \leq 21$	Simplify.
$\dfrac{0.8x}{0.8} \leq \dfrac{21}{0.8}$	Divide both sides by 0.8.
$x \leq 26.25$	Simplify.

Kelly can go for at most 26 rides.

Caution ///////

Sometimes, you must choose a reasonable answer that makes sense. In this case, the greatest number of rides cannot be a decimal, a fraction, or a negative number. It must be a whole number.

Guided Practice

Copy and complete.

2 Grace is at the bookstore with $75 to spend. She plans to buy a reference book that costs $18 and some novels that cost $12 each. Find how many novels Grace can buy along with the reference book.

Let x be the number of novels Grace can buy.   Define the variable.

$$\underline{} + 12x \leq \underline{}$$ Write an inequality.

$$\underline{} + 12x - \underline{} \leq \underline{} - \underline{}$$ Subtract $\underline{}$ from both sides.

$$12x \leq \underline{}$$ Simplify.

$$12x \div \underline{} \leq \underline{} \div \underline{}$$ Divide both sides by $\underline{}$.

$$x \leq \underline{}$$ Simplify.

Grace can buy at most $\underline{}$ novels.

Example 14   **Solve a real-world problem involving algebraic inequalities.**

Theo wants to join a gym. He calls two gyms and is given two different payment plans.

Gym A	Gym B
$100 new membership fee plus $35 per month	$75 new membership fee plus $40 per month

After how many months will Gym A be less expensive than Gym B?

Solution

Let x be the number of months.   Define the variable.

The cost of each option is

new membership fee + cost per month · number of months.

So, Gym A costs $100 + 35 \cdot x = 100 + 35x$

Gym B costs $75 + 40 \cdot x = 75 + 40x$

$$100 + 35x < 75 + 40x$$ Write an inequality.

$$100 + 35x - 40x < 75 + 40x - 40x$$ Subtract 40x from both sides.

$$100 - 5x < 75$$ Simplify.

$$100 - 5x - 100 < 75 - 100$$ Subtract 100 from both sides.

$$-5x < -25$$ Simplify.

$$\frac{-5x}{-5} > \frac{-25}{-5}$$ Divide both sides by −5 and **reverse the symbol**.

$$x > 5$$ Simplify.

Anytime after 5 months, Gym A will be less expensive.

Guided Practice

Copy and complete.

3 While Cheryl is on vacation, she wants to put her dog Cocoa in a kennel that offers an obedience class. She calls two boarding kennels to find their fees for their services.

After how many days will Best Dog Kennel be the cheaper option?

Let x be the number of days.

The cost of a stay at each kennel is

class fee + cost per day · number of days.

So, Happy Dogs Kennel costs 80 + __?__

Best Dogs Kennel costs 100 + __?__

For Best Dog Kennel to be the cheaper option,

$$80 + \underline{} > 100 + \underline{}$$ Write an inequality.

$$80 + \underline{} - \underline{} > 100 + \underline{} - \underline{}$$ Subtract __?__ from both sides.

$$80 + \underline{} > 100$$ Simplify.

$$80 + \underline{} - 80 > 100 - 80$$ Subtract 80 from both sides.

$$\underline{} > 20$$ Simplify.

$$\underline{} \div \underline{} > 20 \div \underline{}$$ Divide both sides by __?__.

$$x > \underline{}$$ Simplify.

Anytime after __?__ days, Best Dog Kennel will be the cheaper option.

Solve. Show your work.

1. The perimeter of an equilateral triangle is at most 45 centimeters. Find the possible length of each side.

2. Roger scored 1,800 points in four rounds of a debate competition. His opponent, Sawyer, scored 324 points in the first round, 530 points in the second round, and 619 points in the third round. How many points must Sawyer score in the final round to surpass Roger's score?

3. Ben plans to sign up for a language class that will cost at least $195. His father gives him $75 and he earns $28 from mowing the lawn for his neighbors. Write and solve an inequality to find out how much more money he needs to save before he can sign up for the class.

4. In her last basketball game, Casey scored 46 points. In the current game, she has scored 24 points so far. How many more two-point baskets must she make if she wants her total score in her current game to be at least as great as her score in the last game?

5. At Middleton Middle School, Marianne must score an average of at least 80 points on 4 tests before she can apply for the scholarship. If she scored 79, 81, and 77 for the first three tests, what must she score on her last test?

6. At the movies, a bag of popcorn costs $3.50 and a bottle of mineral water costs $2.75. If Madeline has $18 and bought only 2 bottles of water, how many bags of popcorn can she buy at most?

7. Party favors are on sale for $2.40 each. You have $380 to spend on the decorations and gifts, and you have already spent $270 on decorations. Write and solve an inequality to find the number of party favors you can buy.

8. Charlie wants to join a golf club. He finds two clubs that have fees as shown in the table.

Golf Club A	Golf Club B
$80 new membership fee plus $45 per month	$110 new membership fee plus $30 per month

After how many months will Golf Club B be less expensive than Golf Club A?

9 Molly can either take her lunch or buy it at school. It costs $1.95 to buy lunch. If she wants to spend no more than $30 each month, how many lunches can she buy at most?

10 Tyson always likes to have at least $150 in his savings account. Currently he has $800 in the account. If he withdraws $35 each week, after how many weeks will the amount in his savings account be less than $150?

11 A cab company charges $0.80 per mile plus $2 for tolls. Melissa has at most $16 to spend on her cab fare. Write and solve an inequality for the maximum distance she can travel if she has at most $16 for cab fare. Can she afford to take a cab from her home to an airport that is 25 miles away?

12 Nine subtracted from four times a number is less than or equal to fifteen. Write an inequality and solve it.

13 Sixteen plus five times a number is more than the number minus eight. Write an inequality and solve it.

14 *Math Journal* Write a word problem that can be solved using an inequality. Write the inequality that represents your problem. Then solve it.

Brain @ Work

A father said, "My son is five times as old as my daughter. My wife is five times as old as my son and I am twice as old as my wife. Grandmother here, who is as old as all of us put together, is celebrating her 81st birthday today." What is the age of the man's son?

Chapter Wrap Up

Concept Map

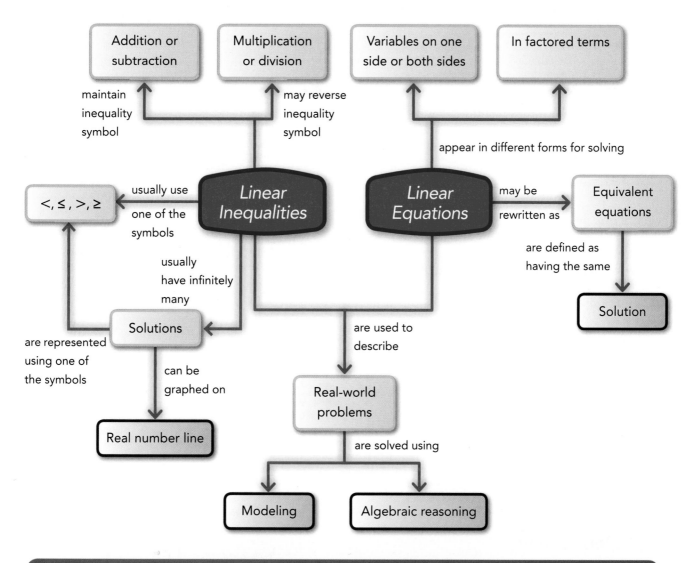

Key Concepts

▶ Equations with the same solution are called equivalent equations.

▶ Solving an equation involves isolating the variable on one side of the equation by writing a series of equivalent equations.

▶ An inequality symbol is used to compare two quantities that are not equal or may not be equal.

▶ The orientation of the inequality symbol must be reversed when both sides of an inequality are multiplied or divided by the same negative number.

Chapter Review/Test

Concepts and Skills

Solve each equation.

1 $8x - 7 = 17$

2 $4 - 6x = 8$

3 $6 - \dfrac{y}{3} = 0$

4 $3 - 3.6x = 4.2$

5 $7x - 5 = 3x + 4$

6 $\dfrac{7}{10}y - \dfrac{1}{5} = \dfrac{3}{5}y + \dfrac{6}{5}$

7 $3.4y - 5.2 - 3y = 2$

8 $15y - 4(2y - 3) = -2$

9 $\dfrac{1}{4}(x + 3) + \dfrac{3}{8}x = \dfrac{13}{4}$

10 $0.4(x + 0.7) = 0.6x - 4.2$

Solve each inequality. Graph each solution set.

11 $4x - 3 > 1$

12 $6 \leq 1 - 5x$

13 $\dfrac{2}{3} - \dfrac{x}{6} \geq -\dfrac{1}{2}$

14 $-6.9 < 8.1 - 1.5x$

15 $9y - 5 \leq 4y + 15$

16 $\dfrac{7}{9}x - \dfrac{2}{3} > \dfrac{1}{6}x + 3$

17 $12.9 < 0.3(5.3 - x)$

18 $3(x + 1) > 5x + 7$

19 $\dfrac{1}{5}(4x - 1) \geq \dfrac{2}{3}x + \dfrac{3}{5}$

20 $4(3 - 0.1x) \leq 15 - 0.6x$

Problem Solving

Write an equation for questions 21 to 25. Solve and show your work.

21 Aiden wrote a riddle: Five less than $\dfrac{1}{5}$ times a number is the same as the sum of the number and $\dfrac{1}{3}$. Find the number.

22 Mary is 6 years older than her sister Kelly. The sum of their ages is 48. How old is Kelly?

23 The sum of the page numbers of two facing pages in a book is 145. What are the page numbers?

24 The perimeter of an equilateral triangle is $6\dfrac{3}{4}$ inches. Find the length of each side of the equilateral triangle.

25 The sum of the interior angle measures of a quadrilateral is 360°. The measure of angle A is three times the measure of angle D. The measure of angle B is four times that of angle D. The measure of angle C is 24° more than angle B. Find the measure of each angle of the quadrilateral.

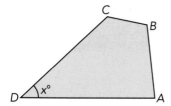

Write an inequality for each question. Solve and show your work.

26 Laura wants the average amount of money she spends each day on her four-day vacation to be no more than $64. On the first three days, she spends $71, $62, and $59. What is the greatest amount of money she can spend on the fourth day?

27 Kevin plans to sign up for p hours of training at a culinary school. The school offers two payment options as shown below.

Option A	Option B
$8 per hour plus $200 for supplies	$18 per hour, no fee for supplies

For how many hours of training is Option B less expensive than Option A?

28 Peter has found a job in a computer store. As shown below, he has two options for how he will be paid. The commission he makes for Option B is based on his weekly sales. For example, if his sales total $1,000 a week, he receives his base salary of $250 plus 8% of $1,000.

Option A	Option B
Fixed salary of $600 per week with no commission	Fixed salary of $250 per week plus commission of 8% of his weekly sales

Peter is thinking about Option B. What would his weekly sales need to be for him to make at least as much as he would for Option A?

29 The school events committee is planning to buy a banner and some helium balloons for graduation night. A store charges them $35 for the banner and $3.50 for each helium balloon. If the committee has at most $125 to spend, how many helium balloons can they buy?

30 The coach of the field hockey team can spend at most $475 on new team uniforms. The coach will order the uniforms online and pay a mailing cost of $6.50. If each uniform costs $29, how many uniforms can the coach order?

CHAPTER 5

Direct and Inverse Proportion

Have you ever painted a mural?

Have you ever created a mural? An artist usually makes a sketch for the mural on a small piece of paper. The artist can then use proportions to enlarge the sketch so that it can be transferred to a wall. For example, suppose an object that is 3 inches tall in the sketch is going to be 8 times as tall in the actual mural. The artist has to make sure that all the lengths in the mural are 8 times the corresponding lengths in the sketch. In this chapter, you will learn more about proportional relationships.

BIG IDEA

▶ Two quantities that are in a proportional relationship can be used to solve real-world and mathematical problems.

Recall Prior Knowledge

Comparing quantities using a ratio

A ratio compares two or more numbers or quantities. You can write a ratio of two quantities, such as 7 and 8, in three ways: 7 to 8, 7 : 8, or $\frac{7}{8}$. The numbers 7 and 8 are the terms of the ratio. You can express a ratio in simplest form by dividing its terms by their greatest common factor (GCF).

✔ Quick Check

Write a ratio to compare quantities.

A store sells 60 headphones, 45 sets of earbuds, and 80 speakers. Write a ratio in simplest form to compare each of the following.

1 The number of speakers to the number of sets of earbuds.

2 The number of headphones to the number of speakers.

Recognizing equivalent ratios

Equivalent ratios show the same comparison of numbers and quantities. They have the same ratio in simplest form. You can obtain equivalent ratios by multiplying or dividing both terms of a ratio by the same number.

$$\times 2 \quad \overset{3 : 20}{\underset{= 6 : 40}{\Large\curvearrowright}} \quad \times 2 \qquad\qquad \div 5 \quad \overset{15 : 100}{\underset{= 3 : 20}{\Large\curvearrowright}} \quad \div 5$$

So, 3 : 20, 6 : 40, and 15 : 100 are equivalent ratios.
3 : 20 is in simplest form because 3 and 20 have no common factors except 1.

✔ Quick Check

Tell whether each pair of ratios are equivalent.

3 9 : 11 and 18 : 22

4 $\frac{1}{33}$ and $\frac{33}{1}$

5 3 to 6 and 9 to 18

Tell whether each ratio is in simplest form. Then write two ratios that are equivalent to the given ratio.

6 4 : 5

7 $\frac{15}{100}$

8 7 to 14

Finding rates and unit rates

A rate compares two quantities with different units.

A unit rate compares a quantity to one unit of another quantity. For example, speed is a unit rate that compares distance traveled to a given unit of time.

Angela reads 7 books in two weeks. Find her reading speed in books per day.

14 days $\longrightarrow$ 7 books

1 day $\longrightarrow \dfrac{7}{14} = \dfrac{1}{2}$ book

Angela reads $\dfrac{1}{2}$ book per day.

✔ Quick Check

Find the unit rate.

9 The winner of the first Tour de France bicycle race in 1903 was Maurice Garin. It took him over 94 hours to complete 2,428 kilometers. Find his approximate average speed. Round your answer to the nearest whole number.

Find and compare unit rates.

The cost of a food item at two different stores is shown. Find the unit price at each store and tell where the item costs less.

10 Store A: $3.20 for 16 oz of walnuts.
Store B: $2.30 for 10 oz of walnuts.

11 Store C: $2.13 for 3 lb of potatoes.
Store D: $3.35 for 5 lb of potatoes.

Identifying and plotting coordinates

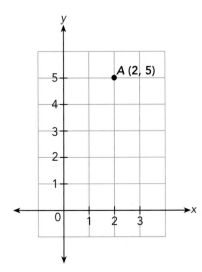

An ordered pair (x, y) is used to represent the location of a point on a graph.

Point A (2, 5) represents the location of a point that is 2 units to the right of the origin, and 5 units up from the origin. The x-coordinate of point A is 2 and the y-coordinate is 5.

The coordinates of the origin are (0, 0).

Use the coordinate plane below.

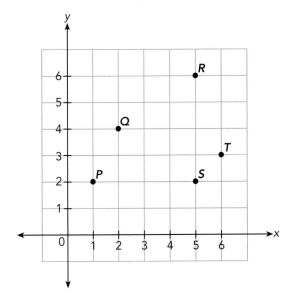

12 Give the coordinates of points *P*, *Q*, *R*, *S*, and *T*.

Solving percent problems

At an art exhibit, 80% of the people were adults, and the rest were children. If there were 600 children, how many people were at the art exhibit?

? people (100%)

Adults
(80%)

600 children
(20%)

From the bar model,

20% ⟶ 600

1% ⟶ $\dfrac{600}{20}$ = 30

100% ⟶ 30 · 100 = 3,000

There were 3,000 people at the art exhibit.

✓ **Quick Check**

Solve word problems involving percent.

13 45% of the beads in a box are blue. If there are 36 blue beads in the box, how many beads are there altogether?

14 Tabitha bought an antique model car priced at $72. She also had to pay 5% sales tax. What was the total amount she paid?

Understanding Direct Proportion

Lesson Objectives

- Identify direct proportion.
- Recognize that a constant of proportionality can be a unit rate.

Identify **Direct Proportion** from a Table.

At a supermarket, each pound of strawberries costs $2.

Strawberries
$2/lb

So, 2 pounds of strawberries cost: $2 · 2 = $4

    3 pounds of strawberries cost: $2 · 3 = $6, and so on.

The table shows the cost, y dollars, for x pounds of strawberries.

Increasing weight →

Weight of Strawberries (x pounds)	1	2	3
Cost (y dollars)	2	4	6

Increasing cost →

Notice what happens when you compare the costs of the strawberries to the number of pounds:

$$\frac{\$2}{1 \text{ lb}} = \frac{\$4}{2 \text{ lb}} = \frac{\$6}{3 \text{ lb}}$$ The rates, cost per pound, are equivalent.

These rates can be associated with ratios: $\frac{2}{1} = \frac{4}{2} = \frac{6}{3}$.

An equation that says two ratios are equivalent is called a **proportion**. $\frac{2}{1} = \frac{4}{2}$ and $\frac{4}{2} = \frac{6}{3}$ are examples of proportions.

> You read the proportion $\frac{4}{2} = \frac{6}{3}$ as "4 is to 2 is as 6 is to 3." The ratios are equivalent because in each ratio, the first term is two times the second term.
>
> $4 = 2 \cdot 2$
> $6 = 2 \cdot 3$

You can see that the cost of the strawberries is always **two times** the number of pounds:

Cost for 1 pound: $2	$2 \cdot 1 = \$2$
Cost for 2 pounds: $4	$2 \cdot 2 = \$4$
Cost for 3 pounds: $6	$2 \cdot 3 = \$6$

The cost of the strawberries and the number of pounds are said to be in direct proportion. If you let y be the cost of the strawberries and x be the number of pounds, you can write two equivalent equations:

$\frac{y}{x} = 2$ and $y = 2x$

If $\frac{y}{x} = k$ or $y = kx$, where k is a constant value, then y is said to be directly proportional to x. The constant value, k, in a direct proportion is called the **constant of proportionality**.

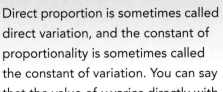

Math Note

Direct proportion is sometimes called direct variation, and the constant of proportionality is sometimes called the constant of variation. You can say that the value of y varies directly with the value of x.

Hands-On Activity

Materials:

• cardboard tube
• 2 yardsticks

IDENTIFY DIRECT PROPORTION IN AN EXPERIMENT

Work in pairs.

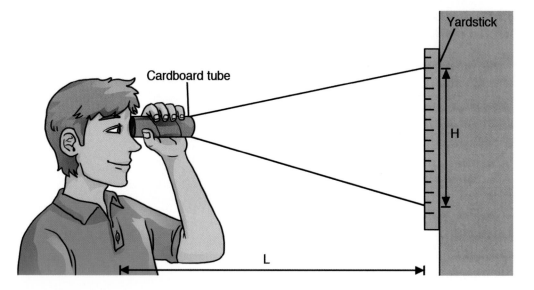

Cardboard tube

Yardstick

H

L

STEP 1 Make a table like the one shown.

Distance from the Wall (L feet)	1	2	3	4	5
Length of Yardstick Seen (H inches)	?	?	?	?	?
$\dfrac{H}{L}$	$\dfrac{?}{1}$	$\dfrac{?}{2}$	$\dfrac{?}{3}$	$\dfrac{?}{4}$	$\dfrac{?}{5}$

STEP 2 Tape a yardstick to the wall.

STEP 3 Stand 1 foot away from the yardstick. Look at the yardstick through the cardboard tube. How many inches of the yardstick can you see? Record the number of inches in the table.

STEP 4 Repeat **STEP 3** for the other values of L shown in the table. Then complete the table.

Math Journal What happens to H as L increases? Based on your observations, do you think H is directly proportional to L? Explain your thinking.

a) A pet store owner uses a table to decide how many of a certain type of fish to put in an aquarium. Tell whether the number of fish, *f*, is directly proportional to the volume of the water, *g* gallons. If so, give the constant of proportionality and tell what it represents in this situation. Then write a direct proportion equation.

Volume of Water (*g* gallons)	4	10	20
Number of Fish (*f*)	6	15	30

Solution

For each pair of values, *f* and *g*:

$$\frac{6 \text{ fish}}{4 \text{ gal}} = \frac{15 \text{ fish}}{10 \text{ gal}} = \frac{30 \text{ fish}}{20 \text{ gal}}$$

The rates are equivalent and can be associated with the ratio 3 : 2.

So, the number of fish is directly proportional to the volume of water.

The constant of proportionality is $\frac{3}{2}$, and represents the number of fish per gallon of water. The direct proportion equation is $f = \frac{3}{2}g$.

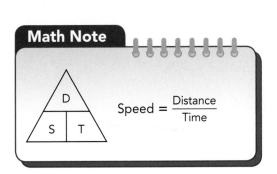

You can also write $f = \frac{3}{2}g$ as $f = 1.5g$.

b) The table shows the distance traveled by a snail, *d* centimeters, after *t* hours. Tell whether *d* is directly proportional to *t*. If so, give the constant of proportionality and tell what it represents in this situation. Then write a direct proportion equation.

Time (*t* hours)	1	2	3
Distance Traveled (*d* centimeters)	9	18	21

Solution

For each pair of values, *d* and *t*:

$$\frac{9 \text{ cm}}{1 \text{ h}} = 9 \qquad \frac{18 \text{ cm}}{2 \text{ h}} = 9 \qquad \frac{21 \text{ cm}}{3 \text{ h}} = 7$$

Because the speeds of the snail are not constant, *d* and *t* are not in direct proportion.

Math Note

$$\text{Speed} = \frac{\text{Distance}}{\text{Time}}$$

Caution ///////

For *y* to be directly proportional to *x*, the ratio $\frac{y}{x}$ must be the same for all the ordered pairs. So, be sure to check all pairs of values in a table.

Guided Practice

Copy and complete to determine whether y is directly proportional to x.

1 The table shows the distance traveled by a school bus, y miles, after x hours.

Time (x hours)	2	3	4
Distance Traveled (y miles)	100	150	200

For each pair of values, x and y:

$$\frac{?\text{ mi}}{?\text{ h}} = \underline{\quad?\quad} \qquad \frac{?\text{ mi}}{?\text{ h}} = \underline{\quad?\quad} \qquad \frac{?\text{ mi}}{?\text{ h}} = \underline{\quad?\quad}$$

So, the distance traveled by the school bus is ___?___ to the number of hours it has traveled.

The constant of proportionality is ___?___ and represents the speed of the bus.
The direct proportion equation is ___?___.

2 The table shows the number of pitches made, y, in x innings of a baseball game.

Number of Innings (x)	1	2	3
Number of Pitches (y)	15	30	50

For each pair of values, x and y:

$$\frac{?\text{ pitches}}{?\text{ innings}} = \underline{\quad?\quad} \qquad \frac{?\text{ pitches}}{?\text{ innings}} = \underline{\quad?\quad} \qquad \frac{?\text{ pitches}}{?\text{ innings}} = \underline{\quad?\quad}$$

So, the number of pitches made is ___?___ to the number of innings of a baseball game.

Identify Direct Proportion from an Equation.

When y is directly proportional to x, you can write $\frac{y}{x} = k$. You can use algebra to write another form of this equation, giving y in terms of x. For example, when $k = 2$, you can multiply both sides of the equation $\frac{y}{x} = 2$ by x to get the equivalent equation $y = 2x$.

$$\frac{y}{x} = 2 \qquad \text{Write an equation.}$$

$$x \cdot \frac{y}{x} = x \cdot 2 \qquad \text{Multiply both sides by } x \text{ to undo the division of } y \text{ by } x.$$

$$y = 2x \qquad \text{Simplify.}$$

You can also use algebra to decide if an equation represents a direct proportion.

Think Math

In the equation $y = 2x$, x represents pounds of strawberries, and y represents the cost of strawberries. How can you use the equation to find the cost of buying 10 pounds of strawberries?

Example 2 **Tell whether quantities are in direct proportion from an equation.**

Tell whether each equation represents a direct proportion. If so, identify the constant of proportionality.

a) $\frac{1}{2}y = 3x$

Try to rewrite the equation as an equivalent equation in the form $y = kx$.

Solution

$\frac{1}{2}y = 3x$

$2 \cdot \frac{1}{2}y = 2 \cdot 3x$ Multiply both sides by 2.

$y = 6x$ Simplify.

Because the original equation $\frac{1}{2}y = 3x$ can be rewritten as an equivalent equation in the form $y = kx$, it represents a direct proportion. The constant of proportionality is **6**.

b) $y - 2 = 5x$

Solution

$y - 2 = 5x$

$y - 2 + 2 = 5x + 2$ Add 2 to both sides.

$y = 5x + 2$ Simplify.

Because the original equation $y - 2 = 5x$ cannot be rewritten as an equivalent equation in the form $y = kx$, it does not represent a direct proportion.

Guided Practice

Tell whether each equation represents a direct proportion. If so, identify the constant of proportionality.

3 $0.4y = x$

$0.4y = x$

$\frac{0.4y}{?} = \frac{x}{?}$ Divide both sides by __?__.

$y = $ __?__   Simplify.

Because the original equation $0.4y = x$ __?__ be rewritten as an equivalent equation in the form $y = kx$, it __?__ a direct proportion. The constant of proportionality is __?__.

Continue on next page

Tell whether each equation represents a direct proportion. If so, find the constant of proportionality.

 4 $x = 1 - 2y$

$$x = 1 - 2y$$
$$x + 2y = 1 - 2y + 2y \qquad \text{Add } 2y \text{ to both sides.}$$
$$x + 2y - \underline{\ ?\ } = 1 - \underline{\ ?\ } \qquad \text{Subtract } \underline{\ ?\ } \text{ from both sides.}$$
$$2y = 1 - \underline{\ ?\ } \qquad \text{Simplify.}$$
$$\frac{2y}{?} = \frac{1}{?} - \frac{?}{?} \qquad \text{Divide both sides by } \underline{\ ?\ }.$$
$$y = \underline{\ ?\ } \qquad \text{Simplify.}$$

Because the original equation $x = 1 - 2y$ ___?___ be rewritten as an equivalent equation in the form $y = kx$, it ___?___ a direct proportion.

> **Think Math**
>
> Adam says the equation $5y + 2y = 7$ represents a direct proportion. Susan disagrees with him. Who is correct?

Recognize that a Constant of Proportionality can be a Unit Rate.

The constant of proportionality in a direct proportion often represents a unit rate. For instance, in the example about buying strawberries, the constant of proportionality 2 represents the unit cost of the strawberries. The total cost of the strawberries, y, is the product of the unit cost and the weight of the strawberries purchased, x pounds.

So, the equation of the direct proportion is: y dollars $= \dfrac{\$2}{1 \text{ pound}} \cdot x$ pounds

$$y = 2x$$

Example 3 **Identify a constant of proportionality from a table.**

The table shows the price, P dollars, for x cans of soup. P is directly proportional to x. Find the constant of proportionality and tell what it represents in this situation. Then write a direct proportion equation.

Number of Cans (x)	1	2	3
Price (P dollars)	1.60	3.20	4.80

Solution

Constant of proportionality: $\dfrac{\$1.60}{1 \text{ can}} = 1.6$

The constant of proportionality is **1.6** and represents the cost, in dollars, per can of soup. The direct proportion equation is $P = 1.6x$.

Guided Practice

Copy and complete.

5 The table shows the number of baseballs, y, made in x days. The number of baseballs made is directly proportional to the number of days of production. Find the constant of proportionality and tell what it represents in this situation. Then write a direct proportion equation.

Number of Days (x)	1	2	3
Number of Baseballs (y)	56	112	168

Constant of proportionality: __?__

The constant of proportionality is __?__ and represents __?__.

The direct proportion equation is __?__.

Example 4 **Identify a constant of proportionality in a verbal description.**

Alina is buying some baseball caps. Each cap costs $8. The amount Alina pays for the caps is directly proportional to the number of caps she buys. Write an equation that represents the direct proportion.

Solution

Let x be the number of baseball caps Alina buys.   Define your variables.
Let y be the amount she pays.

Cost per baseball cap: $**8** per cap.

First define the variables. Then identify the constant of proportionality. Finally, write a direct proportion equation.

The direct proportion equation is $y = 8x$.

Guided Practice

Copy and complete.

6 A cafeteria sells sandwiches for $4 each. The amount Jason pays for some sandwiches is directly proportional to the number he buys. Write an equation that represents the direct proportion.

Let __?__ be the number of sandwiches.
Let __?__ be the amount Jason pays.

Cost per sandwich: $__?__ per sandwich

The direct proportion equation is __?__ = __?__.

Example 5 **Identify the constant of proportionality in an equation.**

Solve. Show your work.

y is directly proportional to x, and $y = 3$ when $x = 9$. Find the constant of proportionality. Then write a direct proportion equation.

> Since y is directly proportional to x, you can use $\frac{y}{x} = k$ to find the constant of proportionality, k.

Solution

Constant of proportionality: $\dfrac{y}{x} = \dfrac{3}{9}$

$\qquad\qquad\qquad\qquad = \dfrac{1}{3}$ Write in simplest form.

The constant of proportionality is $\dfrac{1}{3}$.

The direct proportion equation is $y = \dfrac{1}{3}x$.

Guided Practice

Copy and complete.

7 q is directly proportional to p, and $p = 12$ when $q = 24$. Find the constant of proportionality. Then write a direct proportion equation.

Constant of proportionality: $\dfrac{q}{p} = \dfrac{?}{?}$

$\qquad\qquad\qquad\qquad = \underline{\ \ ?\ \ }$ Write in simplest form.

The constant of proportionality is $\underline{\ \ ?\ \ }$.
The direct proportion equation is $\underline{\ \ ?\ \ }$.

Solve.

8 w is directly proportional to h, and $w = 18$ when $h = 3$. Find the constant of proportionality. Then write a direct proportion equation.

Tell whether _y_ is directly proportional to _x_. If so, find the constant of proportionality. Then write a direct proportion equation.

1

x	1	2	3
y	5	10	15

2

x	2	4	6
y	130	100	70

3

x	3	6	9
y	20	40	50

4

x	2	4	6
y	50	100	150

Tell whether each equation represents a direct proportion. If so, identify the constant of proportionality.

5 $3y = \frac{1}{2}x$

6 $2y - 5 = x$

7 $p = 0.25q$

8 $4.5a = b + 12$

Solve. Show your work.

9 The table shows the the distance traveled, _d_ miles, and the amount of gasoline used, _n_ gallons. Tell whether _d_ is directly proportional to _n_. If so, give the constant of proportionality and tell what it represents in this situation. Then write a direct proportion equation.

Amount of Gasoline (_n_ gallons)	1	2	3
Distance Traveled (_d_ miles)	20	40	60

10 The table shows the number of points scored, _y_, in _x_ basketball games. Tell whether _y_ is directly proportional to _x_. If so, give the constant of proportionality and tell what it represents in this situation. Then write a direct proportion equation.

Number of Games (_x_)	1	2	3
Number of Points (_y_)	24	48	80

11 The table shows the number of tennis balls produced, _y_, by _x_ machines. Tell whether _y_ is directly proportional to _x_. If so, give the constant of proportionality and tell what it represents in this situation. Then write a direct proportion equation.

Number of Machines (_x_)	1	3	5
Number of Tennis Balls (_y_)	20	60	100

12 ✏️ *Math Journal* Describe how can you tell whether two quantities are in direct proportion.

13 ✏️ *Math Journal* An equilateral triangle with a side length of c inches has a perimeter of P inches. The perimeter of the equilateral triangle is described by the equation $P = 3c$. Tell whether P is directly proportional to c. Explain your reasoning.

14 Jim rode his bike at a steady rate of 20 miles per hour. Given that his distance, d miles, is directly proportional to the time he rides, t hours, identify the constant of proportionality and write a direct proportion equation.

15 Emily worked in a florist shop and earned $12 per hour. Given that the amount she earned, w dollars, is directly proportional to the time she worked, t hours, identify the constant of proportionality and write a direct proportion equation.

16 y is directly proportional to x, and $y = 10$ when $x = 15$. Write a direct proportion equation that relates x and y.

17 y is directly proportional to x, and $y = 33$ when $x = 11$. Write a direct proportion equation that relates x and y.

18 Karl hikes 3 miles in 45 minutes. Given that his distance is directly proportional to the time he walks, find the constant of proportionality and write an equation to represent the direct proportion.

19 Paul pays $20 to download 16 songs. Given that the amount he pays is directly proportional to the number of songs he downloads, find the constant of proportionality and write a direct proportion equation.

20 ✏️ *Math Journal* Each table shows the cost of placing an advertisement in a newspaper, C dollars, for t days. Describe how the two tables are alike, and how they are different. Be sure to discuss direct proportion in your answer.

The *Daily Post*

Number of Days (t)	1	2	3	4	5
Total Cost of Advertisement (C dollars)	20	40	60	80	100

The *Evening Star*

Number of Days (t)	1	2	3	4	5
Total Cost of Advertisement (C dollars)	20	40	60	70	80

5.2 Representing Direct Proportion Graphically

Lesson Objective

- Use a graph to interpret direct proportion.

Use a Graph to Interpret Direct Proportion.

Each time the wheel on Mike's unicycle goes around, the unicycle moves forward 2 meters. The distance the unicycle moves forward is directly proportional to the number of revolutions.

The table and the graph show the relationship between the number of revolutions and distance the wheel moves.

Revolutions (x)	1	2	3
Distance (y meters)	2	4	6

$$\frac{\text{Distance}}{\text{Revolutions}} = \frac{2}{1} = \frac{4}{2} = \frac{6}{3} = 2$$

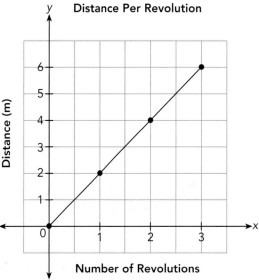

Distance Per Revolution

Distance (m) — Number of Revolutions

The graph of a direct proportion is always a straight line through the origin, (0, 0), that does not lie along the horizontal or vertical axis.

For the graph above, each point (x, y) means that in x revolutions, the unicycle wheel moves y meters. For example, the point (0, 0) means that in 0 revolution, the wheel moves 0 meter. The point (1, 2) means that in 1 revolution, it moves 2 meters.

The point (1, **2**) can be used to find the constant of

proportionality: $\frac{2}{1} = 2$

In general, you can use the point (1, **y**) on a direct proportion graph to find a constant of proportionality.

You can use the constant of proportionality to write a direct proportion equation, y = **2**x.

Think Math

Because $k = \frac{y}{x}$, any point (x, y) except (0, 0) on the line of a direct proportion can be used to find k. Why is the point (1, y) a convenient point to use?

Example 6 **Identify direct proportion from a graph.**

Tell whether each graph represents a direct proportion. If so, find the constant of proportionality. Then write a direct proportion equation.

a)

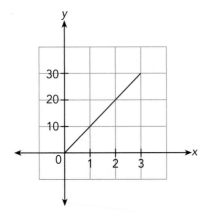

Solution

The graph is a straight line through the origin, and it does not lie along the x- or y-axis. So, it represents a direct proportion.

Because the graph passes through (1, **10**), the constant of proportionality is **10**.

The direct proportion equation is y = **10**x.

> You can use (1, **10**) to find the constant of proportionality.

b)

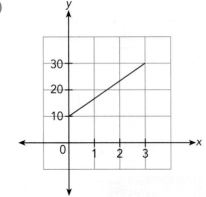

Solution

Although the graph is a straight line that does not lie along the x- or y-axis, it does not pass through the origin. So, the graph does not represent a direct proportion.

c)

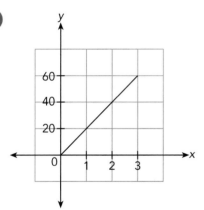

You can see that the graph is not a straight line. It is a curve.

Solution

Although the graph passes through the origin and does not lie along the x- or y-axis, it is not a straight line. So, it does not represent a direct proportion.

Guided Practice

Tell whether each graph represents a direct proportion. If so, find the constant of proportionality. Then write a direct proportion equation.

1

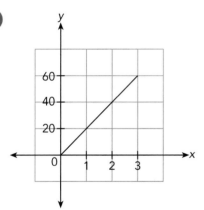

2

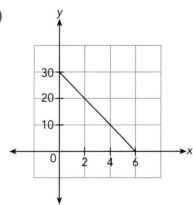

3

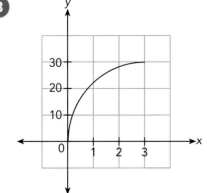

Think Math

Monique thinks that the graph representing a direct proportion can pass through (3, 0). Is she correct? If not, explain why she is incorrect.

Example 7   Interpret a graph of direct proportion.

Jonathan works at a bookstore. The amount of money he earns is directly proportional to the number of hours he works. The graph shows the amount of money, w dollars, he earns in t hours.

a)   Find the constant of proportionality. How much does Jonathan earn per hour?

Solution

Because the graph passes through (1, **15**), the constant of proportionality is **15**.

In this case, the constant of proportionality is the amount of money earned per hour. So, Jonathan earns money at a rate of **$15** per hour.

b)   Write a direct proportion equation.

Solution

The direct proportion equation is $w = 15t$.

c)   Explain what the point (2, 30) represents in this situation.

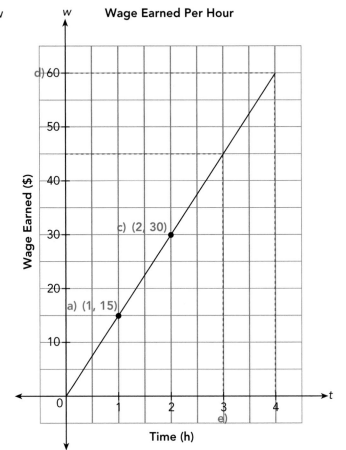

Solution

It means that Jonathan earns $30 in 2 hours.

d)   If Jonathan works 4 hours, how much will he earn?

Solution

From the graph, Jonathan will earn $60 in 4 hours.

e)   If Jonathan wants to earn $45, how long should he work?

Solution

From the graph, Jonathan should work for 3 hours.

Think Math

How can you use the graph to find the number of hours Jonathan should work if he wants to earn $65?

Guided Practice

Complete.

4 Ms. Gray is driving on a long distance trip. The distance she travels is directly proportional to time she travels. The graph shows the distance she travels, *y* miles, after *t* hours.

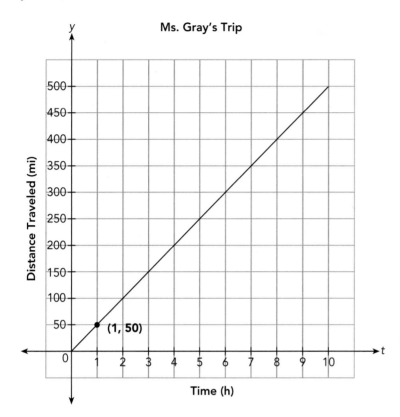

a) Find the constant of proportionality. What is Ms. Gray's driving speed in miles per hour?

Constant of proportionality: $\dfrac{?}{?} = $ ___?___

The constant of proportionality is __?__. So, Ms. Gray's driving speed is ___?___ miles per hour.

b) Write a direct proportion equation.

The direct proportion equation is $y = $ __?__ t.

c) Explain what the point (7, 350) represents in this situation.

It means that Ms. Gray travels __?__ miles in __?__ hours.

d) Find the distance traveled in 3 hours.

From the graph, the distance traveled is __?__ miles.

e) How long does it take Ms. Gray to travel 400 miles?

From the graph, it takes her __?__ hours to travel 400 miles.

Tell whether each graph represents a direct proportion. If so, find the constant of proportionality. Then write a direct proportion equation.

1
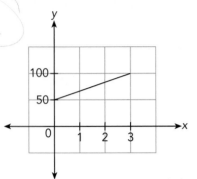

2
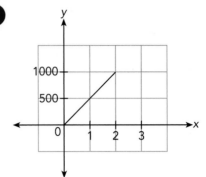

3
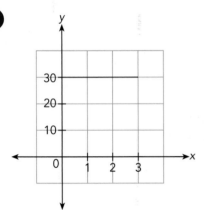

4
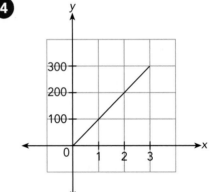

Solve. Show your work.

5 The cost of staying at a motel is directly proportional to the number of nights you stay. The graph shows the cost of staying at a motel, y dollars, for x nights.

a) Find the constant of proportionality. What does this value represent in this situation?

b) How much does it cost to stay at the motel for one week?

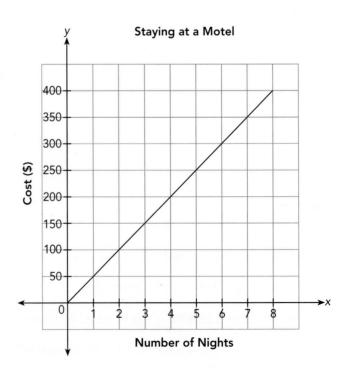

Staying at a Motel

Cost ($)

Number of Nights

6 *Math Journal* Explain how you can tell whether a line represents a direct proportion.

7 When you travel to another country, you can exchange U.S. dollars for the currency of that country. The amount of the new currency you get for your dollars depends on the exchange rate. The graph shows the amount of Mexican pesos, y, you could get if you were to exchange x U.S. dollars for pesos.

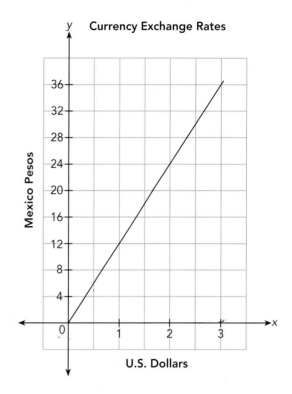

Currency Exchange Rates

a) Is the amount of pesos directly proportional to the amount of U.S. dollars?

b) How many pesos do you get for 3 U.S. dollars?

c) Convert 24 pesos to U.S. dollars.

d) What is the exchange rate when you convert dollars to pesos?

e) Write the direct proportion equation.

Use graph paper. Solve.

8 Beth works at a pottery studio. She is making ceramic pots to sell at a craft fair. Graph the relationship between the number of ceramic pots she makes, y, and the number of days she works at the studio, x. Use 1 unit on the horizontal axis to represent 1 day and 1 unit on the vertical axis to represent 5 ceramic pots.

Number of Days (x)	0	1	2	3	4	5	6
Number of Pots (y)	0	5	10	15	20	25	30

a) Determine whether the graph represents a direct proportion. If so, find the constant of proportionality and write the direct proportion equation.

b) Explain what the point (4, 20) represents in this situation.

c) How many pots can Beth make in 3 days?

d) Beth will not start selling pots until she has made at least 30. How long will it take her to make that many pots?

5.3 Solving Direct Proportion Problems

Lesson Objective

- Solve real-world direct proportion problems.

Vocabulary

cross products

Solve Real-World Direct Proportion Problems.

Because the ratios $\frac{2}{5}$ and $\frac{4}{10}$ are equivalent, you can use them to write a proportion. Notice what happens when you find the **cross products** of the proportion.

Cross products:

$2 \cdot 10 = 4 \cdot 5$ Multiply the numerator of the left fraction by the denominator of the right fraction. Multiply the numerator of the right fraction by the denominator of the left fraction.

$20 = 20$ Simplify.

If you find the cross products of other proportions, you will see that the cross products of a proportion are always equal.

> **Cross products property:**
>
> If $\frac{a}{b} = \frac{c}{d}$, where $b \neq 0$ and $d \neq 0$, then $ad = bc$.

You can use the cross products property to solve problems that involve quantities that are in direct proportion.

For example, suppose you pay $40 for 8 T-shirts at a store. Given that the cost of T-shirts is directly proportional to the number of T-shirts you buy, you can use proportionality reasoning to find the cost of 5 T-shirts.

> You can use a proportion, or you can use a direct proportion equation.

Method 1

Use a proportion.

Let y be the cost of 5 T-shirts.　　Define the variable.

$$\frac{40 \text{ dollars}}{8 \text{ T-shirts}} = \frac{y \text{ dollars}}{5 \text{ T-shirts}}$$　Write a proportion.

$$\frac{40}{8} = \frac{y}{5}$$　　Write ratios as fractions.

$$8 \cdot y = 40 \cdot 5$$　　Write cross products.

$$8y = 200$$　　Simplify.

$$\frac{8y}{8} = \frac{200}{8}$$　　Divide both sides by 8.

$$y = 25$$　　Simplify.

The cost of 5 T-shirts is $25.

> **Caution**
>
> Make sure that both ratios compare quantities in the same order when you write a proportion. In this case, each ratio compares dollars to T-shirts.

Method 2

Use a direct proportion equation.

Let x be the number of T-shirts.　Define the variables.
Let y be the cost of the T-shirts.

Constant of proportionality:

$$\frac{y}{x} = \frac{40}{8}$$　　Substitute $y = 40$ and $x = 8$.

$$= 5$$　　Simplify.

> In this situation, the constant of proportionality is the cost per T-shirt. Because the cost is directly proportional to the number of T-shirts, you can translate the verbal description into a direct proportion equation in the form $y = kx$.

Then write a direct proportion equation.
Direct proportion equation: $y = 5x$　Write an equation.

Finally, find the cost of 5 T-shirts.
When $x = 5$ and $y = 5x$, $y = 5 \cdot 5$　Evaluate $y = 5x$ when $x = 5$.
$$y = 25$$　　Simplify.

The cost of 5 T-shirts is $25.

Check: You can use the unitary method to check the answer.

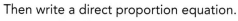

8 T–shirts ⟶ $40

1 T–shirt ⟶ $\frac{\$40}{8} = \$5$

5 T–shirts ⟶ $5 \cdot \$5 = \$25$

Example 8 **Solve a real-world direct proportion problem.**

Belle works at a convenience store. The amount of money she earns is directly proportional to the number of hours she works. She is paid $432 for 18 hours of work. Use a proportion to find how much Belle is paid for 21 hours of work.

Solution

Method 1

Use a proportion.

Let y be the amount of money Belle is paid.   Define the variable.

$$\frac{432 \text{ dollars}}{18 \text{ h}} = \frac{y \text{ dollars}}{21 \text{ h}}$$ Write a proportion.

$$\frac{432}{18} = \frac{y}{21}$$ Write ratios as fractions.

$$y \cdot 18 = 21 \cdot 432$$ Write cross products.

$$18y = 9{,}072$$ Simplify.

$$\frac{18y}{18} = \frac{9{,}072}{18}$$ Divide both sides by 18.

$$y = 504$$ Simplify.

Belle is paid $504 for 21 hours of work.

Method 2

Use a direct proportion equation.

Let x be the number of hours of work.   Define the variables.
Let y be the amount of money Belle is paid.

Constant of proportionality:

$$\frac{y}{x} = \frac{432}{18}$$ Substitute $y = 432$ and $x = 18$.

$$= 24$$ Simplify.

> Because the amount Belle is paid is directly proportional to the number of hours of work, you translate the verbal description into a direct proportion equation in the form $y = kx$.

Direct proportion equation:
$$y = 24x$$ Write an equation.

When $x = 21$ and $y = 24x$, $y = 24 \cdot 21$ Evaluate $y = 24x$ when $x = 21$.

$$y = 504$$ Simplify.

Belle is paid $504 for 21 hours of work.

Guided Practice

Solve.

 At a factory, the number of cars produced is directly proportional to the number of hours factory workers are making the cars. It takes 45 hours to make 60 cars. Use a proportion to find how long it will take to make 250 cars.

Method 1

Use a proportion.

Let x be the number of hours it takes to make 250 cars.   Define the variable.

$$\frac{60 \text{ cars}}{? \text{ hours}} = \frac{? \text{ cars}}{x \text{ hours}}$$ Write a proportion.

$$\frac{60}{?} = \frac{?}{x}$$ Write ratios as fractions.

$$x \cdot 60 = \underline{} \cdot \underline{}$$ Write cross products.

$$60x = \underline{}$$ Simplify.

$$\frac{60x}{?} = \frac{?}{?}$$ Divide both sides by $\underline{}$.

$$x = \underline{}$$ Simplify.

It takes $\underline{}$ hours to make 250 cars.

Method 2

Use a direct proportion equation.

Let x be the number of hours.   Define the variables.
Let y be the number of cars.

Constant of proportionality:

$$\frac{y}{x} = \frac{?}{?}$$ Substitute $y = \underline{}$ and $x = \underline{}$.

$$= \underline{}$$ Simplify.

Direct proportion equation:

$$y = \underline{} x$$ Write an equation.

When $y = 250$ and $y = \underline{} x$, $250 = \underline{} \cdot x$ Evaluate $y = \underline{} x$ when $y = 250$.

$$\underline{} \cdot x = 250$$ Write an equivalent equation.

$$\frac{? \cdot x}{?} = \frac{250}{?}$$ Divide both sides by $\underline{}$.

$$x = \underline{}$$ Simplify.

It takes $\underline{}$ hours to produce 250 cars.

Example 9   Solve a direct proportion problem from a table.

The number of peaches for sale at an orchard, *P*, is directly proportional to the number of crates used to pack the peaches, *C*. The table shows the relationship between the total number of peaches for sale and the number of crates.

Number of Crates (*C*)	15	?	56
Number of Peaches (*P*)	600	1,000	?

a)   Write a direct proportion equation that relates *P* and *C*.

Solution

Number of peaches per crate:

$$\frac{600}{15} = 40$$

The constant of proportionality is the number of peaches per crate.

The direct proportion equation is $P = 40C$.

b)   Find the missing values in the table.

Solution

When $P = 1,000$ and $P = 40C$, $1,000 = 40C$ Evaluate $P = 40C$ when $P = 1,000$.

$$\frac{1,000}{40} = \frac{40C}{40}$$ Divide both sides by 40.

$$25 = C$$ Simplify.

1,000 peaches are packed into 25 crates.

When $C = 56$ and $P = 40C$, $P = 40 \cdot 56$ Evaluate $P = 40C$ when $C = 56$.

$$P = 2,240$$ Simplify.

There are 2,240 peaches in 56 crates.

Guided Practice

Solve.

2 The number of pears for sale at an orchard, *P*, is directly proportional to the number of crates used to pack the pears, *C*. The table shows the relationship between the total number of pears for sale and the number of crates.

Number of Crates (*C*)	8	10	_?_
Number of Pears (*P*)	_?_	200	500

a)   Write a direct proportion equation that relates *P* and *C*.

b)   Find the missing values in the table.

Example 10 **Solve a direct proportion problem involving percent.**

The regular price of a phone was $228. During a sale, its price was marked down by $45.60. Use a proportion to find the percent discount.

Solution

Let x be the percent discount.

$228 (100 percent)

$45.60 (? percent)

Method 1

$$\frac{100 \text{ percent}}{\$228} = \frac{x \text{ percent}}{\$45.60}$$ Write a proportion.

$$\frac{100}{228} = \frac{x}{45.60}$$ Write ratios as fractions.

$x \cdot 228 = 100 \cdot 45.6$ Write cross products.

$228x = 4,560$ Simplify.

$228x \div 228 = 4,560 \div 228$ Divide both sides by 228.

$x = 20$ Simplify.

The percent discount was 20%.

Method 2

Ratio of percents = Ratio of dollar amounts

x percent : 100 percent = $45.60 : $228   Write a proportion.

$$\frac{x}{100} = \frac{45.60}{228}$$ Write ratios as fractions.

$$100 \cdot \frac{x}{100} = \frac{45.60}{228} \cdot 100$$ Multiply both sides by 100.

$x = 20$ Simplify.

The percent discount was 20%.

Think Math

Diego uses a different proportion to solve this problem.

$$\frac{\$45.60}{\$228} = \frac{100 \text{ percent}}{x \text{ percent}}$$

Will he get the correct answer if he uses this proportion? Explain your reasoning.

Guided Practice

Solve.

3 A store owner bought some handbags for $32 each from the manufacturer. Later, the store owner marked up the price of each handbag by $8. Use a proportion to find the percent increase in the price of the handbags.

Practice 5.3

Write a direct variation equation and find the indicated value.

1 m varies directly as n, and $m = 14$ when $n = 7$.

    a) Write an equation that relates m and n.

    b) Find m when $n = 16$.

    c) Find n when $m = 30$.

2 p varies directly as q, and $p = 6$ when $q = 30$.

    a) Write an equation that relates p and q.

    b) Find q when $p = 10$.

    c) Find p when $q = 7$.

In each table, *b* is directly proportional to *a*. Copy and complete the table.

3

a	4	?	19
b	12	15	?

4

a	4	?	16
b	10	25	?

Solve. Show your work.

5 The amount of blood in a person's body, a quarts, is directly proportional to his or her body weight, w pounds. A person who weighs 128 pounds has about 4 quarts of blood.

    a) Find the constant of proportionality.

    b) Write an equation that relates the amount of blood in a person's body to his or her body weight.

    c) Find the weight of a person whose body has about 5 quarts of blood.

6 The height of a stack of books, H inches, is directly proportional to the number of books, n. The height of a stack of 10 books is 12 inches.

    a) Find the constant of proportionality.

    b) Write an equation that relates H and n.

    c) Find the height of a stack of 24 books.

7 The total weight of *n* soccer balls is *m* ounces. *m* is directly proportional to *n*, and *n* = 12 when *m* = 54.

a) Find the weight per soccer ball.

b) Write an equation that relates *n* and *m*.

c) Find the value of *m* when *n* = 30.

8 The cost of CD cases, *C*, is directly proportional to the number of CD cases, *n*. The cost of 6 CD cases is $2.34.

a) Find the cost per CD case.

b) Write an equation that relates *C* and *n*.

c) Find the value of *C* when *n* is 7.

Use a proportion to solve each question. Show your work.

9 Five oranges cost $2. Find the cost of two dozen oranges.

10 It costs $180 to rent a car for 3 days. Find the cost of renting a car for 1 week.

11 John drove 48 miles and used 2 gallons of gasoline. How many gallons of gasoline will he use if he drives 78 miles?

12 Based on past experience, a caterer knows that the ratio of the number of glasses of juice to the number of people at a party should be 3 : 1. If 15 people are coming to a party, how many glasses of juice should the caterer have ready?

13 A recipe for meatloaf requires 10 ounces of ground beef. The recipe serves five people, and you would like to make enough for 8. How much ground beef should you use?

14 George has to pay $30 in taxes for every $100 that he earns. Last summer he earned $3,680. How much did he pay in taxes?

15 Marina wants to buy a sound system that costs $540. The sales tax rate in her state is 8.25%. How much sales tax must she pay?

16 Jason mixes cans of yellow and blue paint to make green paint. The ratio of the number of cans of yellow paint to the number of cans of blue paint is 4 : 3. Jason needs to make more paint. He has 2 cans of yellow paint. How many cans of blue paint does he need to make the same shade of green?

17 The area, *A* square feet, of the wall Ivan is painting is directly proportional to the time he spends painting the wall, *T* hours. It takes Ivan 4 hours to paint 113.6 square feet of the wall. How long will he take to paint 227.2 square feet of the wall?

18 It takes Christy 2 hours to paint 5 model boats.

   a) How long will it take her to paint 10 model boats?

   b) How many model boats can she paint in 10 hours?

19 A commission is an amount of money earned by a sales person, based on the amount of sales the person makes. James works at a shop and earns 5.5% commission on his sales. Last month, he earned $265.32 in commission. Calculate his sales for that month.

20 An initial amount of money deposited in a bank account that earns interest is called the principal. In the table below, *P* stands for principal, and *I* stands for the interest earned by that principal for a period of one year at a particular bank. At this bank, the interest earned for a period of one year is directly proportional to the principal amount deposited.

Principal (*P* dollars)	600	1,000	?
Interest Earned (*I* dollars)	15	?	56

   a) Write a direct proportion equation that relates *I* and *P*.

   b) Copy and complete the table.

21 *Math Journal* *y* varies directly as *x*. Describe how the value of *y* changes when the value of *x* is tripled.

22 *Math Journal* Jenny wants to buy some blackberries. Three stores sell blackberries at different prices:

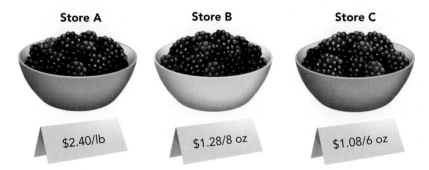

Store A — $2.40/lb

Store B — $1.28/8 oz

Store C — $1.08/6 oz

Which store has the best deal? Give your reasons.

5.4 Understanding Inverse Proportion

Lesson Objectives

- Identify inverse proportion.
- Use a graph to interpret inverse proportion.
- Solve inverse proportion problems.

> **Vocabulary**
>
> inverse proportion

Identify Inverse Proportion from a Table.

Some students want to share some game cards so that each student gets the same number of cards. The table shows the relationship between the number of students, x, and the number of game cards each student gets, y.

Increasing number of students →

Number of Students (x)	1	2	3
Number of Game Cards (y)	120	60	40

Decreasing number of cards →

Because the total number of game cards remains the same, the number of game cards each student receives decreases as the number of students increases.

In this case, you can say that the number of game cards each student receives is inversely proportional to the number of students.

From the table, you can see that the product of x and y is always a constant value.

$$xy = 1 \cdot 120 \qquad xy = 2 \cdot 60 \qquad xy = 3 \cdot 40$$
$$= 120 \qquad\qquad = 120 \qquad\qquad = 120$$

Continue on next page

For any two quantities (x, y) that are in an inverse proportion relationship, their product, xy, is a constant value called the constant of proportionality.

 # Hands-On Activity

Materials:
• algebra tiles

RECOGNIZE INVERSE PROPORTION

Work in pairs.

There are 6 ways of forming a rectangle with 12 algebra tiles. The diagram shows two possible ways.

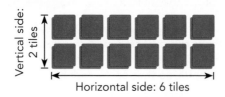

Vertical side: 2 tiles

Horizontal side: 6 tiles

Vertical side: 6 tiles

Horizontal side: 2 tiles

STEP 1 Form a different rectangle by rearranging the 12 algebra tiles. Record your results in a table like the one shown.

Vertical Side (v)	?	2	?	?	6	?
Horizontal Side (h)	?	6	?	?	2	?
v · h	?	12	?	?	12	?

STEP 2 Complete the table by repeating **STEP 1**.

 Math Journal Write down your observations about the values of $v \cdot h$. Describe the relationship between v and h.

Example 11 **Tell whether quantities are in inverse proportion from a table.**

a) The table shows the time it takes, *t* hours, for *n* construction workers to pave a road. Tell whether *t* is inversely proportional to *n*. If so, find the constant of proportionality.

Number of Workers (*n*)	1	2	3
Time (*t* hours)	36	18	12

Solution

For each pair of values, *n* and *t*:

$$nt = 1 \cdot 36 \qquad nt = 2 \cdot 18 \qquad nt = 3 \cdot 12$$
$$= 36 \qquad\qquad = 36 \qquad\qquad = 36$$

The value of *n* increases as the value of *t* decreases, and the product of *n* and *t* is a constant value. So, *t* is inversely proportional to *n*. The constant of proportionality is 36.

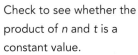

Check to see whether the product of *n* and *t* is a constant value.

b) The table shows the time taken, *y* hours, by *x* students to put a jigsaw puzzle together. Tell whether *y* is inversely proportional to *x*. If so, find the constant of proportionality.

Number of Students (*x*)	1	2	3
Time (*y* hours)	2	1	0.4

Solution

For each pair of values, *x* and *y*:

$$xy = 1 \cdot 2 \qquad xy = 2 \cdot 1 \qquad xy = 3 \cdot 0.4$$
$$= 2 \qquad\qquad = 2 \qquad\qquad = 1.2$$

The value of *x* increases as the value of *y* decreases but the product of *x* and *y* is not a constant value. So, *y* is not inversely proportional to *x*.

If any product of *x* and *y* is different, then *y* is not inversely proportional to *x*.

Caution /////////

For two quantities (*x*, *y*) to be in inverse proportion, the product of *x* and *y* must be the same for all the ordered pairs. So, be sure to check all pairs of values in a table.

Guided Practice

Copy and complete.

1. Some friends want to share the cost of buying a present. The table shows the amount of money that each person has to contribute, y dollars, and the number of people sharing the cost, x. Tell whether y is inversely proportional to x. If so, find the constant of proportionality.

Number of People (x)	1	2	3
Amount Contributed (y dollars)	180	90	60

For each pair of values, x and y:

$1 \cdot 180 = \underline{\ ?\ }$ $\underline{\ ?\ } \cdot 90 = \underline{\ ?\ }$ $\underline{\ ?\ } \cdot \underline{\ ?\ } = \underline{\ ?\ }$

The value of x increases as the value of y decreases, and the product of x and y is a $\underline{\ ?\ }$ value. So, y is inversely proportional to x.

The constant of proportionality is $\underline{\ ?\ }$.

2. Henry drove from Town A to Town B. The table shows the time he took, y hours, if he traveled at various speeds, x miles per hour. Tell whether x and y are in inverse proportion. If so, find the constant of proportionality.

Speed (x miles per hour)	40	50	60
Time (y hours)	9	$7\frac{1}{3}$	6

For each pair of values, x and y:

$40 \cdot 9 = \underline{\ ?\ }$ $50 \cdot \underline{\ ?\ } = \underline{\ ?\ }$ $\underline{\ ?\ } \cdot \underline{\ ?\ } = \underline{\ ?\ }$

The value of x increases as the value of y decreases, but the product of x and y is $\underline{\ ?\ }$ value. So, y is $\underline{\ ?\ }$ inversely proportional to x.

Identify Inverse Proportion from an Equation.

When two quantities, such as y and x, are inversely proportional, their product is a constant value. You can write an algebraic equation relating y and x:

$$xy = k \quad \text{or} \quad y = \frac{k}{x}$$

To see whether the two variables in a given equation are inversely proportional, you can use algebra to rewrite the equation in one or both of these forms.

Example 12 **Identify an inverse proportion equation and find the constant of proportionality.**

Tell whether the equation represents an inverse proportion. If so, find the constant of proportionality.

$$\frac{1}{2}y = \frac{5}{x}$$

> Try to rewrite the equation as an equivalent equation in the form $xy = k$ or $y = \frac{k}{x}$.

Solution

$$\frac{1}{2}y = \frac{5}{x}$$

$$\frac{1}{2}y \cdot 2 = \frac{5}{x} \cdot 2 \qquad \text{Multiply both sides by 2.}$$

$$y = \frac{10}{x} \qquad \text{Simplify.}$$

$$y \cdot x = \frac{10}{x} \cdot x \qquad \text{Multiply both sides by } x.$$

$$xy = 10 \qquad \text{Simplify.}$$

The original equation can be rewritten as two equivalent equations in the form $xy = k$ and $y = \frac{k}{x}$: $xy = 10$ and $y = \frac{10}{x}$. So, the equation represents an inverse proportion. The constant of proportionality is **10**.

Guided Practice

Tell whether the equation represents an inverse proportion. If so, find the constant of proportionality.

3 $\frac{3}{5}y = \frac{6}{x}$

$$\frac{3}{5}y = \frac{6}{x}$$

$$\frac{3}{5}y \cdot \underline{\ ?\ } = \frac{6}{x} \cdot \underline{\ ?\ } \qquad \text{Multiply both sides by } \underline{\ ?\ }.$$

$$y = \frac{?}{x} \qquad \text{Simplify.}$$

$$y \cdot x = \frac{?}{x} \cdot x \qquad \text{Multiply both sides by } x.$$

$$xy = \underline{\ ?\ } \qquad \text{Simplify.}$$

The original equation __?__ be rewritten as two equivalent equations in the form $y = \frac{k}{x}$ and $xy = k$. So, the equation __?__ an inverse proportion. The constant of proportionality is __?__.

Continue on next page

Tell whether the equation represents an inverse proportion. If so, find the constant of proportionality.

4 $y - 3x = 5$

$$y - 3x = 5$$
$$y - 3x + \underline{} = 5 + \underline{} \qquad \text{Add } \underline{} \text{ to both sides.}$$
$$\underline{} = \underline{} \qquad \text{Simplify.}$$

The original equation __?__ be rewritten as two equivalent equations in the form $y = \dfrac{k}{x}$ and $xy = k$. So, the equation __?__ an inverse proportion.

Use a Graph to Interpret Inverse Proportion.

As you saw earlier, the number of game cards each student gets, y, is inversely proportional to the number of students sharing 120 game cards, x. The graph shows this relationship.

Number of Students (x)	1	2	3
Number of Game Cards (y)	120	60	40

The graph of an inverse proportion is a curve.

Because one variable decreases as the other increases, and the product of the variables is a constant value, neither value can be 0. So, the graph of an inverse proportion never crosses the horizontal and vertical axes.

You can use the coordinates of any point (x, y) to find the constant of proportionality.

For example:

$(2, 60) \longrightarrow 2 \cdot 60 = 120$
$(3, 40) \longrightarrow 3 \cdot 40 = 120$
$(4, 30) \longrightarrow 4 \cdot 30 = 120$
$(6, 20) \longrightarrow 6 \cdot 20 = 120$

So, the constant of proportionality is 120.

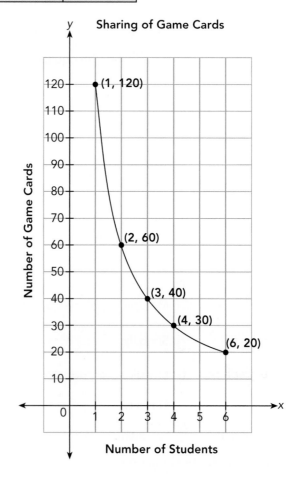

Example 13 **Interpret a graph of inverse proportion.**

The time it takes to clean the windows in an office building is inversely proportional to the number of window cleaners. The graph shows the amount of time, *y* hours, that it takes *x* window cleaners to clean the windows.

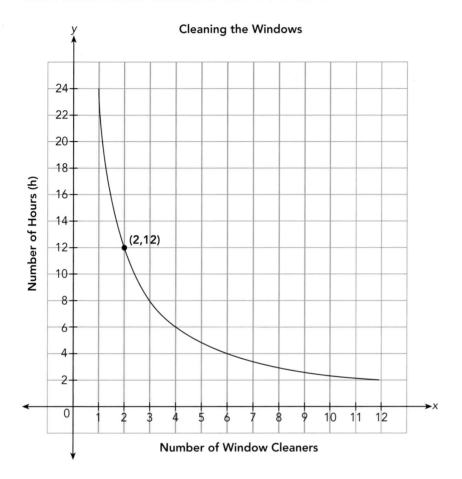

Cleaning the Windows

Number of Hours (h)

Number of Window Cleaners

(2,12)

a) Find the constant of proportionality graphically. Then write an inverse proportion equation.

Solution

Use (2, 12) to find the constant of proportionality:

$x \cdot y = 2 \cdot 12$ Choose the point (2, 12).

$xy = 24$ Multiply.

The constant of proportionality is **24**.
The inverse proportion equation is $xy = 24$.

Choose a point on the graph to find the constant of proportionality. You can choose any point.

b) Explain what the point (2, 12) represents in this situation.

Solution

It means that it will take 2 window cleaners 12 hours to clean the windows.

Guided Practice

Solve an inverse proportion problem graphically.

5) The amount of time needed for volunteers to pick up trash on a beach is inversely proportional to the number of volunteers. The graph shows the amount of time, *y* hours, needed by *x* volunteers.

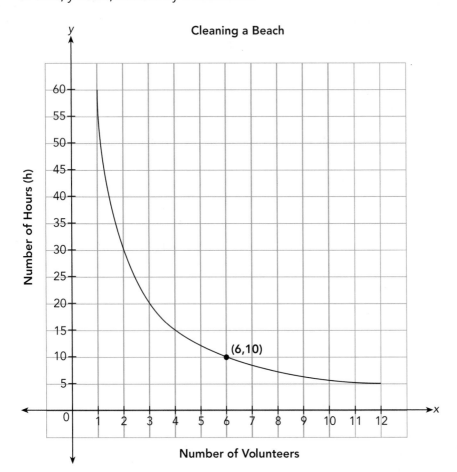

Cleaning a Beach

(6,10)

Number of Hours (h)

Number of Volunteers

a) Find the constant of proportionality graphically. Then write an inverse proportion equation.

Use the point (__?__, __?__) from the graph to find the constant of proportionality:

$x \cdot y = $ __?__ $\cdot$ __?__   Choose the point (__?__, __?__).
$xy = $ __?__   Multiply.

The constant of proportionality is __?__.
The inverse proportion equation is __?__.

b) Explain what the point (6, 10) represents in this situation.

It means that __?__ volunteers can clean the beach in __?__ hours.

Solve Inverse Proportion Problems.

You have learned to write and solve equations. You have also learned to translate verbal descriptions into inverse proportion equations. So, you can write an inverse proportion equation to model mathematical and real-world problems. Then you can use it to find an unknown value.

Example 14 **Identify the constant of proportionality and write an inverse proportion equation.**

Solve. Show your work.

y is inversely proportional to x, and $y = 20$ when $x = 8$.

a) Find the constant of proportionality.

Solution

Constant of proportionality:

$x \cdot y = 20 \cdot 8$
$\quad = 160$

The constant of proportionality is 160.

b) Write an inverse proportion equation that relates x and y.

Solution

Inverse proportion equation:

$xy = 160$ or $y = \dfrac{160}{x}$

The inverse proportion equation is $xy = 160$ or $y = \dfrac{160}{x}$.

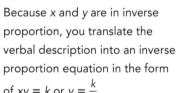

Because x and y are in inverse proportion, you translate the verbal description into an inverse proportion equation in the form of $xy = k$ or $y = \dfrac{k}{x}$.

c) Find the value of y when $x = 5$.

Solution

When $x = 5$ and $y = \dfrac{160}{x}$, $y = \dfrac{160}{5}$ Evaluate $y = \dfrac{160}{x}$ when $x = 5$.

$\quad\quad\quad\quad\quad\quad\quad\quad y = 32$ Simplify.

The value of y is 32.

Guided Practice

Copy and complete.

6 y is inversely proportional to x, and $y = 3$ when $x = 5$.

a) Find the value of the constant of proportionality.

Constant of proportionality:

$$x \cdot y = \underline{\ ?\ } \cdot \underline{\ ?\ }$$
$$= \underline{\ ?\ }$$

The constant of proportionality is $\underline{\ ?\ }$.

b) Write an inverse proportion equation that relates x and y.

Inverse proportion equation:

$$\underline{\ ?\ } = \underline{\ ?\ } \quad \text{or} \quad \underline{\ ?\ } = \underline{\ ?\ }$$

The inverse proportion equation is $\underline{\ ?\ } = \underline{\ ?\ }$ or $\underline{\ ?\ } = \underline{\ ?\ }$.

c) Find the value of x when $y = 10$.

When $x = 10$ and $y = \dfrac{?}{x}$, $y = \dfrac{?}{?}$ Evaluate $y = \dfrac{?}{x}$ when $x = 10$.

$y = \underline{\ ?\ }$.   Simplify.

The value of y is $\underline{\ ?\ }$.

Example 15 **Solve a real-world inverse proportion problem.**

At an auto repair garage, the number of hours, y, it takes to repair a car is inversely proportional to the number of workers, x. It takes 2 workers 6 hours to repair a car. How long will it take 4 workers to repair the same car if they work at the same rate?

Solution

Let x be the number of workers.   Define the variables.
Let y be the number of hours.

Constant of proportionality:

$$x \cdot y = 2 \cdot 6$$
$$= 12$$

Inverse proportion equation:

$$xy = 12 \qquad \text{Write an equation.}$$

> You can translate the verbal description into an inverse proportion equation in the form $xy = k$.

When $y = 4$ and $xy = 12$,

$4 \cdot x = 12$ Evaluate $xy = 12$ when $y = 4$.

$4x = 12$ Simplify.

$\dfrac{4x}{4} = \dfrac{12}{4}$ Divide both sides by 4.

$x = 3$ Simplify.

It will take 4 workers 3 hours to repair a car.

You evaluate $xy = 12$ when $y = 4$ to find the number of hours 4 workers take to repair a car.

Think Math

If two painters can paint a room and a half in a day and a half, how long will it take five painters to paint 20 rooms?

Guided Practice

Solve.

7 Trucks are used to paint dividing lines on a long highway. The number of hours, y, the trucks take to paint the lines is inversely proportional to the number of trucks, x. 15 trucks can paint the highway in 28 hours. How many trucks are needed to paint the same highway in 20 hours?

Let x be the number of trucks.
Let y be the number of hours.

Constant of proportionality:

$x \cdot y = \underline{} \cdot \underline{}$
$ = \underline{}$

Inverse proportion equation:

$xy = \underline{}$ Write an inverse equation.

When $y = 20$ and $xy = \underline{}$,

$20 \cdot x = \underline{}$ Evaluate $xy = \underline{}$ when $y = 20$.

$20x = \underline{}$ Simplify.

$\dfrac{20x}{?} = \dfrac{?}{?}$ Divide both sides by $\underline{}$.

$x = \underline{}$ Simplify.

$\underline{}$ trucks are needed to paint the highway in 20 hours.

Tell whether two quantities are in inverse proportion. If so, find the constant of proportionality.

1

x	25	10	5
y	2	5	10

2

x	7	5	3
y	30	60	70

3

x	4	6	8
y	16	24	32

4

x	6	3	1
y	2	4	12

Tell whether each equation represents an inverse proportion. If so, give the constant of proportionality.

5 $10x = \dfrac{5}{y}$

6 $\dfrac{y}{20} = x$

7 $y + \dfrac{1}{7}x = \dfrac{1}{2}$

8 $0.1x = \dfrac{5}{y}$

Each graph represents an inverse proportion. Find the constant of proportionality.

9

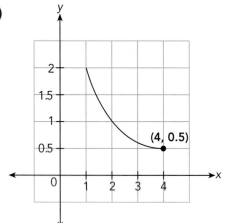

10

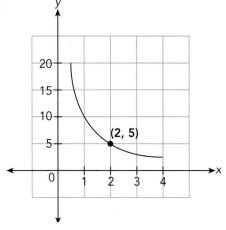

11

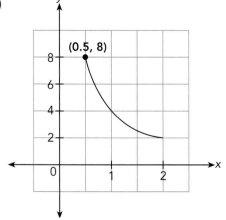

12

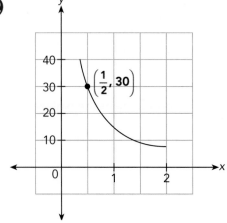

Solve. Show your work.

13 ✏️ *Math Journal* Describe how can you tell whether two quantities are in inverse proportion.

14 The workers at a bakery must mix 12 batches of bagel dough every hour to meet the needs of customers. The number of batches of bagel dough, b, that each worker needs to mix in one hour is inversely proportional to the number of workers, n. The graph shows the relationship between b and n.

  a) Find the constant of proportionality from the graph. Then write an inverse proportion equation.

  b) Explain what the constant of proportionality represents in this situation.

  c) Explain what the point (6, 2) represents in this situation.

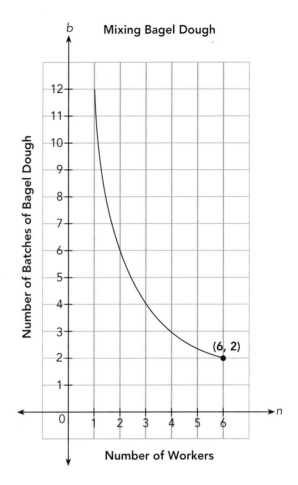

15 A rectangle has a fixed area that does not change. The length, ℓ, of the rectangle is inversely proportional to its width, w. The graph shows the relationship between ℓ and w.

  a) Find the constant of proportionality from the graph. Then write an inverse proportion equation.

  b) Explain what the constant of proportionality represents in this situation.

  c) Explain what the point (3, 8) represents in this situation.

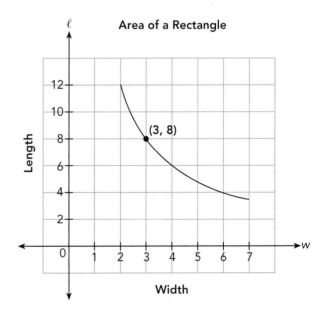

16 y is inversely proportional to x, and $y = 2$ when $x = 5$.

    a) Find the constant of proportionality.

    b) Write an inverse equation relating x and y.

    c) Find the value of x when $y = 4$.

17 y is inversely proportional to x, and $y = \frac{1}{3}$ when $x = \frac{1}{2}$.

    a) Find the constant of proportionality.

    b) Write an inverse proportion equation relating x and y.

    c) Find the value of y when $x = \frac{1}{5}$.

18 *Math Journal* y is inversely proportional to x. Describe how the value of y changes if the value of x is halved.

19 The number of hours it takes to mow nine lawns is inversely proportional to the number of gardeners. It takes three gardeners four hours to mow nine lawns. How many hours would it take one gardener to mow the same nine lawns?

20 The number of minutes it takes to download a file is inversely proportional to the download speed. It takes Jolene 12 minutes to download a file when the download speed is 256 kilobytes per second. How long will it take her to download the same file if the download speed is 512 kilobytes per second?

21 *Math Journal* Each table shows the price, y dollars, that x people have to pay to rent a guest house for one day. Describe how the two tables are alike, and how they are different. Be sure to discuss inverse proportion.

Guest House A

Number of People (x)	1	2	3	4
Price (y dollars)	240	120	80	60

Guest House B

Number of People (x)	1	2	3	4
Price (y dollars)	240	120	85	65

Math Journal **In questions 22 to 25, tell whether each relationship represents a direct or inverse proportion. Explain your answer.**

22 A rectangle with length x inches and width y inches has an area of 50 square inches. The area is given by the equation $xy = 50$.

23 The density of a substance is the mass of the substance per unit of volume. A particular substance with a mass of *m* grams and a volume of *v* cubic centimeters has a density of 3 grams per cubic centimeter. An equation for the density of the substance is $3 = \dfrac{m}{v}$.

24 The music director at a school wants students to sell 200 tickets to the spring musical. The 200 tickets are distributed to the students in equal amounts so that each student gets *y* tickets to sell. The number of tickets each student gets is given by the equation $y = \dfrac{200}{x}$.

25 The sales tax you pay when you buy a new shirt is based on the amount the store charges for the shirt.

Brain @ Work

1 Tom is French, but lives in United States. On a visit to Germany, he saw a book that cost 25.99 euros plus 7% VAT (value-added tax). At that time, one euro was approximately equal to 0.726 U.S. dollars. In the United States, Tom could have bought the same book for 23.99 U.S. dollars plus 6% tax. Should Tom have bought the book in Germany? Explain your answer.

2 Johnny leaves Town P to drive to Town Q, a distance of 350 miles. He hopes to use only 12 gallons of gasoline. After traveling 150 miles, he checks his gauge and estimates that he has used 5 gallons of gasoline. At this rate, will he be able to reach Town Q before stopping for gasoline? Justify your answer.

TOWN P

TOWN Q

350 miles

Chapter Wrap Up

Concept Map

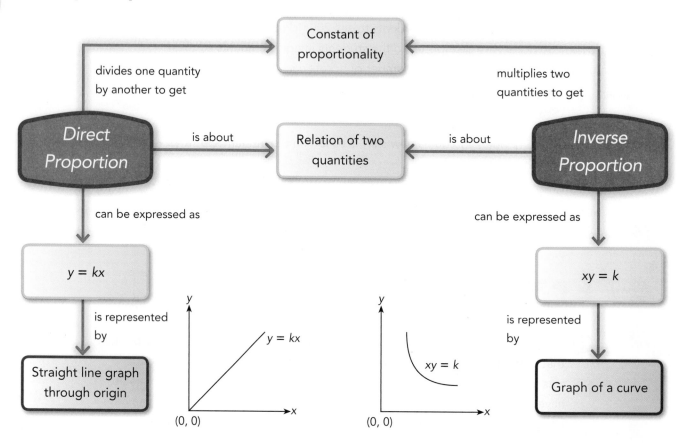

Key Concepts

▶ When y is directly proportional to x, and they have a constant of proportionality, k, you can write an algebraic equation relating y and x:

$$y = kx \qquad \text{or} \qquad \frac{y}{x} = k$$

▶ The graph of a direct proportion is always a straight line that passes through the origin, (0, 0), but does not lie along the horizontal or vertical axis.

▶ When two quantities, such as y and x, are in inverse proportion, and their product is a constant of proportionality, k, you can write an algebraic equation relating y and x:

$$xy = k \qquad \text{or} \qquad y = \frac{k}{x}$$

▶ The graph of an inverse proportion is a curve that never crosses the horizontal and vertical axes.

Chapter Review/Test

Concepts and Skills

Tell whether each table, graph, or equation represents a direct proportion, an inverse proportion, or neither.

1

x	3	5	7
y	4.5	7.5	10.5

2

x	2	4	8
y	50	25	12.5

3

x	6	8	24
y	12	9	3.5

4

x	5	10	15
y	2.5	5	7.5

5
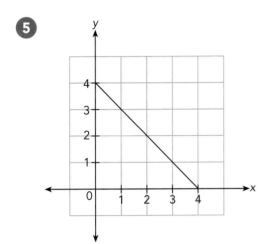

6
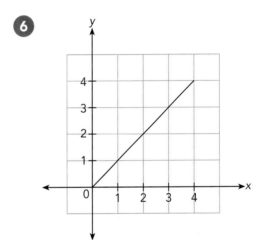

7
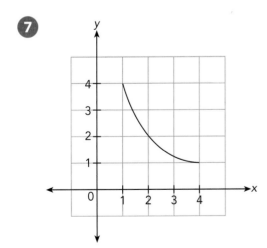

8
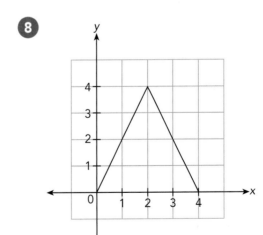

9 $y = \frac{1}{2}x + 5$

10 $\frac{y}{4} = 7x$

11 $-3 + x = y$

12 $\frac{y}{2} = \frac{3}{x}$

In each table, **y** is directly proportional to **x**. Find the constant of proportionality. Then copy and complete the table.

13

x	2	4	?
y	?	16	25

14

x	3	5	?
y	?	2.5	3

In each table, **y** is inversely proportional to **x**. Find the constant of proportionality. Then copy and complete the table.

15

x	2	4	?
y	30	?	10

16

x	2.5	?	5
y	?	2	1.6

Solve using proportionality reasoning.

17 *y* is directly proportional to *x*, and *y* = 56 when *x* = 7. Find the value of *y* when *x* = 4.

18 *y* is inversely proportional to *x*, and *y* = 12 when *x* = 4. Find the value of *x* when *y* = 8.

Problem Solving

Use a proportion to solve each question. Show your work.

19 The graph shows that the cost of gasoline, *y* dollars, is directly proportional to *x* gallons of gasoline.

a)   Find the constant of proportionality. What does this value represent in the context of the problem?

b)   Write a direct proportion equation.

c)   If Umberto spent $24 for gasoline, how many gallons of gasoline did he buy?

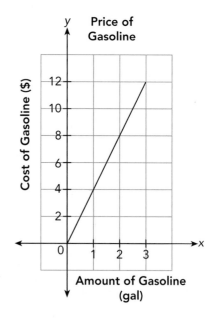

20 Out of every $100 that Judy earns at her part-time job, she saves $25 for college. The amount she saves is directly proportional to the amount she earns. If she earns $3,880 in one year, how much will she save for college?

21 Harry made fruit punch using 2 parts orange juice to 3 parts soda water. The amount of soda water that Harry used is directly proportional to the amount of orange juice he used. How many cups of orange juice should Harry use with 18 cups of soda water?

Use a graph paper. Solve.

22 An initial amount of money deposited in a bank account that earns interest is called the principal. In the table below, P stands for the principal, and I stands for the interest earned by that principal for a period of one year at a particular bank. P is directly proportional to I. Graph the direct proportion relationship between P and I. Use 1 unit on the horizontal axis to represent 1 dollar and 1 unit on the vertical axis to represent $50.

Interest Earned (I dollars)	2	4	6
Principal (P dollars)	100	200	300

a) Using the graph, find the interest earned when the principal is $350.

b) Write an equation relating P and I. Then find the principal when the interest earned is $15.

Use a proportion to solve each question. Show your work.

23 The time taken by some students to deliver 500 flyers, t hours, is inversely proportional to the number of students, n. The graph shows the relationship between n and t.

a) Find the constant of proportionality graphically.

b) Write an equation relating n and t.

c) Describe the relationship between the number of students and the time needed to deliver the flyers.

d) Explain what the point (6, 2) represents in this situation.

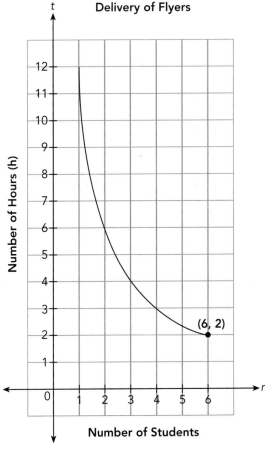

Delivery of Flyers

24 Jerry has set aside a certain amount of money to download applications for his new smart phone. The number of applications he can afford to download is inversely proportional to the cost of each download. With his money, he can afford to download 12 applications that cost $2 each. How many applications can he afford to download if he finds less expensive applications that cost only $1.50 each?

Cumulative Review Chapters 3–5

Concepts and Skills

Simplify each expression. (Lessons 3.1, 3.2, 3.3)

1 $3.9p + 0.9p - 1.8p$

2 $\frac{8}{3}x - \frac{3}{5}y + \frac{2}{5}x + \frac{7}{4}y$

Expand and simplify each expression. (Lesson 3.4)

3 $-0.2(0.8q - 4)$

4 $-\frac{2}{3}\left(-\frac{3}{4}y - \frac{1}{2}\right)$

5 $5\left(\frac{1}{15}x - 6y\right) - \frac{1}{3}x$

6 $2(m - n) - 6(n - 2m)$

Write an algebraic expression for the shaded area shown in questions 7 and 8. Then expand and simplify the expression. (Lesson 3.4)

7
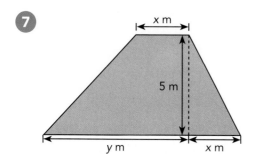

8
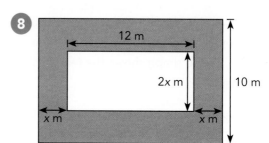

Factor each expression. (Lesson 3.5)

9 $-4k - 36$

10 $9 + 15m - 21n$

Translate each verbal description into an algebraic expression. Simplify the expression when you can. (Lesson 3.6)

11 50% of one-twentieth of the product of 12 and $5z + 5$.

12 21 plus $6p$ minus two-thirds the sum of $14p$ and $3q$.

Tell whether each pair of equations are equivalent. (Lesson 4.1)

13 $x - 7 = 1$ and $x = 6$

14 $0.2x = 0.6$ and $3x + 1 = 10$

Solve each equation. (Lesson 4.2)

15 $11 + 4k = 7$

16 $5p + \frac{2}{15} = \frac{3}{5} + \frac{4}{5}p$

17 $\frac{8}{9}(4x - 3) = \frac{2}{3}$

18 $7(x + 5) - 3x = x - 7$

Solve each inequality. Then graph each solution set on a number line.
(Lesson 4.4)

19 $8x - 7 > 9$

20 $6 + \frac{2}{5}y \leq \frac{1}{3}y + 6\frac{1}{3}$

21 $1.8(x - 5) \geq 0.2(x - 13)$

22 $2(3 - r) + 4(1 + 3r) > -2(3 - 7r)$

Tell whether each table, equation, or graph represents a direct proportion, an inverse proportion, or neither. Find the constant of proportionality for the direct and inverse proportion identified. (Lessons 5.1, 5.2, 5.4)

23

x	1.5	2.5	3.5
y	12	20	28

24

x	10	20	30
y	90	45	30

25

x	3	6	9
y	36	60	84

26 $y = 1.8x + 3.6$

27 $\frac{2}{5}y = \frac{1}{2}x$

28 $3y = \frac{18}{x}$

29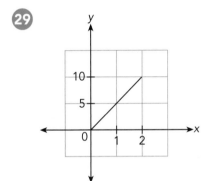

30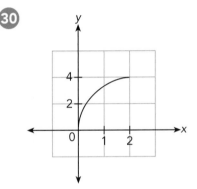

31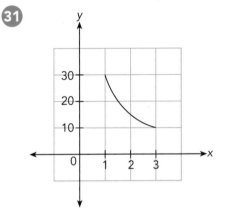

In each table, y is directly proportional to x. Find the constant of proportionality and then complete the table. (Lesson 5.3)

32

x	20	40	?
y	4	?	16

33

x	1	3	?
y	?	27	90

In each table, y is inversely proportional to x. Find the constant of proportionality and then complete the table. (Lesson 5.4)

34

x	12	40	?
y	50	?	10

35

x	1	2	?
y	?	4.5	3

Solve using proportional reasoning. (Lessons 5.3, 5.4)

36 y varies directly as x, and $y = 4.8$ when $x = 0.2$. Find y when $x = 0.8$.

37 P is inversely proportional to Q, and $P = \frac{1}{4}$ when $Q = \frac{1}{2}$. Find P when $Q = 2\frac{1}{2}$.

Problem Solving

Solve. Show your work.

38 The table shows the relationship between the capacity in quarts, x, and the capacity in cups, y. Graph the relationship between y and x. Use 1 unit on the horizontal axis to represent 1 quart and 1 unit on the vertical axis to represent 4 cups. (Chapter 5)

Capacity in Quarts (x quarts)	0	1	2	3	4
Capacity in Cups (y cups)	0	4	8	12	16

a) Is the number of cups directly proportional to the number of quarts? If so, find the constant of proportionality.

b) A soup recipe calls for 5 quarts of stock. How many cups of stock does the soup recipe need?

c) Convert 24 cups of water to quarts of water.

39 A printer takes 2.4 seconds longer to print a page in color than a page in black and white. A page in black and white can be printed in 4 seconds. There are $\left(\frac{5}{8}w + 6\right)$ color pages and $(1.2w + 5)$ black and white pages to print. (Chapters 3, 4)

a) How long does it take to print all the pages?

b) If $w = 40$, how long does it take to print all the pages?

40 Jason has to choose between two offers of a gym club membership as shown below. (Chapter 4)

Gym A	Gym B
$55 per month membership fee plus $15 per hour of training with a personal trainer	$220 per month membership fee and training with a personal trainer at no extra cost

a) After how many hours of training per month would Gym B be a better deal than Gym A?

b) If Jason plans to train for at least 12 hours per month, which gym club membership should he take up? Explain your answers.

41 A commission is an amount of money earned by a sales person, based on the amount of sales the person makes. At a particular home-improvement store, the commission made, C, is directly proportional to the amount of sales, S. A sales person earns $198 when he makes total sales of $3,600. (Chapter 5)

a) Write a direct proportion equation that relates C and S. Then express the store's commission rate as a percent.

b) Find the amount of sales made if his commission is $297.

42 Amy and her friends want to equally share the cost of David's birthday gift. They plan to buy a baseball glove that costs $79.98. The amount of money that each has to contribute, C, is inversely proportional to the number of people sharing the cost, n. (Chapter 5)

a) Write an inverse proportion equation that relates C and n.

b) How much will each person have to pay if 6 people are sharing the cost?

43 The time it takes Tim to cycle to his destination varies inversely as his cycling speed in miles per hour. The graph shows the relationship between y and x. (Chapter 5)

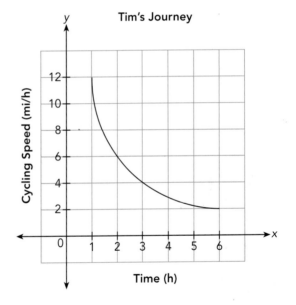

Tim's Journey

a) Find the constant of proportionality. What does this value represent in this situation?

b) Write an equation that relates speed and time taken.

c) Explain what the point (1, 12) represents in this situation.

d) How long does it take Tim to reach his destination if he decreases his speed to 6 miles per hour?

44 Two-thirds of the capacity of jar A is equivalent to eight-fifteenths of the capacity of jar B. Suppose the full capacity of jar B is $(6x - 3)$ liters. (Chapters 3, 4)

a) What is the full capacity of jar A in terms of x?

b) If the capacity of jar A is 18 liters, what is the value of x?

45 A rectangle measures 12 inches by 8 inches. The length of the rectangle is increased by r percent while the width remains unchanged. (Chapters 3, 4)

a) Write an algebraic expression of the area of the expanded rectangle.

b) If the area of the expanded rectangle is 120 square inches, find the value of r.

Selected Answers

CHAPTER 1

Lesson 1.1, Guided Practice (pp. 9–13)

1. $3\frac{2}{7}$ or $\frac{23}{7}$; $\frac{18}{5}$

2.

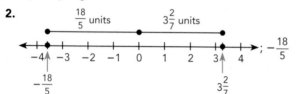

$; -\frac{18}{5}$

3. $\frac{67}{6}$ **4.** $\frac{48}{1}$ **5.** $\frac{-64}{12}$ or $\frac{-16}{3}$ **6.** $\frac{-25}{10}$ or $\frac{-5}{2}$ **7.** $\frac{23}{2}$

8. $\frac{-78}{10}$ or $\frac{-39}{5}$ **9.** $\frac{36}{100}$ or $\frac{9}{25}$ **10.** $\frac{-125}{1,000}$ or $\frac{-1}{8}$

11.

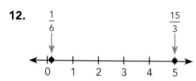

12.

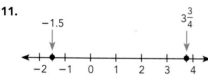

13.

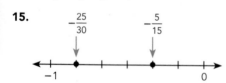

14.

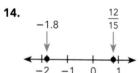

15.

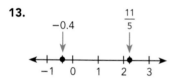

Lesson 1.1, Practice (pp. 14–15)

1. $\frac{7}{10}$;

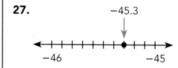

3. $-\frac{5}{13}$;

5. $\frac{67}{1}$ **7.** $\frac{5}{16}$ **9.** $\frac{-1}{5}$ **11.** $\frac{70}{9}$ **13.** $\frac{29}{12}$ **15.** $\frac{2}{5}$

17. $\frac{29}{5}$ **19.** $\frac{-267}{25}$

21.

23. $\frac{305}{20}$

25. $-\frac{21}{12}$

27. -45.3

29. $\frac{23}{8}$; 0; $7\frac{1}{5}$ or $\frac{36}{5}$; 6; $\frac{17}{4}$; 8; 7.8; 9.1   **31.** $0 < \frac{23}{8} < \frac{17}{4}$

$< 6 < 7\frac{1}{5} < 7.8 < 8 < 9.1$ **33.** -9.1 **35.** $-\frac{17}{4}$ min

Lesson 1.2, Guided Practice (pp. 17–24)

1. 0.875   **2.** 4.75   **3.** 1.3   **4.** 10.52   **5.** 0.222…

6. 1.8333…   **7.** 0.4259259…   **8.** 2.108108…

9. $0.8\overline{3}$ **10.** $1.41\overline{6}$ **11.** $\frac{7}{10} < \frac{13}{16}$ **12.** $\frac{24}{7} > \frac{10}{3}$

13. $-\frac{3}{5} > -\frac{4}{5}$ **14.** $-10\frac{3}{4} < -\frac{41}{5}$ **15.** $-4.063 > -4\frac{1}{6}$

Lesson 1.2, Practice (p. 25)

1. 76.5   **3.** -4.7 **5.** 0.35   **7.** $\frac{11}{4}$; 2.75   **9.** $\frac{3}{16}$; 0.1875

11. $-\frac{24}{25}$; -0.96 **13.** $0.83\overline{3}$ **15.** $0.1\overline{45}$ **17.** $-8.9\overline{72}$

19. $-0.\overline{769230}$ **21.** -0.71875; 0.466667; -0.734531;

-0.730769; 0.840909

23. The greater the absolute value of a number, the farther that number is from 0. So, $-\frac{2}{3}$ is farther to the left of 0 than $-\frac{5}{8}$. A number that is to the left of another number on the number line is less than that number. So, $-\frac{2}{3} < -\frac{5}{8}$.

Lesson 1.3, Guided Practice (pp. 31–32)

1. Between 2 and 3; 2.236067977…; 2.24; 2.24; 2.2; 2.3; 2.2;

2. Between -1 and -2; $-1.414213562…$; -1.41; -1.41; -1.4; -1.5; 1.4;

3.

Lesson 1.3, Practice (p. 33)

1.

3.

5.

7.

9.

11.

13.

15.

17. $-\sqrt{132}$

19.

21. 7.681 in.

Lesson 1.4, Guided Practice (p. 36)

1. 208.63   **2.** -12.32 **3.** 12.57

4.

Lesson 1.4, Practice (p. 37)

1. $\sqrt{18} < \sqrt{19}$ **3.** $6.1640 < \sqrt{38}$ **5.** 5.099; 6.775; 3.142; 1.772   **7.** $\sqrt[3]{311} > \sqrt{26} > \pi > \sqrt{\pi}$ **9.** $-\sqrt{8} < \sqrt[3]{8} < \sqrt[3]{27} < \sqrt{10} < \sqrt[3]{64} < \sqrt{25}$ or $\sqrt[3]{125} < \sqrt{100} < \sqrt{1,000} < \sqrt{10,000}$

Lesson 1.5, Guided Practice (pp. 40–46)

1. 2, 3, 0, 0, and 5; 5   **2.** Significant; 3, 6, 7, 9, 4, 1, and 0; 7   **3.** 9 and 4 are significant digits. 2 significant digits.
4. 4, 5, 0, and 0 are significant digits. 4 significant digits.
5. Greater; 350; 340; 350   **6.** 16,900   **7.** 97,000,000
8. 8,254,000   **9.** 7,000   **10.** The significant digits in 6,590,000 are 6, 5, 9, and 0. The significant digits in 200,000 are 2 and 0.   **11.** 5 significant digits; 2 significant digits.   **12.** Less; 1,230.3   **13.** Exactly; 0.877
14. 35.10   **15.** 0.0080100   **16.** 74.0   **17a.** 20.6°C; The digits 2, 0, and 6 are certain.   **17b.** The digit for the second decimal is not significant. The approximate reading of the thermometer is 20.65°C.   **17c.** The approximate reading of the thermometer has 4 significant digits.
18a. 53.5858… cm²   **18b.** 53.6 cm²

Lesson 1.5, Practice (pp. 47–48)

1. 1 and 7; 2   **3.** 3, 0, 0, and 0; 4   **5.** 4, 5, 1, and 3; 4
7. 8,500   **9.** 39,100   **11.** 5,301,000   **13.** 99,000
15. 0.8   **17.** 45.911   **19.** 521   **21a.** 0.1; 100,000
21b. 0.098; 110,000   **21c.** 0.0985; 110,000
23a. Measurement of table A has 1 significant digit; Measurement of table B has 2 significant digits.
23b. Measurement of table A appears to be a rounded figure to the nearest whole number. The digit 0 in the measurement of table B suggests that it is an estimated digit.   **25.** 0.11 mm   **27a.** 44.0°C   **27b.** 3

Lesson 1.5, Brain@Work (p. 48)

a. 3.141692653… (or 3.141492653…)   **b.** Any irrational number between π and a.

c.

or

d. There are infinitely many irrational numbers on the real number line.

Chapter Review/Test (pp. 50–51)

1. $\frac{83}{4}$ **3.** $\frac{58}{13}$ **5.** $\frac{67}{50}$ **7.** 16; 18; -18 **9.** 2.36; 2.7; -2.7 **11.** 0.125   **13.** $9.\overline{09}$ **15.** $-2.1\overline{63}$

17. $5.5 < \sqrt{31} < 5.6$; $-10.6 < -\sqrt{112} < -10.5$;
$5.2 < \sqrt[3]{142} < 5.3$; $-7.8 < -\frac{1}{4}\pi^3 < -7.7$

19.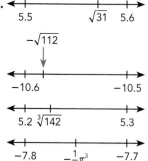

21. 12.375; 12.857; 7.000; 12.806; 8.207

23. $-12\frac{3}{8} < -8.207 < -\sqrt{49} < \sqrt{164} < \frac{90}{7}$

25.

Number	Number of Significant Digits	Answer
0.1350	2	0.14
3,004	3	3,000
22.5	1	20
9.03	2	9.0
4,567	3	4,570
507.01	4	507.0
9,820.036	5	9,820.0
6.999	3	7.00

27. 2.27 g   **29.** 8.5 in.

CHAPTER 2

Lesson 2.1, Guided Practice (pp. 62–72)

1. -5; -5; 3; 2; 3; 2; 5; -5; negative   **2.** -22; -22; 15; 7;
15; 7; 22; -22 **3.** 0   **4.** 0   **5.** -7 **6.** -7 **7.** -12
8. 13   **9.** -15 **10.** 570 ft below sea level

Lesson 2.1, Practice (p. 73)

1. -12 **3.** 0   **5.** -4 **7.** -32 **9.** -22 **11.** -14
13. 1   **15.** -26 **17.** -11 **19.** 16°F   **21.** 257 ft
below sea level   **23.** 3

Lesson 2.2, Guided Practice (pp. 79–83)

1. -30; 9; -30; -9 **2.** 12; -12; $|-35|$; $|-12|$; 47; 12;
-12; -47; 47   **3.** 483 ft   **4.** 4; 21   **5.** -16
6. -6 **7.** 5; 5; (-2); $3 + 2$; 5; 5   **8.** -8; 2,421; 2,421;
-8; $2,421 + 8$; 2,429; 2,429

Lesson 2.2, Practice (pp. 84–85)

1. -11 **3.** -56 **5.** -2 **7.** -26 **9.** -9 **11.** 3
13. 16   **15.** 51   **17.** 25   **19.** -14°C
21. Subtract 590 from 420. Rewrite it as $420 + (-590)$.
Find the difference of the absolute values of 590 and 420.
Assign negative sign to the answer since -590 has a greater
absolute value.   **23.** $(-28) - (-8)$, -20°F   **25a.** 16°F
25b. Freezer A   **27.** 65°F   **29a.** 4; -4; No
29b. 4; 4; Yes   **29c.** Sample answer: Disagree; The
distance between any two integers is a positive number.
So, you need to find $|m - n|$ or $|n - m|$. For example, if
the numbers are 8 and 12, $|8 - 12| = 4$, and $|12 - 8| = 4$.
So, the distance between 8 and 12 is 4. But, $|8| - |12| = 8$
$- 12 = -4$. Since distances must always be positive,
Joe is incorrect.

Lesson 2.3, Guided Practice (pp. 90–92)

1. -72 **2.** 35   **3.** -72 **4.** 4; -24; -24
5. Falls by $18   **6.** 9   **7.** -7 **8.** -15 **9.** -8 ft/min

Lesson 2.3, Practice (p. 93)

1. -35 **3.** -48 **5.** 48   **7.** 0   **9.** -252 **11.** -500
13. 140   **15.** -112 **17.** 0   **19.** 420   **21.** 540
23. -20 **25.** -8 **27.** 6   **29.** 0   **31.** 180 ft below
sea level   **33.** -396 ft   **35.** To evaluate $-12 \div 3 \cdot 2$
$\div (-4)$, Umberto can do it from left to right. Perform any
two operations at one time, and use the rules for sign
multiplication and division: $-12 \div 3 \cdot 2 \div -4 = (-4) \cdot 2$
$\div (-4) = -8 \div (-4) = 2$

Lesson 2.4, Guided Practice (pp. 95–96)

1. 54; -54; -54; -40; -32 **2.** -30; -5; -26 **3.** -26
4. $\frac{3}{2}$; 1; 1; $\frac{3}{2}$; 9; 3; 6; 6

Lesson 2.4, Practice (p. 97)

1. -8 **3.** -39 **5.** -117 **7.** 163   **9.** -22
11. -21 **13.** -10 **15.** 486 in^2 **17.** 40 points

Lesson 2.5, Guided Practice (pp. 101–109)

1. -5; 9; -5; 9; 5; 18; $-\frac{23}{45}$ **2.** $\frac{3}{18}$; $\frac{8}{18}$; $\frac{-3}{18}$; $\frac{8}{18}$; 2;
$\frac{5}{18}$; $2\frac{5}{18}$ **3.** Method 1: $\frac{3}{18}$; $\frac{-10}{18}$; $-\frac{7}{18}$; $-\frac{7}{18}$; $\frac{-6}{18}$;
$\frac{-7 + (-6)}{18}$; $-\frac{13}{18}$; Method 2: $\frac{3}{18}$; $\frac{-10}{18}$; $\frac{-6}{18}$; $\frac{3 + (-10) + (-6)}{18}$;
$-\frac{13}{18}$ **4.** $-\frac{1}{20}$ **5.** $-\frac{1}{40}$ **6.** $-4\frac{7}{12}$ **7.** $-\frac{3}{4}$
8a. $30\frac{7}{10} - 28\frac{1}{2}$ **8b.** $30\frac{7}{10} + \left(-28\frac{1}{2}\right)$ **8c.** $2\frac{1}{5}$ in.

9. $\dfrac{-4 \cdot 20}{5 \cdot 21}$; $\dfrac{-4 \cdot \overset{4}{\cancel{20}}}{\cancel{5} \cdot 21}$; 5; $-\dfrac{16}{21}$ **10.** 13; 8; $\dfrac{13 \cdot \overset{2}{\cancel{8}}}{\cancel{4} \cdot 3}$; 4; $\dfrac{26}{3}$;

$8\dfrac{2}{3}$ **11.** $-\dfrac{7}{8}$ **12.** $2\dfrac{2}{3}$ **13.** $-\dfrac{2}{3}$ **14a.** 12 pancakes

14b. 108 pancakes   **14c.** Yes; 9 cups of flour can make

108 pancakes, which is more than 100 pancakes.

Lesson 2.5, Practice (pp. 110–111)

1. $-\dfrac{1}{3}$ **3.** $\dfrac{-26}{35}$ **5.** $-1\dfrac{13}{42}$ **7.** $-\dfrac{5}{14}$ **9.** $-\dfrac{1}{60}$

11. $-\dfrac{1}{6}$ **13.** $\dfrac{1}{15}$ **15.** $-1\dfrac{3}{4}$ **17.** $-\dfrac{15}{16}$ **19.** 12

21. 3   **23.** $-2\dfrac{1}{2}$ **25.** $-\dfrac{1}{5}$ **27.** $-1\dfrac{1}{2}$ **29.** 3

31. $1\dfrac{1}{5}$ **33.** $9\dfrac{1}{5}$ mi   **35.** $\dfrac{7}{12}$ in.   **37.** Let $a = 2$ and

$b = 3$. Correct answer: $\dfrac{1}{a} + \left(-\dfrac{1}{b}\right) = \dfrac{1}{2} + \left(-\dfrac{1}{3}\right)$

$= \dfrac{3}{2(3)} + \dfrac{-2}{2(3)} = \dfrac{3 + (-2)}{6} = \dfrac{1}{6}$; Peter's method:

$\dfrac{1}{a - b} = \dfrac{1}{2 - 3} = \dfrac{1}{-1} = -1$ **39.** $\dfrac{1}{12}$ h or 5 min

41. $1\dfrac{1}{4}$ oz per wk

Lesson 2.6, Guided Practice (pp. 114–119)

1. $|6.13|$; $|2.35|$; 6.13; 2.35; 3.78; -3.78; negative; -6.13

2. -11.87 **3.** -2.22 **4.** $-1°F$ **5.** -33.258

6. 340.4 **7.** $\$18.40$ **8.** Negative; -31 **9.** Positive;

7.6 **10.** 1.2; 2.5; -1.92; -2; -3.92; -3.92 **11.** 0.2;

0.5; 0.1; 0.4; 0.4 **12.** $\$0.98$ **13.** 9.7% **14.** 26.2 m

Lesson 2.6, Practice (pp. 120–122)

1. -2.35 **3.** -17.82 **5.** -9.086 **7.** -4.64

9. -10.962 **11.** -8.2 **13.** 7.8 **15.** -5.19

17. 44.26 **19.** 5.72 **21.** $93.3°F$ **23.** $\$66.81$

25. 9 T-shirts   **27.** 0.39 g   **29a.** $8.52°F$ **29b.** $1.42°F/h$

31. 12.8 ft   **33.** -20%

Lesson 2.6, Brain@Work (p. 122)

1a. -36.12 **1b.** -3.24 **2a.** $-19.28°F$ **2b.** $12°F$

3. 35.25

Chapter Review/Test (pp. 124–125)

1. 8   **3.** 0   **5.** -41 **7.** -89 **9.** 42   **11.** $5\dfrac{13}{15}$

13. -55 **15.** -24 **17.** -14 **19.** $-\dfrac{1}{3}$ **21.** -9

23. $\dfrac{3}{4}$ **25.** 3.44 **27.** 9.47 **29.** $\dfrac{2}{15}$ **31.** $-24°F$

33. 3.8 lb   **35.** Descent of 790 ft   **37.** -10 points

39. $\$227.70$ **41.** $16\dfrac{2}{3}\%$ increase

Cumulative Review Chapters 1–2
(pp. 126–127)

1. $-\dfrac{87}{100}$ **3.** $-\dfrac{19}{10}$ **5.** 1.4375 **7.** $\sqrt{44}$

9. $\sqrt{162}$ **11.** $\dfrac{\pi}{7}$

13. $\dfrac{244}{7} > 33.9 > \sqrt{345} > \sqrt[3]{675} -\dfrac{86}{3}$ **15.** 0.0961

17. -35 **19.** 25   **21.** -6 **23.** 12   **25.** -96

27. -3 **29.** $\dfrac{1}{8}$ **31.** -32 **33.** -14.3 **35.** 8.64 m/s

37a. 118 points   **37b.** -18 points   **39.** 8,593 ft

41a. $24°C$ **41b.** $12°C$ **41c.** 3 A.M.

CHAPTER 3

Lesson 3.1, Guided Practice (pp. 134–137)

1. $0.2y$; $0.6y$; y; $0.8y$ **2.** $0.8p$; $0.5p$; p; $1.3p$ **3.** $2.2g$

4. x; $\dfrac{3}{4}x$; $2x$; $\dfrac{7}{4}x$ **5.** $\dfrac{1}{2}p$; $\dfrac{2}{5}p$; 10; ten $\dfrac{1}{10}p$; $\dfrac{9}{10}p$

6. $\dfrac{11}{6}m$ **7.** $\dfrac{11}{12}x$ **8.** No, it does not always work. For

example in Example 2b), multiplying the two

denominators, 4 and 6, gives you 24, which is not the least

common denominator.

Lesson 3.1, Practice (pp. 138–139)

1. $0.7y$ **3.** $1.6x$ **5.** $1.6b$ **7.** $2.1k$ **9.** $\dfrac{3}{5}x$

11. $\dfrac{3}{2}m$ **13.** $\dfrac{1}{2}a$ **15.** $\dfrac{11}{10}p$ **17.** $\dfrac{7}{12}a$ **19.** $\dfrac{27}{20}p$

21a. $2\left(4 + \dfrac{2}{3}x\right)$ m or $\left(8 + \dfrac{4}{3}x\right)$ m   **21b.** $\dfrac{35}{9}x$ m

21c. $\left(8 + \dfrac{47}{9}x\right)$ m   **23.** James rewrote the decimal

coefficients as fractions, and Evan rewrote the fractional

coefficients as decimals. Evan's method seems easier and

less time consuming.   **25.** $\left(\dfrac{3}{4}x + \dfrac{3}{2}\right)$ chickens

Lesson 3.2, Guided Practice (pp. 141–143)

1. $0.7y$; $0.4y$; y; $0.3y$ **2.** $0.2a$; $1.1a$; $0.9a$ **3.** $0.2y$

4. $\dfrac{4}{9}x$; $\dfrac{3}{9}x$; 9; nine $\dfrac{1}{9}$; x; $\dfrac{1}{9}x$ **5.** $\dfrac{9}{12}p - \dfrac{2}{12}p$; 12; $\dfrac{7}{12}p$

Lesson 3.2, Practice (p. 144)

1. $0.1y$ **3.** $1.3p$ **5.** $0.8m$ **7.** $\dfrac{2}{3}x$ **9.** $\dfrac{8}{5}x$ **11.** $\dfrac{1}{8}a$

13. $\dfrac{3}{2}b$ **15.** $\dfrac{7}{15}p$ **17.** $\dfrac{15}{14}k$

19. It is correct for Matthew to use a common denominator, but he did not use the LCD. His error is that he did not express the solution in simplest form. The solution should be $\frac{7}{6}x$.

Lesson 3.3, Guided Practice (pp. 146–151)

1. 5.5t; 3　**2.** 0.9m; 2　**3.** 4; $\frac{3}{6}$; 7; $\frac{1}{2}$; 7　**4.** $\frac{4}{12}$; $\frac{11}{12}$;

6　**5.** $\frac{5}{10}$; $\frac{4}{10}$; $\frac{1}{10}$; 5　**6.** 0.8k; 2k　**7.** $\frac{5}{9}p$; $\frac{5}{9}$; $\frac{3}{9}$;

$\frac{2}{9}p$;　**8.** 4a; a; 5a; 12　**9.** $\frac{3}{7}x$; $\frac{2}{7}x$; $\frac{3}{5}$; $\frac{2}{5}$; $\frac{1}{7}x$; $\frac{1}{5}$

10. 6a; a; 7a; 10b　**11.** 3x; 2x; 2y; 3y; x; y

Lesson 3.3, Practice (p. 152)

1. 0.9x + 3　**3.** 0.6x − 5　**5.** 0.9p　**7.** $\frac{11}{12}y$

9. 11x + 6　**11.** 1.1x − 0.6　**13.** 6x + 7y　**15.** 2x + 3y

17. 0.5a + 0.8b　**19.** $a + \frac{1}{3}b$　**21.** 18x cm

23. Like terms are terms that contain the same variables with the same exponents, but can have different numerical coefficients. A group of constant terms are also like terms. Terms with same variable but different exponents are not like terms, such as x and x^2. So, you check to see if two terms have the same variables with the same exponent to identify like terms.

Lesson 3.4, Guided Practice (pp. 155–158)

1. 2x; 3; 2x; 3; 2x; 3; 2x + 3; 8x; 12; 2x + 3　**2.** 3x + 2
3. 5x + 3　**4.** 2x; 5; 0.6x ; 1.5　**5.** 1.4y; +; 2.1; 0.7y; +; 1.05; 0.7y; −; 1.05　**6.** 1.2y + 0.8　**7.** 0.8x − 0.62
8. −12d + 8　**9.** −35k − 7e　**10.** −2.4x + 16
11. $\frac{3}{4}y - \frac{1}{8}$　**12.** 3b; 5b; 4a; 6b; 5b; 4a + 11b
13. $-\frac{7}{2}k + 12$　**14.** 10h − 2k − 14

Lesson 3.4, Practice (pp. 159–160)

1. x + 2　**3.** $\frac{1}{2}p + 1$　**5.** 2k − 3　**7.** $\frac{5}{3}b - \frac{1}{3}$
9. 12x + 0.6　**11.** 0.6x + 0.8　**13.** 0.2m − 0.6
15. 0.6d + 0.2　**17.** −2x − 2　**19.** −12a − 27b
21. −4p − 2　**23.** −10k − 3.4　**25.** −5q + 1.5
27. 6y + 7　**29.** 5x + 4　**31.** $\frac{5}{6}a + 8$　**33.** 0.9x + 0.2
35. −9m − 2　**37.** 1.4r − 2.4　**39.** 10x + 18y
41. 3g + 5v　**43.** 3a + 7b　**45.** d + 10e
47. 2x − 27y　**49.** (15 − h) m; [15(15 − h)] m²;

(225 − 15h) m²　**51.** $\left[\frac{1}{2}(8)(3x - 5y) + 8(6x - y)\right]$ ft²;

(60x − 28y) ft²

Lesson 3.5, Guided Practice (pp. 163–164)

1. 2j; −10k; 2; j; 2; −5k; 2(j − 5k)　**2.** 6(a − 3b)
3. 4(2p − 3q)　**4.** −(5x + 3)　**5.** −3(f + 2)
6. −2(4p + 5q)

Lesson 3.5, Practice (p. 165)

1. 2(x + 4)　**3.** 3(x − 4)　**5.** 2(x + 4y)　**7.** 5(p + 3q)
9. 4(j − 4k)　**11.** 2(a − 5p)　**13.** −(p + 2)
15. −(2d + 7)　**17.** −3(a + 2)　**19.** −5(k + 5)
21. −(1 + 4n)　**23.** −4(3x + 4y)　**25.** 4(x + y + 2)
27. 5(p + 2q + 2)　**29.** 3(s − 3t − 5)
31. 3(4a − 3b − 2)　**33.** (2m − 5n) units

Lesson 3.6, Guided Practice (pp. 169–174)

1. 25; 0.25; w − 0.25w; 0.75w; 0.75w　**2.** 6n; 14; $\frac{6n}{14}$; $\frac{3n}{7}$;

$\frac{3}{7}n$　**3.** $\frac{1}{10}w$; $\frac{2}{5}\left(\frac{1}{2}w\right)$; $\frac{3}{10}w$; $\frac{3}{10}w$　**4.** $\frac{2}{3}b$; $\frac{3}{4}$; $\left(\frac{2}{3}b - \frac{3}{4}\right)$

5. $\left(\frac{2}{5}y + 3\right)$; $\left(\frac{2}{5}y + 3\right)$; 2y; $\frac{14}{5}y + 6$; $\frac{14}{5}y + 6$

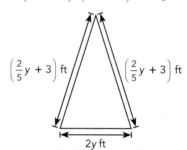

$\left(\frac{2}{5}y + 3\right)$ ft　$\left(\frac{2}{5}y + 3\right)$ ft

2y ft

6.

Diners	Price Per Person	Number of Diners	Cost
Adult	$14.80	m	14.8m dollars
Child	$12	n	12n dollars

14.8m; 12n; 14.8m + 12n

7. (0.25m + 0.05n + 0.1) dollars

8. b; b; 30; 30; $\frac{1}{5}$; b; 30; $\frac{1}{5}b - 6$; $\frac{1}{5}b - 6$

Lesson 3.6, Practice (pp. 176–177)

1. $\frac{1}{6}x + 2.8$　**3.** 0.5q　**5.** 11x

7. 0.24w + 0.5y or $\frac{6}{25}w + \frac{1}{2}y$

9. $\frac{1}{4}(2p + 11)$ or $\left(\frac{1}{2}p + \frac{11}{4}\right)$

11. $\left(6u - \frac{15}{2}\right)$ in.　**13.** $\frac{65}{6}x$ rounds or $10.8\overline{3}x$ rounds

15. (12.4g + 1.24) dollars　**17.** $\frac{9}{11}y$

19. $\left(\dfrac{1}{2}x - 6\right)$ years old   **21.** $(1.08w - 37.8)$ dollars

23a. $(12.5x - 285)$ mi   **23b.** 515 mi

Lesson 3.7, Guided Practice (pp. 180–182)

1. $\dfrac{3}{4}$; $u + 10$; $\dfrac{3}{4}u + \dfrac{15}{2}$; $\dfrac{3}{4}u + \dfrac{15}{2}$ **2.** $25 - w$

2a. 25; w; $(25 - w)$ **2b.** $(25 - w)$; 0.25; $6.25 - 0.25w$;

$(6.25 - 0.25w)$ **3.** $\dfrac{2x}{5} + 1$; $-$; $\dfrac{x}{10}$; $\dfrac{2}{5}x + 1$; $-$; $\dfrac{1}{10}x$;

$\dfrac{2}{5}x - \dfrac{1}{10}x + 1 + 1$; $\dfrac{10}{10}x + \dfrac{4}{10}x + \dfrac{4}{10}x - \dfrac{1}{10}x + 1 + 1$; 10;

$\dfrac{17}{10}x + 2$; $\left(\dfrac{17}{10}x + 2\right)$ **4.** $(25x + 28.8y)$ dollars

Lesson 3.7, Practice (pp. 183–184)

1. $(0.4k + 0.6w)$ L   **3.** $(11.5q + 7)$ dollars

5. $\left(\dfrac{4}{3}x + 50\right)$ min   **7.** $\left(\dfrac{5}{4}b + g\right)$ boys and girls

9. $\dfrac{1}{3}(p + 10)$ years old or $\left(\dfrac{1}{3}p + \dfrac{10}{3}\right)$ years old

11. $(12c + b)$ eggs

13a. $0.3w$ gal   **13b.** 4.65 gal

Lesson 3.7, Brain@Work (p. 184)

From the number line, you see that
180 units in °F ⟶ 100 units in °C

$\therefore$ 1 unit in °F ⟶ $\dfrac{100}{180} = \dfrac{5}{9}$ units in °C

Because 0°C = 32°F, there are
$(F - 32)$° units in a temperature of F °F.

So, $C = \dfrac{5}{9}(F - 32)$.

Chapter Review/Test (pp. 186–187)

1. $0.8w$ **3.** y **5.** $0.3a + 1.4b$ **7.** $2.4p - 3.6$

9. $\dfrac{t}{15} + \dfrac{1}{10}$ **11.** $-4x - 2$ **13.** $5a + 9$ **15.** $8.1m - 5$

17. $4(t - 5s)$ **19.** $4(2i + 3 + j)$ **21.** $-3(3m + n + 2)$

23. $\dfrac{7}{4}x + 7$ **25.** $\dfrac{1}{3}q - \dfrac{4}{3}p - \dfrac{5}{9}$ **27.** $1.65g$ Koi

29a. $1.15m$ dollars   **29b.** $34.50   **31a.** Plan A:
$(10 + 0.214n)$ dollars; Plan B: $(14 + 0.185n)$ dollars

31b. Plan A: $31.40; Plan B: $32.50; Plan A; Because it is cheaper.

CHAPTER 4

Lesson 4.1, Guided Practice (p. 195)

1. 3; 3; 3; 8; cannot; different; not equivalent   **2.** 7; 7; 7;
5; 5; 5; 5; 5; 10; 5 is; same; equivalent   **3.** 6; 6; 6; 14; 14;
14; 14; 14; 16.8; 14 is not; different; not equivalent   **4.** 4;
10 is; same; equivalent

Lesson 4.1, Practice (p. 196)

1. Equivalent   **3.** Equivalent   **5.** d)   **7.** e)   **9.** g)
11. b)

Lesson 4.2, Guided Practice (pp. 202–208)

1. 2; 2; 2; 6x; 6; $\dfrac{6}{6}$; $\dfrac{6}{6}$; 6; 1   **2.** $x = -5$ **3.** $x = 1$

4. $x = 2$ **5.** $-5x$; $-5x$; $-5x$; $\dfrac{-5}{-5}$; $\dfrac{5}{-5}$; -5; -1

6. $y = 18$ **7.** $y = -6$ **8.** $p = 9$ **9.** $q = 35$
10. $x = 9$ **11.** $y = 1$

Lesson 4.2, Practice (pp. 209–210)

1. $b = 2$ **3.** $c = 4$ **5.** $a = 16$ **7.** $y = 4$ **9.** $p = 8$
11. $w = 10$ **13.** The error Priscilla made was to divide
both sides by 4 instead of -4. The correct solution is
$p = \dfrac{1}{2}$.   **15.** $g = 6$ **17.** $j = 2.5$ **19.** $q = -56$

21. $e = \dfrac{4}{3}$ **23.** $y = 18$ **25.** $s = 2$ **27.** $z = 2$

29. $r = 2$ **31.** $d = 0.75$ **33.** $b = 1$ **35.** $a = -3$

37. $w = -8$ **39.** $y = -\dfrac{7}{4}$ **41.** The error that Nelson

made was that the subtraction of 5 from $3(2x + 5)$ gave
$3(2x)$. It should have been as follows:

$$3(2x + 5) - 5 = 17 - 5$$
$$3 \cdot 2x + 3 \cdot 5 - 5 = 17 - 5$$
$$6x + 15 - 5 = 17 - 5$$
$$6x + 10 = 12$$
$$6x + 10 - 10 = 12 - 10$$
$$6x = 2$$
$$6x \div 6 = 2 \div 6$$
$$x = \dfrac{1}{3}$$

Though the remaining steps were correct, the solution was
wrong due to the error made.

Lesson 4.3, Guided Practice (pp. 213–216)

1. -35; -35; -5; -10; -25; -10; -25; x; $\dfrac{2}{5}x$; x; $\dfrac{2}{5}x$; $\dfrac{7}{5}$;

$\dfrac{7}{5}$; $\dfrac{7}{5}$; $\dfrac{7}{5}$; $\dfrac{7}{5}$; -25; -25; -25; -10; -10; -25

2a. Answers vary. Sample: (22,000 + 60x) dollars; (22,000 + 60y) dollars   **2b.** 780 row seats   **3.** +; +; +; 48; 2; +; 48; 2; +; −; 16; 48; −; 16; 2; 32; 2; ÷; 2; 32; ÷; 2; 16; +; 16; +; 32; 32

Lesson 4.3, Practice (pp. 217–219)

1. 35.5   **3.** 120   **5.** 35; 36   **7.** 0.2   **9.** 150 tickets
11. 40 dimes; 28 quarters   **13.** 21 days   **15.** 8 wks
17. 350 mi   **19.** Weekend: $7.50; Weekday: $5

Lesson 4.4, Guided Practice (pp. 224–232)

1. x; x; 3; 3; 3; x; 1

2. x; x; 1; 1; 1; x; 1
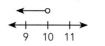

3. x < 10

4. x ≥ 7

5. x < −4

6. w ≥ −10

7. m < −3

8. y > −20

9. 7; 7; 7; 20; 4; 20; 4; 4; 5

10. 9; 9; 9; 30; (−5); 30; (−5); −5; −6

11. x ≥ 8.5

12. y < −7

13. y ≥ 7

14. y ≤ −3

Lesson 4.4, Practice (pp. 233–234)

1. x > 6

3. x > −2

5. x > 15

7. x ≤ 6

9. x < 5

11. x ≥ 7

13. x < 11

15.   8 + 2x ≥ 12
     8 + 2x − 8 ≥ 12 − 8
          2x ≥ 4
        2x ÷ 2 ≥ 4 ÷ 2
           x ≥ 2

The value 2 is a solution of 8 + 2x ≥ 12, but not a solution of 8 + 2x > 12

17. x ≥ −1

19. x ≥ −10

21. x ≤ −30

23. y > 2

25. x ≥ 3$\frac{1}{4}$

27. x < 10

29. x > −2

31. x ≤ 9

33. x > 3

35. y ≤ 4   **37.** a ≤ 7   **39.** x < −1   **41.** y > −5
43. x ≥ $\frac{1}{5}$ **45.** x ≤ −4

47. Similarities: You can apply DSBS when solving both inequalities and equations; Adding or subtracting the same number to both sides of the equation does not change the solution of an equation or the solution set of an inequality; Both inequalities and equations are solved by isolating the variable on one side.
Differences: When solving inequalities, you reverse the inequality symbol when you multiply or divide both sides by the same negative number, but not when you solve equations; Each linear equation usually has only one solution, but each inequality usually has an infinite number of solutions.   **49.** a ≤ 1.4

Lesson 4.5, Guided Practice (pp. 236–238)

1. At least 94 **2.** 18; 75; 18; 18; 75; 18; 18; 57; 12; 57; 12; 12; 4.75; 4 **3.** 20x; 15x; 20x; 15x; 20x; 15x; 15x; 15x; 15x; 5x; 5x; 5x; 5x; 5; 5; 5; 4; 4

Lesson 4.5, Practice (pp. 239–240)

1. At most 15 cm **3.** Answers vary. Sample: $x + 75 + 28 \geq 195$; At least $92 more **5.** At least 83 points **7.** Answers vary. Sample: $2.4x + 270 \leq 380$; At most 45 favors **9.** At most 15 lunches **11.** Answers vary. Sample: $2 + 0.8x \leq 16$; At most 17.5 mi; No **13.** Answers vary. Sample: $16 + 5x > x - 8$; $x > -6$

Lesson 4.5, Brain@Work (p. 240)

5 years old

Chapter Review/Test (pp. 242–243)

1. $x = 3$ **3.** $y = 18$ **5.** $x = 2\frac{1}{4}$ **7.** $y = 18$ **9.** $x = 4$

11. $x > 1$

13. $x \leq 7$

15. $y \leq 4$

17. $x < -37.7$

19. $x \geq 6$

21. Answers vary. Sample: $\frac{x}{5} - 5 = x + \frac{1}{3}$; $-6\frac{2}{3}$

23. Answers vary. Sample: $x + (x + 1) = 145$; 72; 73

25. $3x + 4x + (4x + 24) + x = 360$; m∠A: 84°; m∠B: 112°; m∠C: 136°; m∠D: 28°

27. $18p < 8p + 200$; Option B is less expensive for less than 20 hours of training.

29. Answers vary. Sample: $35 + 3.5h \leq 125$; At most 25 balloons

CHAPTER 5

Lesson 5.1, Guided Practice (pp. 252–256)

1. $\frac{100}{2}$; 50; $\frac{150}{3}$; 50; $\frac{200}{4}$; 50; directly proportional; 50; $y = 50x$ **2.** $\frac{15}{1}$; 15; $\frac{30}{2}$; 15; $\frac{50}{3}$; $16\frac{2}{3}$; not directly proportional **3.** 0.4; 0.4; 0.4; 2.5x; can; represents; 2.5

4. x; x; x; x; 2; 2; $\frac{x}{2}$; 2; $\frac{1}{2} - \frac{x}{2}$ cannot; does not represent

5. 56; 56; daily production rate of baseballs; $y = 56x$

6. Answers vary. Sample: n; x; Answers vary. Sample: A; y; 4; Answers vary. Sample: A; 4n; y; 4x **7.** $\frac{24}{12}$; 2; 2; $q = 2p$

8. 6; $w = 6h$

Lesson 5.1, Practice (pp. 257–258)

1. Yes; 5; $y = 5x$ **3.** No **5.** Yes; $\frac{1}{6}$ **7.** Yes; 0.25

9. Yes; 20; It represents the miles traveled per gallon of gasoline; $d = 20n$ **11.** Yes; 20; It represents the number of tennis balls produced per machine; $y = 20x$ **13.** Yes; Yes. Because $\frac{P}{c}$ is equal to a constant value 3, P and c are in direct proportion. **15.** 12; $w = 12t$ **17.** $y = 3x$ **19.** $\frac{5}{4}$; Answers vary. Sample: $P = \frac{5}{4}n$; $y = \frac{5}{4}x$

Lesson 5.2, Guided Practice (pp. 261–263)

1. Yes; 20; $y = 20x$ **2.** No **3.** No **4a.** $\frac{50}{1}$; 50; 50; 50

4b. 50 **4c.** 350; 7 **4d.** 150 **4e.** 8

Lesson 5.2, Practice (pp. 264–265)

1. No **3.** No **5a.** 50; It represents the cost per night. **5b.** $350 **7a.** Yes **7b.** 36 pesos **7c.** 2 U.S. dollars **7d.** 12 pesos per U.S. dollar **7e.** $y = 12x$

Lesson 5.3, Guided Practice (pp. 269–271)

1. Method 1: 45; 250; 45; 250; 45; 250; 11,250; 60; $\frac{11,250}{60}$; 60; 187.5; 187.5; Method 2: $\frac{60}{45}$; 60; 45; $\frac{4}{3}$; $\frac{4}{3}$; $\frac{4}{3}$; $\frac{4}{3}$; $\frac{4}{3}$; $\frac{4}{3}$; $\frac{4}{3}$; $\frac{4}{3}$; $\frac{4}{3}$; $\frac{4}{3}$; 187.5; 187.5 **2a.** $P = 20C$

2b.

Number of Crates (C)	8	10	25
Number of Pears (P)	160	200	500

3. 25%

Lesson 5.3, Practice (pp. 272–274)

1a. $m = 2n$ **1b.** 32 **1c.** 15

3.

a	4	5	19
b	12	15	57

5a. $\frac{1}{32}$ **5b.** $a = \frac{1}{32}w$ **5c.** 160 lb **7a.** 4.5 oz **7b.** $m = 4.5n$ **7c.** 135 **9.** $9.60 **11.** 3.25 gal **13.** 16 oz **15.** $44.55 **17.** 8 h **19.** $4,824

21. The value of y will triple as well because x and y are in direct proportion.

Lesson 5.4, Guided Practice (pp. 278–285)

1. 180; 2; 180; 3; 60; 180; constant; 180   **2.** 360; $7\frac{1}{3}$;

$366\frac{2}{3}$; 60; 6; 360; not a constant; not   **3.** $\frac{5}{3}$; $\frac{5}{3}$; $\frac{5}{3}$; 10;

10; 10; can; represents; 10   **4.** 3x; 3x; 3x; y; 5 + 3x;

cannot; does not represent   **5a.** Answers vary. Sample:

6, 10; Answers vary. Sample: 6, 10; 60; 60; xy = 60; 6; 10

6a. 5; 3; 15; 15   **6b.** xy; 15; y; $\frac{15}{x}$; xy; 15; y; $\frac{15}{x}$

6c. 15; $\frac{15}{10}$; 15; 1.5; 1.5   **7.** 15; 28; 420; 420; 420; 420;

420; 420; 20; $\frac{420}{20}$; 20; 21; 21

Lesson 5.4, Practice (pp. 286–289)

1. Yes; 50   **3.** No   **5.** Yes; $\frac{1}{2}$ **7.** No   **9.** 2   **11.** 4

13. Two quantities are in inverse proportion when one quantity decreases and the other increases in such a way that the product of the two quantities remains constant. So, you can tell whether two quantities are in inverse proportion by checking whether the product of the two quantities remains constant.   **15a.** 24; $\ell w = 24$ or $\ell = \frac{24}{w}$

15b. Area of a rectangle   **15c.** It means that the rectangle with a fixed area of 24 square units has a length of 8 units when the width is 3 units.   **17a.** $\frac{1}{6}$

17b. $xy = \frac{1}{6}$ or $y = \frac{1}{6x}$ **17c.** $\frac{5}{6}$ **19.** 12 h

21. Both tables show the amount paid by each person in the house per day; The products of x and y are the same until each house has 2 people. Because xy is constant for Guest House A, the amount paid by each person in the house per day is inversely proportional to the number of people in the house. Because xy is not a constant for Guest House B, the amount paid by each person in the house per day is not inversely proportional to the number of people in the house.   **23.** As the equation is in the form $\frac{m}{v} = k$,

$\frac{m}{v} = 3$ represents a direct proportion.   **25.** The amount of sales tax depends on the number of shirt purchased. Sales tax amount = Shirt price · Sales tax. The sales tax amount is directly proportional to the number of shirts purchased.

Lesson 5.4, Brain@Work (p. 289)

1. Tom should have bought the book in Germany, as it was cheaper.

2. He needs $6\frac{2}{3}$ gallons to travel the remaining journey.

So, Johnny is able to drive to Town Q before stopping for gasoline.

Chapter Review/Test (pp. 291–293)

1. Direct proportion   **3.** Neither   **5.** Neither

7. Inverse proportion   **9.** Neither   **11.** Neither

13.

x	2	4	6.25
y	8	16	25

The constant of proportionality is 4.

15.

x	2	4	6
y	30	15	10

The constant of proportionality is 60.

17. 32   **19a.** 4; It represents the unit cost per gallon of gasoline.

19b. $y = 4x$ **19c.** 6 gal   **21.** 12 cups   **23a.** 12

23b. $nt = 12$ or $t = \frac{12}{n}$ **23c.** Answers vary. Sample:

The number of students increases as the amount of time decreases; The number of students decreases as the amount of time increases.   **23d.** 6 students take 2 hours to deliver 500 flyers.

Cumulative Review Chapters 3–5 (pp. 294–297)

1. 3p   **3.** $-0.16q + 0.8$ **5.** $-30y$ **7.** $\left[\frac{5}{2}(y + 2x)\right]$ m²;

$\left(\frac{5}{2}y + 5x\right)$ m²   **9.** $-4(k + 9)$ **11.** $\frac{5}{2}(z + 1)$

13. Not equivalent   **15.** $k = -1$ **17.** $x = \frac{15}{16}$

15. $x > 2$ **21.** $x \geq 4$

23. Direct proportion; 8   **25.** Neither

27. Direct proportion; $\frac{5}{4}$ **29.** Direct proportion; 5

31. Inverse proportion; 30

33.

x	1	3	10
y	9	27	90

Constant of proportionality = 9

35.

x	1	2	3
y	9	4.5	3

Constant of proportionality = 9

37. $\frac{1}{20}$ **39a.** (8.8w + 58.4) s   **39b.** 410.4 s

41a. $C = \frac{11}{200}S$ or C = 0.05S; 5.5%   **41b.** $5,400

43a. 12; Distance traveled by Tim   **43b.** xy = 12

43c. When Tim cycles at a speed of 12 miles per hour, he will take 1 hour to cycle to his destination.   **43d.** 2 h

45a. 96 + 0.96r   **45b.** 25

Glossary

A

absolute value

The distance of a number from 0 on a number line.

additive inverse

The additive inverse of a number x is the number that, when added to x, yields zero.

Example: 2 and -2 are additive inverses.

algebraic expression

A mathematical expression that contains at least one variable.

Examples: $2x$ and $0.5y^3 + 4$

approximate

Close to the actual value of a number. The numbers 1.4, 1.41, and 1.4142 are approximate values for $\sqrt{2}$.

C

coefficient

A numeric factor in a term of an algebraic expression.

Example: In the expression $6x^3$, 6 is the coefficient of x^3.

complex fraction

A fraction in which the numerator, the denominator, or both the numerator and the denominator contain a fraction.

Examples: $\dfrac{\left(\frac{2}{7}\right)}{8}$, $\dfrac{3}{-\left(\frac{5}{2}\right)}$, and $\dfrac{-\left(4\frac{1}{2}\right)}{-\left(1\frac{5}{16}\right)}$ are complex fractions.

constant of proportionality

The constant value of the ratio of two quantities x and y that are in direct proportion. When x and y are inversely proportional, the constant of proportionality is the product of x and y.

Example: In the direct proportion equation $y = 2x$, 2 is the constant of proportionality. In the inverse proportion equation $xy = 4$, 4 is the constant of proportionality.

cross product

A product found by multiplying the numerator of one fraction by the denominator of another fraction. If two fractions are equal, then their cross products are also equal.

Example: $\dfrac{3}{4} = \dfrac{9}{12}$, so $3 \cdot 12 = 4 \cdot 9$.

cube root

A number that when cubed is equal to a given number.

Examples: $\sqrt[3]{64} = 4$ and $\sqrt[3]{-64} = -4$, because $4^3 = 64$ and $(-4)^3 = -64$.

D

direct proportion

A relationship between two quantities in which both quantities increase or decrease by the same factor.

E

equivalent equations

Algebraic equations with the same solution.

Example: $2(6 - x)$ and $12 - 2x$ are equivalent equations.

equivalent expressions

Two algebraic expressions that are equal for all values of the variables in the expression.

Example: $2x + 5x$ and $7x$ are equivalent expressions.

equivalent inequalities

Algebraic inequalities with the same solution set.

Example: $2x < 8$ and $x - 1 < 3$ are equivalent inequalities.

I

inverse proportion

A relationship between two quantities in which one quantity decreases as the other increases and vice versa so that the product of the two quantities remains constant.

irrational number

A number that cannot be written as $\frac{m}{n}$ where m and n are integers with n being a nonzero integer.

Examples: π and $\sqrt{5}$ are irrational numbers.

L

least common denominator

The common multiple of the denominators of two or more fractions that has the least value.

Example: The least common denominator of $\frac{1}{2}$ and $\frac{1}{5}$ is 10.

N

negative fractions

A set of fractions to the left of 0 on a number line.

Examples: $-\frac{1}{2}$, $-\frac{13}{5}$, and $-\frac{10}{3}$ are negative fractions.

negative integers.

The set of integers to the left of 0 on a number line: ..., $-4, -3, -2, -1$.

Examples: $-5, -17$, and -98 are negative integers.

O

opposites

Two numbers that are the same distance from 0 but are on opposite sides of 0 on the number line. 0 is its own opposite.

Example: 2 and -2 are opposites.

P

positive integers

The set of integers to the right of 0 on a number line: 1, 2, 3, 4, ...

Examples: 2, 10, and 51 are positive integers.

precise

A word describing the level of detail a measuring tool can measure.

proportion

An equation that says two ratios are equivalent.

Examples: $\frac{5}{2} = \frac{10}{4}$ and $\frac{8}{3} = \frac{24}{9}$ are proportions.

R

rational number

A number that can be written as $\frac{m}{n}$ where m and n are integers with n being a nonzero integer.

Examples: 8, $\frac{7}{11}$, and $-\frac{63}{253}$ are rational numbers.

real numbers

A set of numbers that consists of rational and irrational numbers.

Examples: -10, $-\frac{7}{11}$, 0, 5, 9.9, π, $\sqrt{5}$, and 123 are real numbers.

real number line

A number line containing all real numbers.

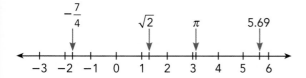

repeating decimal

A decimal that has a group of one or more digits that repeat endlessly.

Examples: $0.111\ldots$, $0.030303\ldots$, and $0.16333\ldots$ are repeating decimals.

S

set of integers

The set of negative integers, 0, and positive integers: $\ldots, -4, -3, -2, -1, 0, 1, 2, 3, 4, \ldots$

significant digits

The digits that are certain and the digit that is estimated in a number.

solution set

A set of values that make an inequality true.

Example:
$$x + 3 > 4$$
$$x + 3 - 3 > 4 - 3$$
$$x > 1$$
$x > 1$ is the solution set.

square root

A number which, when squared, is equal to a given number.

Examples: $\sqrt{49} = 7$ and $-\sqrt{49} = -7$

T

terminating decimal

A decimal that has a finite number of nonzero decimal places.

Examples: 0.5, 0.28, and 0.75 are terminating decimals.

W

whole numbers

The set of counting numbers and 0.

Examples: $0, 1, 2, 3, \ldots$ are whole numbers.

Z

zero pair

A pairing of the integers 1 and -1, whose sum is 0.

Example: $2 + (-3)$ has two zero pairs:
$$2 + (-3) = 1 + 1 + (-1) + (-1) + (-1)$$
$$= [1 + (-1)] + [1 + (-1)] + (-1)$$

Table of Measures, Formulas, and Symbols

METRIC | CUSTOMARY

Length

METRIC	CUSTOMARY
1 kilometer (km) = 1,000 meters (m)	1 mile (mi) = 1,760 yards (yd)
1 meter = 10 decimeters (dm)	1 mile = 5,280 feet (ft)
1 meter = 100 centimeters (cm)	1 yard = 3 feet
1 meter = 1,000 millimeters (mm)	1 yard = 36 inches (in.)
1 centimeter = 10 millimeters	1 foot = 12 inches

Capacity

METRIC	CUSTOMARY
1 liter (L) = 1,000 milliliters (mL)	1 gallon (gal) = 4 quarts (qt)
	1 gallon = 16 cups (c)
	1 gallon = 128 fluid ounces (fl oz)
	1 quart = 2 pints (pt)
	1 quart = 4 cups
	1 pint = 2 cups
	1 cup = 8 fluid ounces

Mass and Weight

METRIC	CUSTOMARY
1 kilogram (kg) = 1,000 grams (g)	1 ton (T) = 2,000 pounds (lb)
1 gram = 1,000 milligrams (mg)	1 pound = 16 ounces (oz)

TIME

1 year (yr) = 365 days	1 week = 7 days
1 year = 12 months (mo)	1 day = 24 hours (h)
1 year = 52 weeks (wk)	1 hour = 60 minutes (min)
leap year = 366 days	1 minute = 60 seconds (s)

CONVERTING MEASUREMENTS

You can use the information below to convert measurements from one unit to another.

To convert from a smaller unit to a larger unit, divide.	To convert from a larger unit to a smaller unit, multiply.
Example: 48 in. = ___?___ ft	Example: 0.3 m = ___?___ cm

Recall: 12 in. = 1 ft
48 ÷ 12 = 4
48 in. = 4 ft

Recall: 1 m = 100 cm
0.3 · 100 = 30
0.3 m = 30 cm

PERIMETER, CIRCUMFERENCE, AND AREA

Square

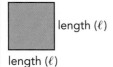

length (ℓ)

length (ℓ)

Perimeter = 4ℓ
Area = ℓ^2

Rectangle

width (w)

length (ℓ)

Perimeter = $2\ell + 2w$
= $2(\ell + w)$
Area = ℓw

Circle

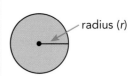

radius (r)

Circumference = πd
= $2\pi r$
Area = πr^2

Triangle

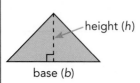

height (h)

base (b)

Area = $\frac{1}{2} bh$

Parallelogram

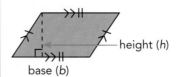

height (h)

base (b)

Area = bh

Trapezoid

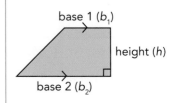

base 1 (b_1)

height (h)

base 2 (b_2)

Area = $\frac{1}{2} h(b_1 + b_2)$

SURFACE AREA AND VOLUME

Cube

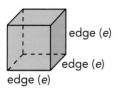

edge (*e*)
edge (*e*)
edge (*e*)

Surface area = $6e^2$
Volume = e^3

Rectangular Prism

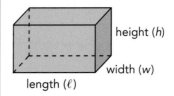

height (*h*)
width (*w*)
length (*ℓ*)

Surface area = $2(\ell w + wh + \ell h)$
Volume = $\ell wh = Bh*$

Prism

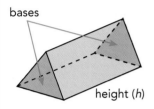

bases
height (*h*)

Surface area
= Sum of the areas of the faces
= Perimeter of base · Height + Area of two bases
Volume = $Bh*$

Pyramid

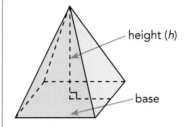

height (*h*)
base

Surface area = Sum of the areas of the faces
Volume = $\frac{1}{3} Bh*$

Cylinder

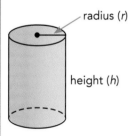

radius (*r*)
height (*h*)

Surface area = $2\pi r^2 + 2\pi rh$
Volume = $\pi r^2 h$

Cone

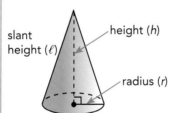

slant
height (*ℓ*)
height (*h*)
radius (*r*)

Surface area = $\pi r(\ell + r)$,
where ℓ is the slant height
Volume = $\frac{1}{3} \pi r^2 h$

Sphere

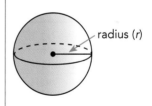

radius (*r*)

Surface area = $4\pi r^2$
Volume = $\frac{4}{3} \pi r^3$

*B represents the area of the base of a solid figure.

Centimeters

PYTHAGOREAN THEOREM

Right Triangle

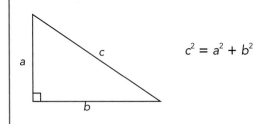

$$c^2 = a^2 + b^2$$

PROBABILITY

Probability of an event A occurring:

$$P(A) = \frac{\text{Number of favorable outcomes}}{\text{Total number of equally likely outcomes}}$$

Probability of an event A not occurring:
$P(A') = 1 - P(A)$

LINEAR GRAPHS

The slope, m, of a line segment joining points $P(x_1, y_1)$ and $Q(x_2, y_2)$ is given by

$m = \dfrac{y_2 - y_1}{x_2 - x_1}$ or $m = \dfrac{y_1 - y_2}{x_1 - x_2}$.

Given the slope, m, the equation of a line intersecting the y-axis at $(0, b)$ is given by $y = mx + b$.

The distance, d, between two points $P(x_1, y_1)$ and $Q(x_2, y_2)$ is given by

$d = \sqrt{(x_2 - x_1)^2 + (y_2 - y_1)^2}$ or $d = \sqrt{(x_1 - x_2)^2 + (y_1 - y_2)^2}$.

RATE

Distance = Speed · Time

Average speed = $\dfrac{\text{Total distance traveled}}{\text{Total time}}$

Interest = Principal · Rate · Time

TEMPERATURE

Celsius (°C) $C = \dfrac{5}{9} \cdot (F - 32)$

Fahrenheit (°F) $F = \left(\dfrac{5}{9} \cdot C\right) + 32$

$<$	is less than	$|a|$	absolute value of the number a
$>$	is greater than	(x, y)	ordered pair
$\leq$	is less than or equal to	$1 : 2$	ratio of 1 to 2
$\geq$	is greater than or equal to	$/$	per
$\neq$	is not equal to	$\%$	percent
$\approx$	is approximately equal to	$\perp$	is perpendicular to
$\cong$	is congruent to	$||$	is parallel to
$\sim$	is similar to	$\overleftrightarrow{AB}$	line AB
10^2	ten squared	$\overrightarrow{AB}$	ray AB
10^3	ten cubed	$\overline{AB}$	line segment AB
2^6	two to the sixth power	$\angle ABC$	angle ABC
$2.\overline{6}$	repeating decimal 2.66666...	$m\angle A$	measure of angle A
7	positive 7	$\triangle ABC$	triangle ABC
-7	negative 7	$°$	degree
$\sqrt{a}$	positive square root of the number a	π	pi; $\pi \approx 3.14$ or $\pi \approx \frac{22}{7}$
$\sqrt[3]{a}$	cube root of the number a	$P(A)$	the probability of the event A happening

Graphing Calculator Guide

A graphing calculator has different sets of function keys you can use for mathematical calculations and graphing. The screen supports both text and graphic displays.

Four Operations

Enter expressions into the Home Screen. Then press **ENTER** to evaluate.

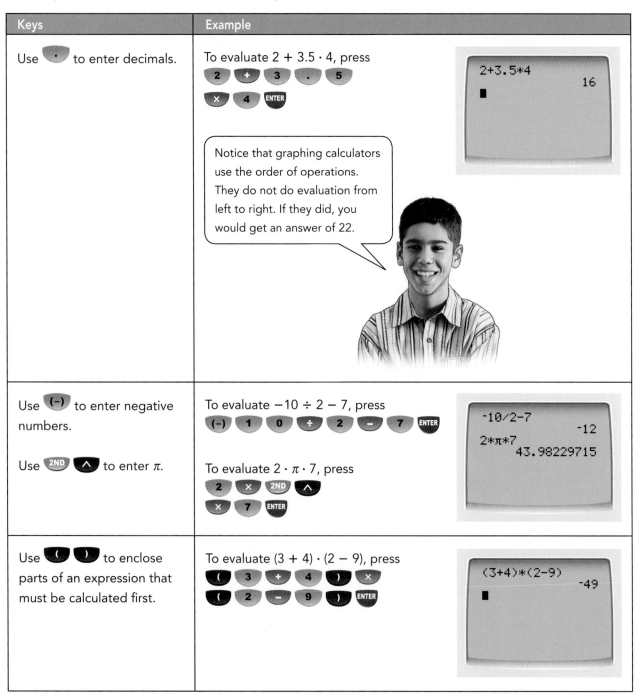

Keys	Example
Use **.** to enter decimals.	To evaluate $2 + 3.5 \cdot 4$, press **2** **+** **3** **.** **5** **×** **4** **ENTER** Notice that graphing calculators use the order of operations. They do not do evaluation from left to right. If they did, you would get an answer of 22. `2+3.5*4` `16`
Use **(−)** to enter negative numbers. Use **2ND** **∧** to enter π.	To evaluate $-10 \div 2 - 7$, press **(−)** **1** **0** **÷** **2** **−** **7** **ENTER** To evaluate $2 \cdot \pi \cdot 7$, press **2** **×** **2ND** **∧** **×** **7** **ENTER** `-10/2-7` `-12` `2*π*7` `43.98229715`
Use **(** **)** to enclose parts of an expression that must be calculated first.	To evaluate $(3 + 4) \cdot (2 - 9)$, press **(** **3** **+** **4** **)** **×** **(** **2** **−** **9** **)** **ENTER** `(3+4)*(2-9)` `-49`

Fractions

Use **MATH** to enter and convert fractions.

Keys	Example	
Use **MATH** to access Frac to enter fractions.	To enter $\frac{2}{5}$, press **2** **÷** **5** **MATH** then select 1: Frac and press **ENTER** To enter $\frac{5}{2}$, press **5** **÷** **2** **MATH** then select 1: Frac and press **ENTER**	```2/5▸Frac 2/5``` ```5/2▸Frac 5/2``` ```■```
Use **MATH** to access Frac and Dec to swap between fractions and decimals.	To convert 0.25 to a fraction, press **.** **2** **5** **MATH** then select 1: Frac and press **ENTER** To convert the fraction back to a decimal, press **MATH** then select 2: Dec and press **ENTER**	```.25▸Frac 1/4``` ```Ans▸Dec .25``` ```■```

Squares and Cubes of Numbers

Use **^** to enter squares and cubes.

Keys	Example	
Use x^2 to find the square of numbers. Use **^** to find the cube of numbers.	To evaluate 3^2, press **3** x^2 **ENTER** To evaluate 5^3, press **5** **^** **3** **ENTER**	```3² 9``` ```5³ 125```
Use **2ND** x^2 to find the square root of numbers. Use **MATH** to find the cube root of numbers.	To evaluate $\sqrt{25}$, press **2ND** x^2 **2** **5** **ENTER** To evaluate $\sqrt[3]{27}$, press **MATH** then select 4: $\sqrt[3]{(}$ and press **2** **7** **ENTER**	```√25 5``` ```³√27 3``` ```■```

Exponents

Use $\wedge$ to enter numbers in exponential notation.

Keys	Example	
Use $\wedge$ to enter positive exponents.	To evaluate $2^2 \cdot 5^0$, press [2] [∧] [2] [ )] [×] [5] [∧] [0] [ENTER] To evaluate $(4^2)^3$, press [( ] [4] [∧] [2] [ )] [ )] [∧] [3] [ENTER]	2^2*5^0 $\qquad\qquad$ 4 $(4^2)^3$ $\qquad\qquad$ 4096
Use $\wedge$ and [(−)] to enter negative exponents.	To evaluate $2^{-2} \cdot 10$, press [2] [∧] [(−)] [2] [ )] [×] [1] [0] [ENTER]	$2^{-2}*10$ $\qquad\qquad$ 2.5

Scientific Notation

Use [2ND] [,] to enter numbers in scientific notation.

Keys	Example	
Use [2ND] [,] to enter powers of 10.	To evaluate $3.4 \cdot 10^2 + 1.5 \cdot 10^3$, press [3] [.] [4] [2ND] [,] [2] [+] [1] [.] [5] [2ND] [,] [3] [ENTER] To evaluate $1.4 \cdot 10^3 \div 2.4 \cdot 10^{-6}$, press [1] [.] [4] [2ND] [,] [3] [÷] [2] [.] [4] [2ND] [,] [(−)] [6] [ENTER]	3.4ε2+1.5ε3 $\qquad\qquad$ 1840 1.4ε3/2.4ε⁻6 $\qquad$ 583333333.3 ■

Probability

Use **MATH** to generate random numbers.

Keys	Example

Use **MATH** to access randInt(under PRB to simulate tossing a fair coin multiple times.	To simulate the tossing of a fair coin 20 times and store the outcomes, press **MATH** then select 5: randInt(under PRB and press **0** **,** **1** **,** **2** **0** **)** **ENTER**
	
	`randInt(0,1,20)`
	`(1 0 1 0 0 0 0 ▶`
	`Ans→L₁`
	`(1 0 1 0 0 0 0 ▶`
	
	 Here 0 indicates a tail, 1 indicates a head, and 20 indicates the number of times the coin is tossed.

Use **STO▶** to store values.	To store the results in a list L1, continue to press **STO▶** **2ND** **1** **ENTER**

Use **STAT** to access Edit to enter data.	To view the list in a table, press **STAT** then select 1: Edit
	
	 To get back to the Home Screen, press **2ND** **MODE**
	
	 `L1    L2    L3    1`
	`1     ----- -----`
	`0`
	`1`
	`0`
	`0`
	`0`
	`0`
	`L1(1)=1`

Use **MATH** to access randInt(under PRB to simulate rolling a fair number die multiple times.	To simulate the rolling of a fair number die 10 times and store the outcomes in a list L2, press **MATH** then select 5: randInt(under PRB and press **1** **,** **6** **,** **1** **0** **)** **STO▶** **2ND** **2** **ENTER**
	
	`randInt(1,6,10)▶`
	`(4 4 6 3 2 2 5 ▶`
	
	 Here 1 and 6 indicate the least and greatest possible results, and 10 indicates the number of times the number die is rolled.

Use **MATH** to access randBin(under PRB to simulate tossing a biased coin multiple times.	To simulate the tossing of a biased coin 20 times and store the outcomes in a list L3, press **MATH** then select 7: randBin(under PRB and press **1** **,** **.** **7** **,** **2** **0** **)** **STO▶** **2ND** **3** **ENTER**
	
	`randBin(1,.7,20▶`
	`(1 0 1 0 1 1 1 ▶`
	
	 Here 1 indicates heads 0.7 indicates the probability of landing on heads, 20 indicates the number of times the coin is tossed.

Credits

Index

COMMON CORE STATE STANDARDS FOR MATHEMATICAL CONTENT

	STANDARDS	CITATIONS
7.RP RATIOS AND PROPORTIONAL RELATIONSHIPS		
Analyze proportional relationships and use them to solve real-world and mathematical problems.		
7.RP.1	Compute unit rates associated with ratios of fractions, including ratios of lengths, areas and other quantities measured in like or different units.	SE Course 2A: 171–172, 174–175, 246, 250–251, 253–256 SE Course 2B: 102–110
7.RP.2	Recognize and represent proportional relationships between quantities.	SE Course 2A: 245, 248–253, 275–287 SE Course 2B: 102–110, 243, 261–262
7.RP.2a	Decide whether two quantities are in a proportional relationship, e.g., by testing for equivalent ratios in a table or graphing on a coordinate plane and observing whether the graph is a straight line through the origin.	SE Course 2A: 245, 248, 250–252, 259–263, 271, 276–278, 280–282 SE Course 2B: 102–110
7.RP.2b	Identify the constant of proportionality (unit rate) in tables, graphs, equations, diagrams, and verbal descriptions of proportional relationships.	SE Course 2A: 246, 248–250, 252–256, 259–263, 276–278, 280–282 SE Course 2B: 102–106, 109–110
7.RP.2c	Represent proportional relationships by equations.	SE Course 2A: 249–254, 259–263, 278–280 SE Course 2B: 253–254
7.RP.2d	Explain what a point (x, y) on the graph of a proportional relationship means in terms of the situation, with special attention to the points $(0, 0)$ and $(1, r)$ where r is the unit rate.	SE Course 2A: 246–247, 259–263, 280–282
7.RP.3	Use proportional relationships to solve multistep ratio and percent problems.	SE Course 2A: 57, 118, 167–168, 179, 182, 245, 247, 266–274, 284–285, 289 SE Course 2B: 13–16, 24–25, 102–104, 107–110, 241, 243, 251, 253–254, 256, 260–262, 270–271
7.NS THE NUMBER SYSTEM		
Apply and extend previous understandings of operations with fractions to add, subtract, multiply, and divide rational numbers.		
7.NS.1	Apply and extend previous understandings of addition and subtraction to add and subtract rational numbers; represent addition and subtraction on a horizontal or vertical number line diagram.	SE Course 2A: 53–55, 58–59, 61, 63–69, 71–72, 74–81, 98–105, 112–115
7.NS.1a	Describe situations in which opposite quantities combine to make 0.	SE Course 2A: 63–64, 66, 74–77, 94–95

COMMON CORE STATE STANDARDS FOR MATHEMATICAL CONTENT

	STANDARDS	CITATIONS
7.NS.1b	Understand $p + q$ as the number located a distance $|q|$ from p, in the positive or negative direction depending on whether q is positive or negative. Show that a number and its opposite have a sum of 0 (are additive inverses). Interpret sums of rational numbers by describing real-world contexts.	SE Course 2A: 59–60, 63–64, 66, 71–72, 98–101, 112–114
7.NS.1c	Understand subtraction of rational numbers as adding the additive inverse, $p - q = p + (-q)$. Show that the distance between two rational numbers on the number line is the absolute value of their difference, and apply this principle in real-world contexts.	SE Course 2A: 76–83, 94–95, 102–105, 114–115
7.NS.1d	Apply properties of operations as strategies to add and subtract rational numbers.	SE Course 2A: 58, 72, 94, 95, 99, 103
7.NS.2	Apply and extend previous understandings of multiplication and division and of fractions to multiply and divide rational numbers	SE Course 2A: 55–56, 106–109, 107–109, 115–117, 200
7.NS.2a	Understand that multiplication is extended from fractions to rational numbers by requiring that operations continue to satisfy the properties of operations, particularly the distributive property, leading to products such as $(-1)(-1) = 1$ and the rules for multiplying signed numbers. Interpret products of rational numbers by describing real-world contexts.	SE Course 2A: 55–56, 86–90, 94–96, 106, 115–116
7.NS.2b	Understand that integers can be divided, provided that the divisor is not zero, and every quotient of integers (with nonzero divisor) is a rational number. If p and q are integers, then $-\left(\dfrac{p}{q}\right) = \dfrac{(-p)}{q} = \dfrac{p}{(-q)}$. Interpret quotients of rational numbers by describing real world contexts.	SE Course 2A: 91–92, 107–109, 200
7.NS.2c	Apply properties of operations as strategies to multiply and divide rational numbers.	SE Course 2A: 86–90, 94–96, 115–116, 119
7.NS.2d	Convert a rational number to a decimal using long division; know that the decimal form of a rational number terminates in 0s or eventually repeats.	SE Course 2A: 16–20
7.NS.3	Solve real-world and mathematical problems involving the four operations with rational numbers[1].	SE Course 2A: 45–46, 57, 64, 71–72, 90, 91, 118

[1]Computations with rational numbers extend the rules for manipulating fractions to complex fractions.

COMMON CORE STATE STANDARDS FOR MATHEMATICAL CONTENT

	STANDARDS	CITATIONS

7.EE EXPRESSIONS AND EQUATIONS

Use properties of operations to generate equivalent expressions.

7.EE.1	Apply properties of operations as strategies to add, subtract, factor, and expand linear expressions with rational coefficients.	SE Course 2A: 130–137, 140–144, 148–151, 153–160, 161–165, 193
7.EE.2	Understand that rewriting an expression in different forms in a problem context can shed light on the problem and how the quantities in it are related.	SE Course 2A: 166–177, 179, 182, 193–195, 211–219

Solve real-life and mathematical problems using numerical and algebraic expressions and equations.

7.EE.3	Solve multi-step real-life and mathematical problems posed with positive and negative rational numbers in any form (whole numbers, fractions, and decimals), using tools strategically. Apply properties of operations to calculate with numbers in any form; convert between forms as appropriate; and assess the reasonableness of answers using mental computation and estimation strategies.	SE Course 2A: 16–21, 29–32, 34–36, 38, 42–46, 57, 58–59, 74–76, 91, 94–95, 102–109, 112–119
7.EE.4	Use variables to represent quantities in a real-world or mathematical problem, and construct simple equations and inequalities to solve problems by reasoning about the quantities.	SE Course 2A: 166–167, 211–216, 235–240 SE Course 2B: 20–23, 26–27, 36–37, 44–50, 133–137, 141, 147–149, 163–166
7.EE.4a	Solve word problems leading to equations of the form $px + q = r$ and $p(x + q) = r$, where p, q, and r are specific rational numbers. Solve equations of these forms fluently. Compare an algebraic solution to an arithmetic solution, identifying the sequence of the operations used in each approach.	SE Course 2A: 178–184, 197–202, 204–208, 211–219, 222
7.EE.4b	Solve word problems leading to inequalities of the form $px + q > r$ or $px + q < r$, where p, q, and r are specific rational numbers. Graph the solution set of the inequality and interpret it in the context of the problem.	SE Course 2A: 190–191, 220–235

7.G GEOMETRY

Draw, construct, and describe geometrical figures and describe the relationships between them.

7.G.1	Solve problems involving scale drawings of geometric figures, including computing actual lengths and areas from a scale drawing and reproducing a scale drawing at a different scale.	SE Course 2B: 102–110

COMMON CORE STATE STANDARDS FOR MATHEMATICAL CONTENT

	STANDARDS	CITATIONS
7.G.2	Draw (freehand, with ruler and protractor, and with technology) geometric shapes with given conditions. Focus on constructing triangles from three measures of angles or sides, noticing when the conditions determine a unique triangle, more than one triangle, or no triangle.	SE Course 2B: 6, 9, 26, 34–35, 67–68, 71–74, 76, 81, 85–92, 94–100
7.G.3	Describe the two-dimensional figures that result from slicing three-dimensional figures, as in plane sections of right rectangular prisms and right rectangular pyramids.	SE Course 2B: 126–129, 140–141

Solve real-life and mathematical problems involving angle measure, area, surface area, and volume.

	STANDARDS	CITATIONS
7.G.4	Know the formulas for the area and circumference of a circle and use them to solve problems; give an informal derivation of the relationship between the circumference and area of a circle.	SE Course 2A: 46 SE Course 2B: 124, 125, 133–135, 141, 144, 147, 163–164
7.G.5	Use facts about supplementary, complementary, vertical, and adjacent angles in a multi-step problem to write and solve simple equations for an unknown angle in a figure.	SE Course 2B: 6, 9, 11, 20–23, 26–27, 36–37, 44–45, 47–49, 74–75, 82
7.G.6	Solve real-world and mathematical problems involving area, volume and surface area of two- and three-dimensional objects composed of triangles, quadrilaterals, polygons, cubes, and right prisms.	SE Course 2B: 109–110, 121–122, 133–137, 140, 147–151, 158–160, 163–166

7.SP STATISTICS AND PROBABILITY

Use random sampling to draw inferences about a population.

	STANDARDS	CITATIONS
7.SP.1	Understand that statistics can be used to gain information about a population by examining a sample of the population; generalizations about a population from a sample are valid only if the sample is representative of that population. Understand that random sampling tends to produce representative samples and support valid inferences.	SE Course 2B: 212–219, 222–234
7.SP.2	Use data from a random sample to draw inferences about a population with an unknown characteristic of interest. Generate multiple samples (or simulated samples) of the same size to gauge the variation in estimates or predictions.	SE Course 2B: 215–219, 222–226

Draw informal comparative inferences about two populations.

	STANDARDS	CITATIONS
7.SP.3	Informally assess the degree of visual overlap of two numerical data distributions with similar variabilities, measuring the difference between the centers by expressing it as a multiple of a measure of variability.	SE Course 2B: 184, 186–189, 193–194, 202–205, 227–231

COMMON CORE STATE STANDARDS FOR MATHEMATICAL CONTENT

	STANDARDS	CITATIONS
7.SP.4	Use measures of center and measures of variability for numerical data from random samples to draw informal comparative inferences about two populations.	SE Course 2B: 184–189, 193–199, 202–209, 224–225, 227–228
Investigate chance processes and develop, use, and evaluate probability models.		
7.SP.5	Understand that the probability of a chance event is a number between 0 and 1 that expresses the likelihood of the event occurring. Larger numbers indicate greater likelihood. A probability near 0 indicates an unlikely event, a probability around $\frac{1}{2}$ indicates an event that is neither unlikely nor likely, and a probability near 1 indicates a likely event.	SE Course 2B: 251–254, 256
7.SP.6	Approximate the probability of a chance event by collecting data on the chance process that produces it and observing its long-run relative frequency, and predict the approximate relative frequency given the probability.	SE Course 2B: 251–259, 266–275
7.SP.7	Develop a probability model and use it to find probabilities of events. Compare probabilities from a model to observed frequencies; if the agreement is not good, explain possible sources of the discrepancy.	SE Course 2B: 279–288
7.SP.7a	Develop a uniform probability model by assigning equal probability to all outcomes, and use the model to determine probabilities of events.	SE Course 2B: 279–288
7.SP.7b	Develop a probability model (which may not be uniform) by observing frequencies in data generated from a chance process.	SE Course 2B: 279–288
7.SP.8	Find probabilities of compound events using organized lists, tables, tree diagrams, and simulation.	SE Course 2B: 245–248
7.SP.8a	Understand that, just as with simple events, the probability of a compound event is the fraction of outcomes in the sample space for which the compound event occurs.	SE Course 2B: 254–262
7.SP.8b	Represent sample spaces for compound events using methods such as organized lists, tables and tree diagrams. For an event described in everyday language (e.g., "rolling double sixes"), identify the outcomes in the sample space which compose the event.	SE Course 2B: 254–262
7.SP.8c	Design and use a simulation to generate frequencies for compound events.	SE Course 2B: 287–288

COMMON CORE STATE STANDARDS FOR MATHEMATICAL PRACTICE

Math in Focus®, Course 2 aligns to the Common Core State Standards for Mathematical Practice throughout.

	CITATIONS

1. MAKE SENSE OF PROBLEMS AND PERSEVERE IN SOLVING THEM.

How *Math in Focus*® Aligns:

*Problem Solving is at the heart of the **Math in Focus**® curriculum. Students use problem solving to build skills and persevere to solve routine and nonroutine problems that include real-world and mathematical applications in proportionality, number sense, algebra, geometry, measurement, data analysis, and probability.*

For example:

SE Course 2A: 35, 38, 45–46, 48, 71–72, 90, 122, 128, 132–137, 140–147, 150–151, 153–155, 161–162, 170, 173–175, 178–184, 191, 193–194, 197–199, 211–216, 220–232, 235–240, 245, 247, 248–253, 255–256, 259–263, 266–274, 278–282, 284–285, 289

SE Course 2B: 15–16, 20–23, 24–25, 26–27, 47–50, 54, 74–75, 82, 90–92, 101–104, 109–110, 114, 122, 133–137, 141, 148–149, 163–166, 168, 184, 203, 205, 217, 222–226, 227–231, 234, 260–261, 272–276, 291

2. REASON ABSTRACTLY AND QUANTITATIVELY.

How *Math in Focus*® Aligns:

*In **Math in Focus**®, concrete to pictorial to abstract progression helps students develop a deep mastery of concepts. Students analyze and solve nonroutine problems, formulate conjectures through explorations, hands-on and technology activities, and observations, identify and explain mathematical situations and relationships, and relate symbols such as negative numbers and variables to real-world situations.*

For example:

SE Course 2A: 20–21, 26–27, 48, 65, 74–76, 86–89, 122, 145–146, 150–151, 153–155, 161–162, 173–175, 178–184, 211–219, 226–227, 235–240, 247, 249, 250, 289

SE Course 2B: 9, 34–35, 43–44, 70, 79, 91, 103, 107–108, 127, 135–136, 140–141, 148–149, 158–159, 189, 209, 215, 219, 226, 266–267, 246, 275, 287–288

3. CONSTRUCT VIABLE ARGUMENTS AND CRITIQUE THE REASONING OF OTHERS.

How *Math in Focus*® Aligns:

*In **Math in Focus**®, students communicate in Math Journals and Think Math's. They demonstrate and explain mathematical steps using a variety of appropriate materials, models, properties, and skills. They share and critique mathematical ideas with others during class in 5-minute Warm-Up and Hands-On, Technology, and group activities, Guided Practice Exercises, Ticket Out the Door exercises, Projects, and other Differentiated Instruction activities.*

For example:

SE Course 2A: 21, 25, 27, 33; 51, 58, 65, 72, 73, 76, 84, 85, 86, 88, 89, 93–95, 97, 111, 130, 137, 139; 152, 155, 156, 161, 177, 196, 206, 209, 210, 222, 224, 225, 226, 227, 228, 233, 234, 240, 250, 258, 266, 267, 274, 276, 287, 288

SE Course 2B: 15–16, 24–25, 34–35, 43–44, 70, 79, 91, 103, 107–108, 127, 135–136, 140–141, 148–149, 158–159, 178, 183–184, 189, 209, 215, 219, 226, 229–231, 246, 266–267, 272–273, 275, 287–288

	CITATIONS

4. MODEL WITH MATHEMATICS.

How *Math in Focus*® Aligns:

In **Math in Focus**®, students and teachers represent mathematical ideas, model and record quantities using multiple representations, such as concrete materials, manipulatives, and technology; visual models such as number lines, bar models, drawings, tables, and coordinate graphs; and symbols such as algebraic expressions, equations, inequalities, and formulas.

For example:

SE Course 2A: 20−21, 27, 36, 45, 46, 58−59, 63−67, 69, 71, 74−76, 77, 132−147, 150−151, 153−155, 161−162, 166−172, 173−175, 178−184, 190, 193−194, 198−199, 211−219, 221−226, 227−232, 235−240, 246−247, 250−252, 255−256, 259−263, 271, 275−278, 280−282

SE Course 2B: 15−16, 20−27, 36−37, 44−50, 71−74, 76 81, 86, 88−89, 94−98, 101−103, 105, 121−123, 124, 133−137, 140, 141, 147−149, 178, 181, 184, 189, 193−196, 202−206, 209, 213−214, 215−219, 224, 227−231, 240, 246, 251, 254−262, 266−267, 272, 274−276

5. USE APPROPRIATE TOOLS STRATEGICALLY.

How *Math in Focus*®Aligns:

Math in Focus® helps students explore the different mathematical tools that are available to them, such as pencil and paper, geometry drawing tools, concrete and visual models such as number lines and grids, or technology to model developing skills and interpret everyday situations that involve proportionality, geometric construction and formulas, variation, data distribution, and probability.

For example:

SE Course 2A: 7−15, 18, 20−21, 23−24, 26−27, 30−31, 34, 36, 48, 53, 65, 58−59, 63−67, 69, 71, 74−76, 86−88, 132−137, 140−143, 145−147, 150−151, 170−172, 174−175, 190−194, 198−199, 211, 214−215, 221−232, 250, 257−263, 276, 280−282

SE Course 2B: 6, 9, 34−35, 66−68, 71−74, 76, 81, 86, 88−89, 94−98, 178, 180−181, 186−187, 189, 193, 197−198, 209, 212, 213−219, 240, 246, 251, 266−267, 275

6. ATTEND TO PRECISION.

How *Math in Focus*® Aligns:

In **Math in Focus**®, students check answers, define, highlight, review, and use mathematical vocabulary, define and interpret symbols, use appropriate forms of numbers and expressions, label bar and geometric models correctly, and compute with appropriate formulas and units in solving problems and explaining reasoning.

For example:

SE Course 2A: 9−10, 16−21, 34, 38, 42−46, 54, 116, 117, 132−147, 150−151, 153−155, 161−162, 173−174, 184, 190, 193−194, 197−202, 206−208, 212−213, 222, 224, 225, 228, 247, 251, 266, 267, 271

SE Course 2B: 5, 7−8, 10−11, 13, 16, 24−25, 33−37, 43, 46−50, 54, 74−75, 82, 85, 87−89, 94, 98, 101−103, 105, 114, 121, 122, 126, 133−137, 141, 147−149, 163−166, 168, 178, 184, 203, 205, 217, 224, 227−231, 234, 240, 243, 244, 251, 254−262, 267−271, 272, 274−275, 291

COMMON CORE STATE STANDARDS FOR MATHEMATICAL PRACTICE

CITATIONS

7. LOOK FOR AND MAKE USE OF STRUCTURE.

How *Math in Focus*® Aligns:

*The inherent pedagogy of **Math in Focus**® allows students to look for and make use of structure. Students recognize patterns and structure and make connections from one mathematical idea to another through, Best Practices, Big Ideas, Math Notes, Think Maths, and Cautions. Also occurs as skills and concepts are interconnected in prior knowledge activities, concept traces, and chapter concept maps.*

For example:

SE Course 2A: 2–6; 9, 16, 28, 32, 36, 39, 49, 52–58, 63, 65, 86, 89, 90, 91, 94, 98, 99, 103, 106, 107, 108, 112, 123, 128, 132, 134, 151, 155, 156, 158, 166, 167, 168, 169, 174, 185, 195, 198, 200, 201, 207, 216, 221, 225, 228, 231, 236, 241, 249, 251, 252, 254, 259, 261, 262, 267, 271, 276, 277, 283, 290

SE Course 2B: 15–16, 20–23, 26–27, 44–50, 55–56, 63–64, 86–90, 102, 105, 107–108, 115–116, 120, 121, 141, 148–149, 169, 178, 197–198, 202–205, 215–219, 227–231, 235–236, 240, 243–244, 247, 251, 254–258, 266–267, 269–270, 272–276, 292–293

8. LOOK FOR AND EXPRESS REGULARITY IN REPEATED REASONING.

How *Math in Focus*® Aligns:

*In **Math in Focus**®, students are given consistent tools for solving problems, such as bar models, algebraic variables, tables, coordinate grids, standard algorithms with rational numbers, numerical and geometric properties, and formulas so they see the similarities in how different problems are solved and understand efficient means for solving.*

For example:

SE Course 2A: 39–40, 46, 58, 63–64, 66, 72, 86, 89, 94, 95, 99, 103, 106, 107, 128, 130, 131, 145–146, 150–151, 153–155, 156, 161, 170, 184, 189, 191, 193–194, 197–200, 206, 211–213, 220–232, 245, 247, 251, 266, 271

SE Course 2B: 5–6, 8–9, 11, 13, 20–27, 32–37, 43–50, 52, 63–64, 86–90, 97, 121–122, 135–137, 141, 147–149, 164–165, 178B, 180–181, 183–184, 186–189, 197–198, 202–209, 215–219, 227–231, 240, 251–254, 258–262, 266, 272–276

BLANK

BLANK

BLANK

BLANK